the Lyle
official
ANTIQUES
review

DRAWINGS BY

PETER KNOX
STUART BARTON
JANE BARTON
ALISON MORRISON

the Lyle
official
ANTIQUES
review
1978

Compiled by
Margo Rutherford

Edited by Tony Curtis

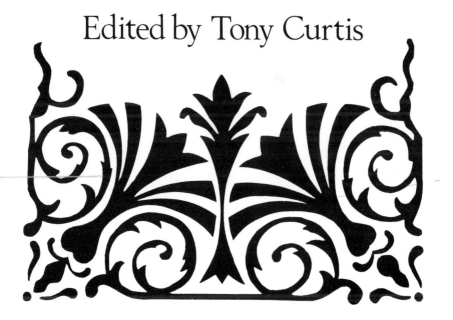

Acknowledgements

The Publishers wish to express their sincere thanks to the hundreds of contributors - Auctioneers, Dealers, Trade Warehouses - throughout the U.K., without whose help and co-operation this book could not have been produced.

And special thanks to
Tweeddale Press
John McQueen & Son
Annette Hogg
May Mutch
Lynn Hall
Josephine McLaren
Janice Moncrieff

SBN 0-902921-58-4

Copyright© Lyle Publications 1977   8th year of Issue

Published by Lyle Publications Glenmayne Galashiels Selkirkshire Scotland

Printed by Apollo Press, Unit 5, Dominion Way, Worthing, Sussex

CONTENTS

ANTIQUES REVIEW

Everyone from the office tea lady to the directors of the leading Auction Houses, knows that 'there's money in antiques'.

There is also a great deal of mystique, one-upmanship and, for want of a better word, plain, old fashioned bull. There are those, still, to whom an 'Antique' is something special; something which is not simply old, but which has great intrinsic value. These are the people who are aware of the worth of craftsmanship in its highest sense, and who, not infrequently, make the elementary mistake of equating craftsmanship with art. They will recognise the 'Antiqueness' of a Reisener bureau or a good Dutch marquetry display cabinet, but they may question the word's applicability to an eighteenth century cricket table or doughbin. They are the people who recognise only the curiosity value of something which is merely old, and who tend to believe that Antiques are never found in houses other than those belonging to the titled, the wealthy and the famous.

Fortunately, the amount of publicity given to the antiques trade in news-papers, magazines, and on television and radio, has done much to educate the general public and provide the house-wife and the man in the street with a soundly-based understanding of current values. This has done much to save attics full of accumulated 'junk' which might otherwise have found its way to the municipal rubbish tip or Guy Fawkes' bonfire. But, of course, every coin is double-sided. Sometimes a legitimate Dealer nowadays finds him-self, when making a perfectly fair offer for an object of only moderate worth, having to defend himself against accusations of dishonesty levelled by its owner who saw 'the identical thing' (in a book, magazine or television programme) valued at many times the offer in question.

Although such instances, when they occur, prove extremely annoying to the Dealer, he can usually explain quite satisfactorily the difference between the item under consideration and its more valuable counterpart - and here, his reputation for fair dealing will weigh heavily in his favour. In extreme circumstances he can always establish his credibility by offering to accept the judgement of a local Auctioneer and Valuer of repute.

Another difficulty experienced by Dealers and, indeed, private individuals (not to mention publishers of books such as the Lyle Official Antiques Review) when attempting to establish a mutually agreeable value for an item is that of regional variations in taste and supply. Some four years ago, to give a simple example, Lyle Publications moved from the South Coast of England to the Scottish Borders. At that time, you may remember, the demand for stripped pine was particularly great in the South. In the Borders, it was virtually unwanted. In consequence, pine furniture could be picked up almost for pennies in local auctions, while Dealers in the South were forced, through the laws of supply and demand, to pay (and charge) prices several hundred percent higher.

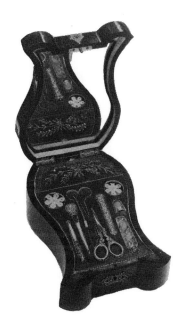

Anything rare or unusual will reflect these qualities in its price. This fine Regency musical-box etui is lyre-shaped, its satinwood and walnut case embellished with an ormolu trim. It plays two melodies and sold to the tune of £410.

Taken overall, however, with the growth of international trade and the increasing mobility of buyers made possible by virtue of containerisation and other bulk transport facilities, regional variations in value are becoming ever less marked. It should be obvious to everyone, however, that the High Street Dealer with his largely private clientele faces an entirely different set of problems in this respect to those which confront the bulk buyer and a shipper. By virtue of his method of trading, the High Street man, buying locally and selling locally to (mainly) established customers is going to be much harder pressed when it comes to obtaining the right goods for his relatively specialised business than the man who can select from all that the country has to offer to sell to an equally wide market. He is, therefore, risking having a rather myopic vision of the state of the market in general, and of the values of goods as they relate to his small corner of the market in particular. The only way he can gain a truer, over-all picture of the state of the trade in the wider sense - and this is becoming ever more essential to survival - is to lose no chance to broaden his outlook and gain as extensive a knowledge as possible of the market as a national (or even international) whole.

One certain way, open to virtually every Dealer in the country, to extend trading capability and keep in touch with national and international market trends is to join an organisation such as LAPADA. Besides fulfilling the immediately useful function of issuing newsletters containing lists of members (both at home and overseas), the Association publishes lists of wanted items, lists of stolen items and generally does a great deal toward disseminating the kind of information which no Dealer should be without.

Additionally, and here are perhaps the main functions of LAPADA in relation to the daily business of Antiques trading, the Association fights to establish and maintain standards which will benefit everyone who ever has anything to do with the buying or selling of

Only nineteenth century marquetry, but this bureau bookcase sold for £3,500.

antiques. Besides establishing standards of trading, the Association has proved extremely helpful to many members by assisting with problems concerning VAT, shipping goods, valuation and authentication. Not only that, they not infrequently arbitrate in cases of dispute between their members and other Dealers, Auctioneers and private buyers. So far their proud boast is that they have never yet been beaten by any problem they have attempted to solve. Currently, they are looking deeply into the relationship between Dealers and Auction Houses following a large number of complaints received claiming that certain of the latter are careless with goods handled, advertise in an unfair way which knocks the trade, impose unacceptable conditions of sale and, generally, adopt a high-handed attitude toward Dealers.

Any Association which is outward-looking enough to take up such a gauntlet on behalf of its members deserves, in my opinion, all the support it can get - and that includes increased membership, for it should not be over-looked that any improvements won for LAPADA members are, ultimately, going to benefit every legitimate trader in the country, whether a member or not. But on no account should quarrels betweer some dealers and some auction houses be allowed to upset the finely balanced relationship which exists generally between these two essential and interdependent branches of the trade.

Besides a rapidly-growing membership in the U.K., LAPADA claims a strong overseas membership, particularly among importers. Naturally enough, overseas members will tend to patronise Dealers recommended by the Assoc-

A nice little work table, and likely to be always in demand, sold for £260.

iation in this country since, by doing so, they will feel that they have some guarantee of fair trading, quite apart from the fact that they will have some advance knowledge of the kind of goods and extent of stock that is likely to be offered for their consideration.

But this is not intended to be a commercial for LAPADA. Every Dealer in the country must know about the Association by now, and every one of them is as aware of the advantages of joining as they are of the truth of my original statement - 'there's money in antiques'.

Of course there is. At one end of the scale we have an exclusive company of large Auction Houses and Dealers making seemingly fabulous profits year after year, buying and selling the world's most exquisite treasures to

Museums, Art Galleries, Trades Unions, 'Private American Buyers' and each other for sums we ordinary mortals can hardly comprehend. At the other end, we have a small number of hard-faced rip-off merchants and con-men who make fat pickings off the gullible, the careless and the greedy.

But in between, we have the mass of Dealers, Auctioneers, Restorers, Packers and Shippers who work long, hard hours, with varying degrees of success, to make as good a living as trade and conscience will allow.

In the main, the past few years have been pretty good to the average trader, despite the burden of extra work imposed by the vatman - and even the rigours of inflation were ameliorated to some extent by the encouragement overseas buyers have received from the failure of the pound to hold its place against other currencies. But the boom conditions which prevailed during 1976 and the early part of 1977 have tapered off to a point where a few Dealers (and Shippers, particularly), especially those who simply rode the crest of the wave without too much concern for the future, have had to reassess their trading philosophies.

The hard fact is that a Dealer now needs to make 40% more money than last year just to stand still - such has been the rise in value of good stock and the increased cost of overheads. To this has to be added the very real problem of a shortage of the right quality goods at the right prices and, far removed as it may seem from the average High Street shop, the worldwide state of economic uncertainty which, by causing delays in buying decisions overseas, slows down the turnover of stocks in Brighton, Bath, Widdicombe-in-the-Mold or wherever.

There have been a few complaints, mainly in the media, that our British Heritage is being shipped abroad, and that we will soon be living in a land bereft of art and antiques, but this view has never seriously been subscribed to by the majority. The general feeling on this score was best (if rather simplisticly) summed up by a South Coast Dealer who said 'It's happened before and it'll happen again, but the pendulum keeps swinging and the chances are that we'll soon be over the hump, then we'll be out there buying everything back - and a bit more besides - until the next time.'

Quite a large number of Dealers who

Early oak is rising nicely in value. This 17th century box-seat settle sold for £450

have clearly accepted that times change, and have done something about it, are those who have taken shop or stall premises in one of the Collective Markets which are appearing all over the country. Of course, this is a trend which has been going on for some time, but there are now around two hundred such setups in the country and, without a discoverable exception, they are all thriving. The logic is simple and unarguable; by combining under a single roof, each Dealer can obtain a prime trading site for a cost likely to be lower than that of premises in a less desirable area. By having a number of different dealers in close proximity, trade buyers and private individuals know they stand a better chance of finding what they want with a minimum amount of effort and, of course, each of the individual traders stands to gain from the various spin-off deals which such co-operation generates automatically.

As time goes by, and as competition for trade grows more fierce, it becomes increasingly evident that, to sustain a viable growth rate Dealers are going to be forced into adopting a positive and active approach to the question of Marketing. Here again the collective market can score every time over the individual trader. London's Bermondsey Market, for instance, sends people abroad to consolidate existing export connections and establish new markets for the benefit of all their traders. Small ads and three column-inch displays in the local paper serve an undeniably useful purpose in the immediate area, but today's market for trade is worldwide, and how many Middle Eastern buyers make a point of reading the Dunoon Bugle from cover to cover every week?

Despite the slight levelling-off of trade, there can be no mistaking the fact that the British antiques market is in an extremely healthy state, with good business being reported from all over the country, both in the private and trade sectors. Certainly, the amount of rubbish changing hands at inflated prices has fallen, but the market for really good quality goods is as strong as ever and we are once again hearing the heartfelt cry of 'I just can't get enough good quality stock to satisfy my customers......'.

This, of course, is where the subject of restoration has to be raised. The only way to keep a high standard of good quality stock in circulation is by keeping our restorers busy. Car body filler and Araldite have their place - but it is not around the loose leg of a Queen Anne display cabinet. Every Dealer knows this, but so many botch up their own repairs with the excuse that proper restoration would take too long or be uneconomical. This would not be quite so bad were it not for the virtual indestructibility of modern fillers and adhesives which, once used, create all kinds of additional problems and expense for the man who would like the job done properly later.

Needless to say, though, restorers are all reporting excellent business - quite a few receiving a large proportion of their work from overseas buyers who tell them that, not only is their standard of work as high as any done on the Continent, but their charges are far lower.

Continental buyers (Germans and the

Pieces such as this early nineteenth century, French, bow-fronted chest of six drawers, with its marble top, cross-banded rosewood and gilt metal enrichments (£560) are finding favour with buyers from the Middle East.

Dutch, particularly) are still to be found in large numbers over here, both at auctions and travelling round the country to visit individual Dealers in search of good quality stocks. The German Dealers, particularly, being still on the lookout for clocks. Both Canada and the Middle East are being increasingly represented, Arab buyers tending to be on the lookout for 19th century French furniture whose ormolu embellishment finds favour with their customers at home. It has been suggested, however, that they are slowly moving toward the better, eighteenth century furniture. The Canadians, of course, now allow goods over fifty years old to enter duty-free (not including wines and spirits!), a factor which is making many a British authenticator have to burn the midnight oil while doing a whole lot of extra homework.

At home, the taste for good Edwardian furniture is becoming more widespread, dealers all over the country reporting growing interest on the part of private, as well as trade, buyers. Most dealers, of course, have acknowledged for years that even the better Edwardian pieces have been undervalued, so it is particularly satisfying to report that an item like an inlaid corner whatnot which most dealers would have passed by with a shrug just a short time ago, can now take its rightful place in the scheme of things and command a respectable price at auction just about anywhere in the U.K.

Auction Houses right across the country are reporting the level of private buying to be, if not actually on the increase, at least consistently high, particularly as regards pieces having investment potential. Here again, the move in furniture is towards the Edwardian taste partly, I suspect, because it is beginning to have a fashionable appeal, and partly having been for so long undervalued, word has spread to the private market that it has a good chance of rising in value faster than other, similarly-priced articles. The chief reason should be, however, that much Edwardian furniture is tastefully stylish, elegantly proportioned and extremely well made, besides being still not overvalued —

more than can be said for many antique, and most modern, pieces of furniture.

Good oak, of course, has always commanded a certain amount of respect - and prices to match - but recent sales indicate that this is another area where prices are rising a little faster than average. Carved pieces, in particular, are doing especially well at the moment (some have doubled) and look set fair to continue in the same way.

Victorian furniture, it is generally recognised, has passed its fashionable peak by now, but that is not to say that it is lagging behind the rest of the market in any way, and at least one South Coast Auctioneer reports that the demand is as great as ever for any good quality pieces passing through his salerooms. Even the largest of pieces are eagerly sought after, including those huge breakfronted wardrobes which, a few years ago merited little interest, and are now selling for hundreds of pounds.

Five-piece Victorian silver tea and coffee service. £820. Good investment potential for private buyers.

Thought weighty a few years ago, and not fully appreciated. Now this nineteenth century walnut credenza attracts nearly £1300.

valuations to carry over from one year to the next and, when estimating values, to take full account of the rise over the past few years and project this forward sensibly for the year ahead.

Although this problem has great bearing on the subject of furniture valuation, it is likely to be even more tricky when applied to collectables, since these are sometimes subject to meteoric rises in value over relatively short periods of time. Consider the effects of fashionable attention on such hitherto undesirable items as Advertising Signs, Toys, Postcards, Lead Soldiers, Kitchen Utensils, Printed Packages, early photographs and empty bottles. Examples of all of these are almost certainly lying in dustbins at this very moment, having been thrown out by beavering housewives clearing out loft, cellar or garden shed. Their values are set by the demand created by

One particular problem resulting from inflation and the consequent rise in antiques prices is, as many firms are discovering, that of valuing for probate or insurance purposes. Dealers, private buyers and auctioneers - in fact anyone concerned with the day-to-day business of buying and selling antiques, paintings or, indeed, any other collectable commodities can set a figure on an item, based on experience and on intelligent use of books such as this. The problem arises when a figure has to be set on an item which is not for immediate sale. A piece which is worth, say, £500 today can fairly be expected with inflation to have risen in value to around £600 by this time next year. But will it? Or will it have shot up still higher? Needless to say, the lesson to be learned here, particularly by the private individual, is never simply to allow insurance

Instruments of all kinds are doing well. This nineteenth century, two-day, marine chronometer by Parkinson and Frodsham sells for around £500.

enthusiastic collectors, and are then inflated by the scarcity which results from relatively large numbers of people, encouraged by articles in Sunday supplements, drawing on the limited number of items available. After a time, values level off and fairly reliable estimates of a collection's worth may be made - which will be subject only to the normal, year-by-year increases but, during the period of fashionable adherance (particularly when that coincides, as now, with a period of inflation) prices are likely to disappear into the stratosphere and make any realistic appraisal of values impossible.

But that situation really only exists with regard to 'craze' type collectables. Normally, the collectable market can be expected to have the same kind of stability as any other section of the antiques market in general. Which means that, at the moment, the overall picture is good worldwide.

Silver is creeping back up to its rightful place in the scheme of things, and reports across the country suggest that Georgian, and older, silver is no longer held to be quite so far above the pocket of the private buyer as it was even a year ago.

Experience suggests, however, that it is unlikely to see for some time another boom period such as it had just a few years ago. It is, nevertheless, generally considered to be a good investment area at the present, and prices are expected to keep well enough ahead of inflation to satisfy the most demanding investor.

Cameras and scientific instruments are still doing fairly well, particularly the latter, many of which are sought after for their decorative value as much as their scientific and historical relevance. Despite this, country sales in particular still have bargains to offer the occasional addict of 'box and contents' lots.

Art Nouveau, it is widely agreed, has now gone through the roof, closely followed by Art Deco but, again, the country sales are more likely to yield small, attractive items at still reasonable prices than the better patronised sales in towns and 'good' areas.

Taken by and large, the year ahead offers exciting prospects of continued growth in trade on both the domestic and the overseas fronts. But, with the economic situation as it is, no dealer who wishes to carve himself a slice of the cake will be able to afford to sit back and expect the world to come flocking to him. He will have to adopt as aggressive a marketing policy as he can and, since such programmes take time and money, we can expect to see a continued increase in the number of collective markets as more Dealers realise the benefits that can accrue from such co-operative enterprises.

It is likely, too, that Shippers, in order to meet the increasing cost of transport, etc., will have to concentrate on improving the standard of goods in containers - all the indications are that the boom in rubbish is over. But there is no doubt whatever that, for those who tackle the problems of increasing competition and inflation in a realistic manner, there will continue to be money in antiques for many years to come.

TONY CURTIS

All photographs in this article by kind permission of King & Chasemore.

GOOD COMPANIONS

FOR THE TRUE PROFESSIONAL

Wonderful value at only £6.00 each

23

There are a great many antique shippers in Britain

but few, if any, who are as quality conscious as Norman Lefton, Chairman and Managing Director of British Antique Exporters Ltd. of Newhaven, Sussex. Fourteen years experience of shipping goods to all parts of the globe have confirmed his original belief that the way to build clients' confidence in his services is to supply them only with goods which are in first class saleable condition. To this end, he employs a full-time staff of over 40, from highly skilled packers, joiners, cabinet makers, polishers and restorers, to representative buyers and executives. Through their knowledgeable hands

BRITISH ANTIQUE EXPORTERS LTD

SHOWROOMS & CONTAINER DEPOT,
NEW ROAD INDUSTRIAL ESTATE, NEWHAVEN,
SUSSEX, ENGLAND.

Cables ANTIQUES NEWHAVEN.

Telephone NEWHAVEN (07912) 5561

24

passes each piece of furniture before it leaves the B.A.E. warehouses, ensuring that the overseas buyer will only receive the best and most saleable merchandise for their particular market. This attention to detail is obvious on a visit to the New-haven warehouses where potential customers can view what must be the most varied assortment of Georgian, Victorian, Edwardian and 1930's furniture in the area. One cannot fail to be impressed by, not only the varied range of merchandise but by the fact that each piece is in perfect condition awaiting shipment. As one would expect, packing is considered somewhat of an art at B.A.E. and David Gilbert, the factory manager, ensures that each piece will reach its final destination in the condition a customer would wish. B.A.E. set a very high standard and, as a further means of improving each container load Mr. Gilbert, who also deals with customer/container liaison, asks each customer to return detailed infor-mation on the saleability of each

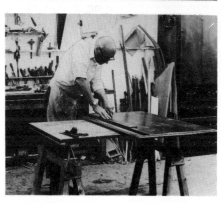

piece in the container thereby ensuring successful future shipments. This feedback of information is the all important factor which guarantees the profitability of future containers "By this method" Mr. Lefton explains, "we have established that an average £6000 container will, immediately it is unpacked at its final destination, realise in the region of £9000·£12000 for our clients selling the goods on a quick wholesale turnover basis". These figures are confirmed by the Chartered Accountant, Mr. A. E. C. Wheeler who whilst officially the Company Accountant is also very involved in promoting good customer relationships and could be called B.A.E.'s public relations genius. He is always ready to discuss the financial aspects of the shipments and proves a valued member of this highly successful Company. Other employees you will meet on a visit to Newhaven are Tracy Ware, who deals with documentation/customer liaison, Michael Schneider who is a buyer as well as generally looking after overseas visitors.

In any average 20-foot container, B.A.E. put approximately six really fine pieces, some 20 quality pieces, 20 "run of the mill" items and as many as 400 to 500 smaller pieces of bric-a-brac, all in eminently saleable condition.

Based at the south coast port of Newhaven – 10 miles from Brighton and on a direct rail link with London (only 50 minutes journey) the Company is ideally situated to ship containers to all parts of the world. The showrooms, restoration and packing departments are open to overseas buyers and no visit to purchase antiques for re-sale in other countries is complete without a visit to their Newhaven premises where a welcome is always found.

A selection of antiques

28

from a container load

29

30

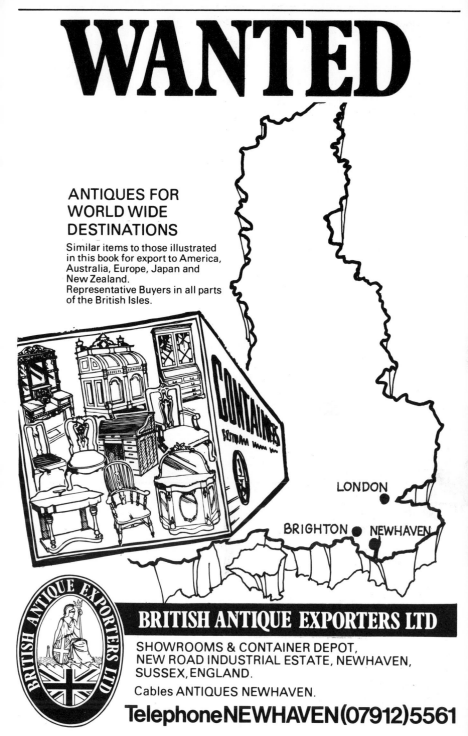
31

32

THE QUALITY CONSCIOUS SHIPPERS

BRITISH ANTIQUE EXPORTERS LTD

EXPORTERS   PACKERS   SHIPPERS

HEAD OFFICE: NEW ROAD INDUSTRIAL ESTATE · NEWHAVEN · EAST SUSSEX BN9 0EN ENGLAND

TELEPHONE: NEWHAVEN (07913) 5561   CABLES: ANTIQUES NEWHAVEN ENGLAND

1 9 7 8

Dear Overseas Importer,

We can supply you with a container full of Antiques, which will be ideally suitable to your particular market.

Our buyers are strategically placed throughout England, Ireland, Scotland and Wales, in order to take full advantage of regional pricing. We are, therefore, highly competitive.

You can purchase a container from us for as little as £3,000 ex works. This would be filled with mostly 1930s furniture and chinaware; you could expect to pay approximately £7,000 - £10,000 for a quality shipment of Georgian and Victorian furniture and porcelain. However, we are entirely flexible in our dealings and we do ship containers up to a value of £60,000.

Whichever type of container you buy from us we guarantee, as far as we are able, that you will make a most satisfactory profit.

We assure you of our best attention at all times.

Yours faithfully,
BRITISH ANTIQUE EXPORTERS LTD.

N. Lefton
Chairman & Managing Director

DIRECTORS: N. LEFTON (Chairman & Managing), P. V. LEFTON, G. LEFTON, THE RT. HON. THE VISCOUNT EXMOUTH, A. FIELD, MSC FBOA DCLP FSMC FAAO, B. LEWIS
REGISTERED OFFICE: 12/13 SHIP STREET, BRIGHTON   REGISTERED NO 893406 ENGLAND
BANKERS: NATIONAL WESTMINSTER BANK LTD. 155 NORTH STREET, BRIGHTON, SUSSEX   THE CHASE MANHATTAN BANK, N.A., 410 PARK AVENUE, NEW YORK

BRITISH ANTIQUE EXPORTERS LTD

SHOWROOMS & CONTAINER DEPOT,
NEW ROAD INDUSTRIAL ESTATE, NEWHAVEN,
SUSSEX, ENGLAND.

Cables ANTIQUES NEWHAVEN.

Telephone NEWHAVEN (07912) 5561

34

35

36

We name names...

Holbrook's GUIDE TO THE ANTIQUE TRADE IN SCOTLAND – Scotland's only directory of the trade – is a unique collection of interesting and informative facts about antiques, essential to both collectors and the trade.

HOLBROOK'S

guide
to the
Antique
trade
in scotland

This invaluable publication is available from reputable booksellers & stationers. In case of difficulty, contact
ABERDEEN ADVERTISER 123 CROWN STREET
ABERDEEN AB1 2HN Telephone (0224) 56665

Only £1

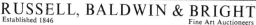

42

Spencers

OF RETFORD

THE FINE ART AUCTIONEERS OF THE NORTH

Above:
A Royal Worcester vase.
Painted by C. Baldwyn.
Realised £850

Below:
Still life. Oil on panel.
Attributed to Dirk Van Der Aa.
12 x 9 inches.
Realised £15,500

A set of four George III candlesticks.
London 1764.   Realised £1,200

A set of four embossed bird pictures,
attributed to Samuel Dixon.
Realised £1,050

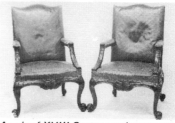

A pair of XVIII Century mahogany open
armchairs of Chippendale style.
Realised £2,200

A selection of items sold by us during the past season.

HENRY SPENCER AND SONS LIMITED 20, The Square, Retford, Nottinghamshire
Telephone (0777) 2531
IN ASSOCIATION WITH SOTHEBY'S

43

44

INTRODUCTION

The Lyle Official Antiques Review is published on the first of November of every year, enabling you to begin each new year with an up to date knowledge of the current trends, together with the verified values of antiques of all descriptions.

We have endeavoured to obtain a balance between the more expensive collector's items and those which, although not in their true sense antiques, are handled daily by the antique trade.

The illustrations and prices in the following sections have been arranged to make it easy for the reader to assess the period and value of all items with speed.

You will find illustrations for almost every category of antique and curio, together with a corresponding price collated during the last twelve months, from auction rooms and retail outlets throughout Britain.

When dealing with the more popular trade pieces, a calculation of an average price has been estimated from the varying accounts researched. As regards prices when 'one of a pair' is given in the description the price quoted is for a pair, for with the limited space we have at our disposal we feel only one illustration is necessary.

ANIMALIA

Victorian stuffed
hedgehog.   £15

Part of a collection of
foreign moths and
butterflies in a maho-
gany cabinet. £1,900

19th century
stuffed curlew.
£15

African grey
parrot under
a glass dome.
£40

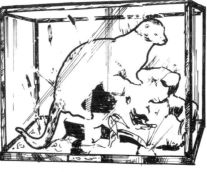

Victorian stuffed otter in its
natural habitat.   £60

A lacquered
and decorated
ostrich egg. £450

A large stuffed
moose head.
£60

Stuffed and mounted
pelican in glass fronted
case, 2ft. 7in. high. £200

Brown bear,
72in. high.
£230

A late 19th century suit of armour in the 15th century style. £1,150

A 17th century Cromwellian trooper's helmet, skull formed in two pieces. £160

Italian 17th century suit of horseman's armour with close helmet. £1,200

A suit of 17th century Cromwellian armour. £750

An Indo-Persian suit of chain mail, 16/17th century. £310

19th century Japanese suit of armour. £1,800

A composite full suit of armour in the 16th century style. £2,800

19th century Samurai suit of armour. £570

AUTOMATON FIGURES

An English amusing cat tea party automaton, the cardboard construction operated by a clockwork mechanism at the rear. **£130**

Musical automaton of a rabbit which rises from the lettuce. **£260**

A French musical pianist automaton with maker's plaque G. Vichy Fils, 1ft. 3in. wide, circa 1900. **£850**

A French automaton of a negro musician from the third quarter of the 19th century, 3ft. high. **£1,500**

Mid 19th century French monkey trio barrel organ automaton, 3ft. high. **£1,750**

A French musician automaton, the figure with composition head, wearing a scarlet long-tailed coat, circa 1900, 1ft. 11in. high. **£750**

A French gilt metal clock automaton stamped on the back plate H.L., circa 1900. **£1,100**

A late 19th century French magician's 'Cups and Balls' clock automaton, signed P. Garnier, Paris, 1ft.9in. high. **£1,500**

A late 19th century French musician automaton, 1ft.10in. wide. **£700**

A levitation automaton depicting Snow White lying on a couch, 45in. x 38in., circa 1920.
£650

Late 19th century French cymbalist automaton, the bisque headed doll impressed on the back VTE Jumeau S.O.D.G.
£850

Early 20th century French musical automaton group of three clowns, 1ft.4in. high.
£100

Early 20th century French dancing girl automaton, the bisque headed doll with glass eyes, 1ft.10in. high.
£800

An unusual French presentation timepiece automaton by Cooke and Knelvey, Paris, 1ft. 7in. high.   £550

Early 20th century German flower girl automaton, 1ft.8in. high.
£650

Late 19th century French musical ballerina automaton, 1ft.10in. high. £750

An early 20th century French sleeping doll automaton, 1ft.2in. wide.
£420

Early 20th century seascape automaton under a glass dome, 1ft.3in. high.
£180

BAROMETERS

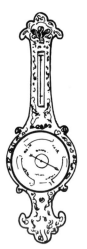

Mahogany wheel barometer with shell inlay by A. Pagani, Nottingham, circa 1810. £155

George III mahogany stick barometer, 3ft. 5in. high, by Knie, Edinburgh.£620

Rosewood and mother-of-pearl inlaid barometer, 19th century. £340

A rare walnut pillar barometer by Daniel Quare, 3ft. high. £2,500

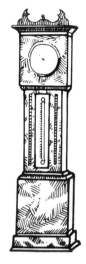

Wheel barometer in rosewood, circa 1845, 3ft. 2½in. long. £130

Miniature oak grandfather clock and barometer, 16in. high. £45

Rosewood wheel barometer by Emilio Zuccani of London, circa 1840, 44in. high. £285

Mahogany 8in. wheel barometer, circa 1790, engraved B. Corty, Glasgow. £185

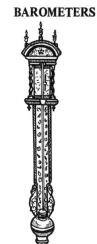

Rosewood cased wheel barometer, circa 1840, 36in. high. **£110**

Mahogany stick barometer by Ciceri & Pini, Edinburgh, circa 1855. **£230**

Sheraton wheel barometer by A. Benzoni, circa 1800. **£155**

Late 17th century walnut stick barometer with marquetry panels and engraved brass scale. **£1,200**

Walnut cased cistern stick barometer by J. Perse, Winchester, circa 1845, 39½in. high. **£195**

Large mahogany banjo barometer, 40in. high, maker's name F. Harrison, Hexham, circa 1830. **£155**

Rare late 17th century ebonised column barometer by Thomas Tompion, 3ft. 5in. high. **£1,900**

Mahogany eight inch wheel barometer, circa 1820, 3ft. 2½in. long. **£200**

BAROMETERS

Rosewood wheel barometer with silvered dial, by J. Somalvico & Son, circa 1820, 38in. high. £385

George II mahogany stick barometer by Carls. Aiano, 3ft.4in. high. £380

Rosewood wheel barometer, circa 1820, 10in. dial. £110

Burr walnut stick barometer, circa 1800.£195

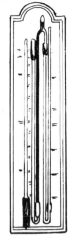

Rare George III double tube barometer, 1ft. 11in. high.£400

Wheel barometer by J. T. Jeffs of Luton, 38in. high, circa 1850. £95

Rosewood stick barometer by Lancaster & Sons, circa 1830. £185

Rosewood wheel barometer with 10in. dial, circa 1860. £105

BAROMETERS

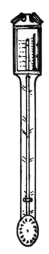

Fine grained walnut Victorian wheel barometer. £95

Late George III yew wood stick barometer signed Jas. Corte, Glasgow, 3ft. 2½in. high.£500

19th century rosewood wheel barometer, 37in. high, circa 1830. £125

Early 19th century mahogany stick barometer signed T. Dunn, Edinburgh, 3ft. 1in. high. £360

George II walnut barometer with circular silvered register plate, 3ft.8in. high. £540

Late 18th century mahogany wheel barometer with silvered dial, circa 1790, 37in. high. £225

George II walnut barometer, 3ft. 5in. high. £450

Wheel barometer by M. Barnuk in faded mahogany case, 39in. high, circa 1795.£175

BIRDCAGES

Victorian brass birdcage.   £30

Magician's bird-cage canister, circa 1900. £35

Late Victorian brass birdcage with etched glass decoration.   £25

Late 18th century Russian painted birdcage.   £520

19th century blue and white Delft earthenware birdcage.   £275

Mid 19th century 'Crystal Palace' brass birdcage.   £55

19th century bird-cage automaton.   £340

19th century ormolu birdcage with ogee top, 24in. high.   £1,400

19th century brass parrot cage.   £60

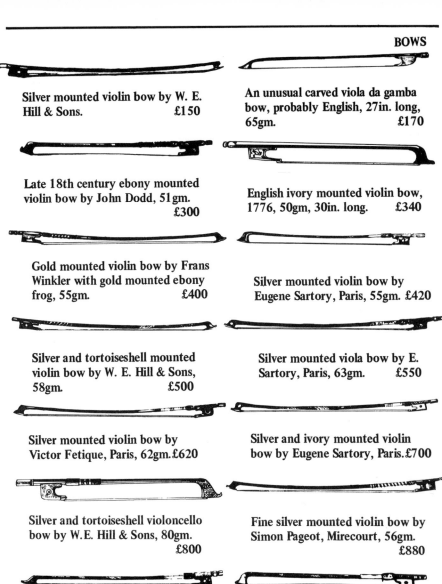

Silver mounted violin bow by W. E. Hill & Sons. £150

An unusual carved viola da gamba bow, probably English, 27in. long, 65gm. £170

Late 18th century ebony mounted violin bow by John Dodd, 51gm. £300

English ivory mounted violin bow, 1776, 50gm, 30in. long. £340

Gold mounted violin bow by Frans Winkler with gold mounted ebony frog, 55gm. £400

Silver mounted violin bow by Eugene Sartory, Paris, 55gm. £420

Silver and tortoiseshell mounted violin bow by W. E. Hill & Sons, 58gm. £500

Silver mounted viola bow by E. Sartory, Paris, 63gm. £550

Silver mounted violin bow by Victor Fetique, Paris, 62gm.£620

Silver and ivory mounted violin bow by Eugene Sartory, Paris.£700

Silver and tortoiseshell violoncello bow by W.E. Hill & Sons, 80gm. £800

Fine silver mounted violin bow by Simon Pageot, Mirecourt, 56gm. £880

Early 19th century gold mounted violin bow by Jacques Lafleur, Paris, 57gm. £1,000

Gold mounted violin bow by Georges Mougenot, Brussels, circa 1875, 66gm. £1,200

Early 19th century gold and ivory mounted violin bow, 61gm, by John Dodd. £1,600

Gold mounted violin bow by Francois Tourte, 60gm. £2,700

BRONZE

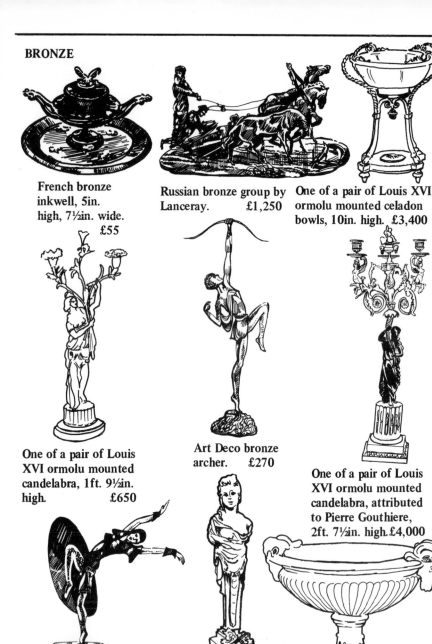

French bronze
inkwell, 5in.
high, 7½in. wide.
£55

Russian bronze group by
Lanceray.   £1,250

One of a pair of Louis XVI
ormolu mounted celadon
bowls, 10in. high. £3,400

One of a pair of Louis
XVI ormolu mounted
candelabra, 1ft. 9½in.
high.   £650

Art Deco bronze
archer.   £270

One of a pair of Louis
XVI ormolu mounted
candelabra, attributed
to Pierre Gouthiere,
2ft. 7½in. high.£4,000

Bronze and ivory figure
by Demetre Chiparus.
              £5,200

Louis XV ormolu
portrait of Madame
de Pompadour, 1ft.
high.   £800

One of a pair of fine porphyry
tazze of oval form, 1ft. 5in.
high.   £2,700

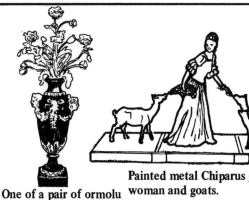

One of a pair of ormolu mounted porphyry candelabra, 1ft. 9½in. high. £900

Painted metal Chiparus group of woman and goats. £550

Bronze figure of a cat, signed Jean Earril, 19in. high. £550

Art Deco bronze and ivory figure of an air-woman, by F. Preiss. £1,200

Art Deco ivory and gilt bronze figure by Chiparus. £780

One of a pair of Louis XVI ormolu mounted onyx urns, 9in. high. £650

One of a pair of Louis XVI ormolu candle-sticks on white marble plinths, 9in. high. £650

One of a pair of Louis XVI ormolu chenets on leaf-cast plinths, 1ft. high. £500

Art Deco ivory and gilt bronze figure by Chiparus. £780

BRONZE

Bronze model of an owl perched on ink-well stump. £75

16in. tall bronze figure of an athlete, signed Schmidt Felling, 1905. £140

Late 19th century bronze lion, signed Barye. £220

Bronze figure of Cupid, signed Auguste Moreau. £320

Cambodian gilded bronze antelope, reclining, circa 1880. £195

Chinese, Shang/early Western Chou dynasty, bronze pole finial, 15cm. high. £80,000

Elegant bronze Art Nouveau lamp, 15in. high. £80

Late 19th century Seiya bronze of an elephant, Japanese, 14in. long. £160

Bronze figure of Diana by Louis-Ernest Barries, late 19th century, 17in. high. £540

Japanese red bronze box, signed Yoshiaki, 10.8cm. £1,000

Bronze and ivory dancer, by Cl.J.R. Colinet, 14½in. high. £380

Late 19th century bronze of two horses 'L 'Accolade', signed by P.J. Mene, 8in. high. £750

Japanese bronze vase, signed by Dai Nihon Kyoto ju Bunryu. £1,000

A bronzed eagle with outstretched wings, perched on a branch, signed A. Thorburn, early 20th century, 4½in. long. £150

Bronzed metal figure of Cupid, signed Palcomet, circa 1870, 1ft. 4½in. high. £140

A well modelled heavy bronze figure of Goering, 15in. high. £230

Bronze model of a stallion, 12in. high. £520

Victorian bronze bust of Byron. £100

BRONZE

A bronze cow with raised head, signed I. Bonheur, circa 1870, 6¼in. high. **£360**

Art Nouveau spelter bust, signed, circa 1900. **£100**

French bronze bulldog on a square base, 11in. long, signed P. Dinby, circa 1900. **£200**

A bronze retriever with pheasant in mouth, 15½in. high, signed J. Moigniez. **£360**

Elaborate bronze figure of an Egyptian priestess. **£450**

Early 18th century Dutch bronze cannon with a pale green patina overall, 33in. long. **£650**

Early 17th century Dutch bronze pestle and mortar. **£340**

Chiparus bronze and ivory dancer, **£2,100**

Late 19th century Japanese bronze figure of a tiger, 28in. long, signed. **£390**

One of a pair of bronze figures of cock and hen pheasants, 11¾in. high. £170

West African cast bronze figure of a seated smoker, 6½in. tall. £40

A bronze model of a retriever with its right paw raised, signed P. J. Mene, mid 19th century, 4½in. long. £150

A bronze racehorse and jockey, signed I. Bonheur, circa 1860, 18½in. long. £1,050

Signed Art Nouveau bronze figure. £240

One of a pair of French 19th century bronze Marley horses, 24in. high. £540

Elaborate Shibayama vase and cover, mother-of-pearl flower-heads, 6in. high, late 19th century. £720

Louis XVI ormolu mounted white marble brule parfum, 1ft. 5in. high. £950

Late Victorian bronze group by E. Piat, 20in., long. £975

BRONZE

Late 19th century French bronze of Hercules, 14in. high. £480

T'ang gilt bronze figure of a striding lion, 6½in. high. £100,000

Bronze figure of Peace by Edward Onslow Ford, 22in. high. £450

Bronze figure of Juno by Antoine-Louis Barye, 11in. high. £1,500

A pair of French 19th century bronze Marley horses. £320

One of a pair of Komai style bronze vases, 17½in. high. £3,600

A small late 19th century bust of Judith, 7in. high. £60

Bronze of two duelling musketeers by E. Drouot, 17½in. long. £360

Late 19th century bronze figure of a Moroccan falconer, 24in. high. £420

Gilt bronze figure of the dancer Louie Fuller by Raoul Larche, 18¼in. high. £3,600

Late 19th century bronze bull, 8in. wide, signed I. Bonheur. £250

Japanese bronze figure of a running bull, pad mark with incised character marks, 29in. long, on wooden stand. £440

One of a pair of 19th century candelabra made by Emile Guillemin, Paris, 9ft. 9in. high. £29,000

Pair of bronze partridges by E. Pautrot, signed, 13½in. high. £450

Bronze figure of 'The Sluggard' by Lord Leighton, 1886, 17in. high. £950

'The Javelin Thrower' by F. Preiss, 12in. high. £900

Early 20th century bronze racing group, 12 x 38in., signed Yves Benois Gironier. £1,200

Bronze Florentine lute player by A. E. Gaudez, 18in. high. £350

BRONZE

Bronze incense burner and cover, 11 in. high.
£77

Italian bronze group by A. Pandiani of Milan, circa 1880.
£520

Japanese bronze figure of an eagle, 29 in. wingspan, on a wooden base.
£430

Bronze and ivory figure of the the 'Torch Dancer' by Preiss, 15¾ in. tall.
£1,540

Bronze group of a centaur attacking a warrior, 21 in. high.
£290

Bronze fish eagle with shakudo beak and crystal eyes, signed Mitani, 42.5 cm. high.
£425

Large bronze muffin man's handbell by Mears and Son. £35

Mid 19th century bronze figure of a racehorse, 19 in. high.
£680

Bronze statuette of Joan of Arc in full armour, 9 in. high. £90

64

Late 19th century bronze elephant attacked by tigers, 39cm. long. £1,100

Art Deco bronze nude dancer signed Bouraine, 23in. high. £240

Late 19th century bronze panther, signed Van de Kemp, 4½in. high. £240

Bearded nude man carrying a dead boar, bronze, 16½in. high, on rouge marble plinth. £420

A French bronze group of two pointers with a dead hare, signed P.J. Mene, dated 1872, 8in. iong. £520

Well modelled bronze of Venus, 34in. high, circa 1860. £395

19th century Nepalese bronze Bhudda, 8in., high. £55

Bronze group of Russian soldiers, 14½in. high. £850

19th century tribal Kond in bronze depicting the goddess seated on an elephant, 8in. high. £80

BRONZE

Art Nouveau solid bronze inkwell, circa 1900, 7in. long. £24

Late 19th century Russian model of a lady. £90

16th century Venetian bronze inwell. £700

Early 15th century Ming bronze figure of Golden Boy, 6.5in. high. £680

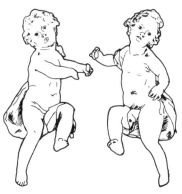

Pair of Louis XV gilt bronze putti by Philippe Caffieri, 13in. high. £1,600

Untypical ivory and bronze figure by Franz Preiss. £1,250

Large Egyptian bronze statue of a cat. £26,000

A pair of 19th century Italian bronze figures, 10½in. high. £440

Late 19th century French bronzed spelter figure of a Harlequin, 38in. tall. £350

BRONZE

Late Victorian bronze
elephant paperweight,
3½in. high.   £26

Small late Victorian
spelter figure of a
cricketer.   £15

Spelter figure of a girl
on an onyx and marble
base, circa 1920, 1ft.
6in. long.   £130

Preiss bronze and
ivory figure of a
dancing girl, 15in.
high.   £1,100

19th century Japanese
bronze figure of a
Samurai warrior, 10in.
high.   £600

Bronze figure of a
miner by Constantin
Meunier, 22½in. high.
          £1,250

Oriental bronze figure
of a man, on a wooden
base, circa 1890, 9in.
high.   £35

Pair of French bronze
figures of Cavaliers,
21in. high.   £420

One of a pair of Regency
bronze and white marble
tazze, 10½in. high. £400

67

BUCKETS AND HODS

Early 19th century
copper coal bucket.
£70

18th century lead
cistern, dated 1755,
41in. wide. £250

Regency period
brass coal box
with an embossed
flap.   £45

Late Victorian
bread bin. £5

Brass banded oak
butter tub, circa
1840.   £48

Wooden flour bin
made by a cooper.
£6

Late 19th century
oak coal box, with
a brass handle and
fittings.   £18

A brass handled and
banded mahogany
plate pail, circa 1755.
£200

French ormolu
coal scuttle, 24in.
high.   £100

Early 19th century
copper coal scuttle.
£35

Dutch circular copper
bucket with swing
handle, 15in. diameter.
£70

Copper coal
helmet. £22

19th century brass
bound bucket. £44

Kingwood ormolu mounted
jardiniere inset with porcelain
marquetry flowers, circa 1840,
46cm. wide.   £345

Art Nouveau brass
coal bucket with
lid and liner, circa
1880.   £31

Copper coal bucket,
circa 1820, 13in.
high.   £32

Bushel corn
measure, iron
banded, circa
1840.   £37

Victorian copper
coal bucket. £37

CADDIES AND BOXES

A small oak bible box dated 1613. £50

One of a pair of Regency black and gold lacquer boxes. £65

Mid Victorian mahogany companion inkwell stand, 12 x 10in. £30

Jacob & Co., Coronation coach biscuit box, 1937. £28

Oak country house letter box formed as a miniature pillar box, 16in. high. £130

Huntley and Palmer book biscuit tin. £15

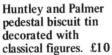

Huntley and Palmer pedestal biscuit tin decorated with classical figures. £10

Late 18th century Sheraton mahogany tea caddy with boxwood inlay. £50

Huntley and Palmer library biscuit tin, circa 1905. £24

Yellow lacquer casket
with two companion
smaller boxes, probably
Italian.   £60

George III mahogany
cheese boat.   £38

Italian marquetry
writing cabinet,
circa 1880, 1ft.
6¼in. long. £105

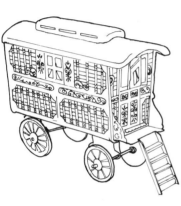

Jacob's gypsy caravan
biscuit tin, circa 1905.
£28

Taper box
with gilt
decoration
on green.£3

Huntley and Palmer book
biscuit tin, circa 1903. £18

17th century tortoiseshell
powder box with inlaid
decoration.   £200

Victorian pochette with
silver and gold thread
decoration of a peacock.
£6

Huntley and Palmer
laundry basket
biscuit tin, circa 1904.
£15

CADDIES AND BOXES

A good 18th century pierced ivory tea caddy. £470

Victorian leather covered jewellery case with silver fittings. £1,250

Late 18th century Pontypool oval tea caddy with red and gilt decoration. £195

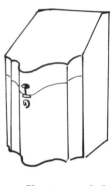

Late 18th century mahogany urn shaped caddy with boxwood string inlay. £265

Superb cased set of nine late 17th century cordial or spirit clear glass bottles in a wrought iron banded oak case, circa 1690.£450

Sheraton period inlaid mahogany knife box with cutlery compartments. £95

Late 18th century mother-of-pearl tea caddy with silver fittings, 6½in. high. £500

George III inlaid satinwood tea caddy, circa 1780, 5in. high. £70

Late 19th century Indian ivory and ebony box. £15

Decorated mustard tin showing National Games. £14

George III harewood and marquetry caddy with flower vignettes, about 1790, 5in. high. £180

A Kashmir lacquered box. £50

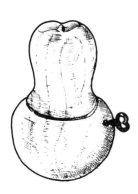

Georgian fruitwood tea caddy in the shape of a pear, and with its original lock and key. £120

Lacquered work box with lift-up lid and four drawers. £160

Late 18th century mahogany knife box. £70

Late Georgian lacquer box with silver carrying handle. £95

Tunbridgeware box which bears the trade label of Edmund Nye, early 19th century. £45

Early mahogany caddy case with original tin caddies inside, 4in. high. £185

CADDIES AND BOXES

An excellent quality late 18th century tea caddy with rolled paper decoration, 5in. high. £350

Victorian papier mache tea caddy with floral decoration. £55

Late 18th century decagonal tea caddy of tortoiseshell with ivory banding and a silvered plaque, 5in. high. £235

Japanned spice box, black with gilt decoration. £7

Miniature Japanese cabinet in lacquer, with bird designs. £45

English box and counters, 1755-1760, enamelled on copper, 6½cm. wide. £1,700

19th century English lacquer box by Jennens and Bettridge. £170

Victorian mahogany games box of circa 1880, including chess and dominoes. £75

Early 19th century tea caddy with penwork decoration. £195

Small yew wood spice
box, crossbanded and
with double herring-
bone inlay, circa 1700.
£300

Sarcophagus shaped black
and gold lacquer box with
a scene of Chinese figures
in a landscape.   £20

Burr yew tree
tea caddy,
circa 1830. £25

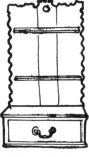

Early 19th century
lacquer games box
with six lidded
boxes and nine
trays.   £70

George I oak
and walnut
spoon rack,
26in. high.
          £185

Table square spice box
with named sectioned
interior, circa 1840. £34

19th century Indonesian
casket inlaid with bone,
20in. long.   £110

Coromandel wood
toilet box with
Sheffield Plate
fittings.   £90

Rosewood and ivory
cigar box, circa 1840.
          £38

CADDIES AND BOXES

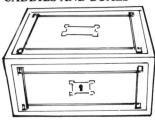

Mahogany brass bound Regency writing box. £38

One of a pair of Tole green chestnut vases and covers, 12in. high, circa 1800. £120

Early Georgian silver mounted caddy covered in shagreen. £275

George III shagreen cased apothecary's chest, circa 1760. £175

Early 19th century Japanese lacquer inro by Shibata Zeshin, 4¾in. long. £7,000

Mid 19th century English kingwood and mother-of-pearl bombe liqueur cabinet, 11 x 13½in. £340

Late 18th century mahogany knife-box with ornate brass keyhole escutcheon. £105

19th century mahogany specimen cabinet of six drawers, with boxwood string inlay, 16½in. wide. £60

Silver pipe case with engraved foliate decoration, Birmingham 1903. £65

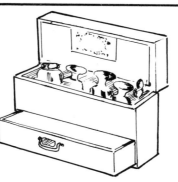

Late 18th century
mahogany knife-
box.   £65

Georgian apothecary's box
in mahogany with fitted
drawer, circa 1810.   £245

Mahogany inlaid
Art Nouveau
tobacco cabinet,
circa 1900. £35

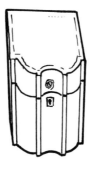

French Empire ormolu
and mother-of-pearl
necessaire casket, with
musical box.   £460

Georgian mahogany
fitted knife-box,
circa 1790.   £110

A good 18th century
French papier mache
writing box with
fitted interior. £125

18th century
Scandinavian
marriage box.
      £400

Small, Victorian tooled
leather stationery box
with fitted interior.£20

A good five case black
lacquered inro signed
Inagawa.   £375

CADDIES AND BOXES

18th century brass coin-opening tobacco box, 9½in. long. £130

An English tin container, in the form of a commode chest, circa 1890-1910. £15

Art Nouveau smoker's cabinet with brass facings, circa 1920, 1ft. 9in. high. £38

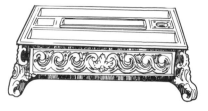

Indian ivory and ebony chess and backgammon board. £620

Louis XV ormolu encrier with brass inlaid ebony frieze, 1ft. 11in. wide. £2,000

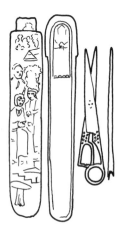

Victorian papier mache spectacle case with pewter decoration. £8

Persian lacquered pen box. £350

Lacquer pen case in the style of Ali Quli Jabbadar. £7,200

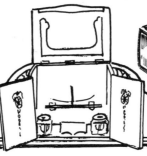

Rare George II palissander wood tea caddy, 6¾in. high by 11in. wide. £380

Oak inlaid stationery box, circa 1905. £33

Unusual enamelled silver box in the form of an outsize matchbox, London 1905. £420

18th-19th century papier mache Qalamdan, Persian, 9½in. long.£900

French miniature musical box in tortoiseshell case. £460

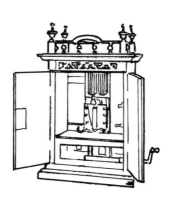

Victorian, Chinese style, tin tea caddy. £6

Edwardian smoker's cabinet Alexandra disc musical box. £620

18th century oak candle box with sliding front, 16in. high. £80

CAMERAS

A whole plate model of a field camera by Rouch of the Strand, circa 1887. £175

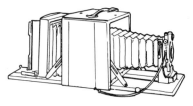

American Folmer & Schwing 'graphic' camera, circa 1920. £65

Brass bound Ross stereoscopic camera, circa 1870. £700

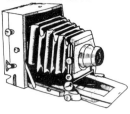

Quarter-plate camera by J. Lancaster, circa 1893. £60

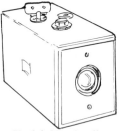

Kodak No. 1 roll film camera in black leather case, 1888. £1,300

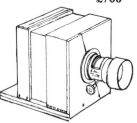

A sliding-box Daguerreo type camera, circa 1850. £780

Early sliding-box wet-type or Daguerreo type camera, circa 1855. £640

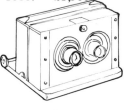

Smith, Beck and Beck achromatic stereoscope, 1860's, sold with cards. £130

Square bellows tail-board, 5 x 5 wet-plate Daguerreo type, about 1850. £700

London Stereoscopic Co., whole plate camera, circa 1890.£85

J. Lizars 'Challenge' stereoscopic camera, circa 1900. £550

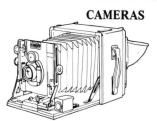

Very early Daguerreo type camera by Clarke, Strand, circa 1841. £2,200

Mahogany brass bellows camera by the Tella Camera Co., circa 1890.£30

Houghton Ltd., 'Sanderson' hand camera, circa 1910. £48

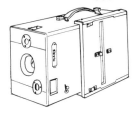

19th century mahogany and brass dry plate camera engraved 'Patent Thornton Pickard'.£100

Stirn's small waistcoat detective camera, in brass, second model, circa 1888. £400

Mars detective camera, 5 x 4½ x 10in., German, circa 1895. £150

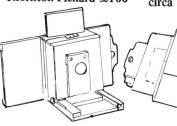

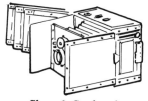

Rare multiple image camera by Billcliff of Manchester, circa 1880. £250

Shew & Co. hand camera, English, circa 1910. £85

Sanderson hand camera. £34

Rare Johnson pantoscopic camera, circa 1860. £3,200

Swiss compass camera, 2½ x 2¼ x 1¼in., circa 1940. £300

CAR MASCOTS

Red Ashay's bird in flight. £195

Golfing mascot by Desmo. £20

Flying eagle by Desmo. £20

Old Bill by Bruce Bairnsfather. £45

Bentley mascot. £230

Kingfisher enamelled mascot.£95

Telco Pup car mascot. £100

Chromium plated Mercury.£30

Chromium plated Minerva. £100

Spirit of Ecstasy mascot. £80

Winged Maiden, car mascot. £50

Lalique cockerels head.£320

Cockatoo by Bour-cart. £30

Nickel plated Flying Boat.£55

Lalique Seagull in Flight. £100

Lalique falcon's head.£80

Brass Astor car mascot. £25

Lalique St. Christopher. £220

Lalique Falcon mascot. £400

Snipe car mascot. £22

Lalique Vitesse mascot. £220

Lalique Dragonfly mascot. £375

Lalique Spirit of the Wind. £250

Nickel plated Minerva mascot.   £85

CARVED WOOD

17th century carved oak panel, 30 x 9in. £65

Complete set of wooden skittles, circa 1875. £12

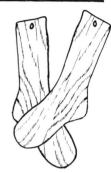

A pair of wooden sock stretchers. £5

18th century carved fruitwood nut-crackers. £10

Early 20th century English polychromed carved wood fairground galloper, 2ft. 10in. wide. £100

Early Flemish painted carved wood figure, 25in. high. £550

19th century Buddha decorated with gold lacquer, paste and mirror glass. £300

Early 19th century lacquered panel in Indian red and gilt, 63 x 33in. £780

19th century carved, bear pipe rack, 11in. tall. £15

Chinese lacquer
figure of Weng
Chong, 36in.
high.   £950

19th century German wooden
dolls in a shoe, 5.5cm. high.£260

A Malay carved
wood kris stand,
18in. high. £70

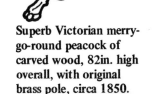

Late 16th/early 17th
century carved wood
and gilt gesso figure
of St. George.£1,150

Superb Victorian merry-
go-round peacock of
carved wood, 82in. high
overall, with original
brass pole, circa 1850.
          £475

Elm bellows with brass
centre decoration piece,
25in. long, circa 1790.
          £35

17th century Flemish
carving of a young
man, 25in. high,
circa 1620.   £475

Maori carved wood
present box, 5½in.
long.   £1,500

16th century carved
oak caryatid, 31in.
high.   £185

CARVED WOOD

Carved wood figure of Eliah and the ravens, 9in. high. £16

Carved wood Malay kris stand, 21in. high. £34

Tlingit mask representing a hawk. £500

Victorian wooden paper knife with floral decoration. £1.50p.

Finely carved pinewood cockerel, circa 1820, 18in. diameter. £165

Victorian transfer printed wooden scent bottle case. £8

Walnut octagonal bowl, 12in. diam. £29

Yoruba figure, 9½in. tall, of mother and child. £4,840

Rare wood drum with sharkskin covering, 11½in. high. £62,000

Wood canoe stern ornament from the Taranaki district, 56in. high. £38,000

Ekoi wood and hide headdress. £400

Scandinavian wooden tankard with inscribed and dated silver plaque, 1743. £300

18th century carved wood angel. £820

Japanese carved wood figure of a man holding a shoe, 53cm. high. £54

Zombo wood fetish figure, 23in. tall. £3,250

A good late 17th century German carved oak figure, 3ft. 7in. high. £850

Maori figure, the face carved with Moko patterns, 14in. high. £5,400

South Cameroon wooden reliquary figure. £28,000

CARVED WOOD

Carved oak sternboard from the boat of an 18th century Dutch flagship, 33in. wide. £540

New Guinea Sepic River wood mask, 18in. high. £46

Hand carved beech grain shovel. £18

Carved walnut figure group of two cavaliers, 41in. high. £510

Late 19th century Arabian blackamoor figure. £42

Late 19th century Arabian blackamoor figure, 36in. tall. £38

Oak cider jug, with oval body, 13in. high. £260

Early Nigerian wood carving of twin figures, 11¾in. high. £450

Mid 18th century carved giltwood bracket. £500

Carved wooden begging-
bowl.   £260

19th century
turned wood
goblet.   £14

Carved wooden
native food hook.
                £100

A Bali carved wood
kris stand, 28in.
high.   £150

Malay kris stand,
17in. high.   £75

19th century papier
mache figure of a
man smoking a pipe,
10in. high.   £15

Fine George II
carved pinewood
wall bracket, 1ft. 8in.
high with later marble
shelf.   £450

Early Nigerian wood carving
of an ancestral figure, 15¾in.
high.   £600

17th century Spanish
carved wood and pain-
ted polychrome reli-
gious group, 19in.
high.   £3,000

BELLEEK

A lobed oval tureen stand, moulded with hunting scenes and with gilt scroll and trellis work, 14½in. diameter. £160

One of a pair of First Period Belleek menu holders. £100

Belleek basket, circa 1880, 2½in. high, 5in. wide. £35

Rare Belleek figure of a tinker woman, her clothes sparsely tinted with yellow. £135

Early Belleek basket with lattice work side and a handle of entwined branches, 11in. wide. £90

Belleek spill vase, the fluted cornucopia with a bronzed putto kneeling at the foot. £260

Large circular dish, 15¼in. diameter, moulded and outlined in brown with a dragon in the centre. £100

Second period Belleek jardiniere, 11in. high. £110

An attractive Belleek lattice work basket. £65

One of a pair of kidney shaped Bloor Derby dessert dishes, 10in. diameter. £540

Bloor Derby floral encrusted bough pot and cover. £315

One of a pair of Bloor Derby dessert dishes on scroll feet, 11½in. diam. £460

One of a pair of Bloor Derby dessert dishes, 9¼in. £140

Bloor Derby figure of John Liston as Paul Pry, by Samuel Keys, late 19th century, 5¾in. high. £100

One of a set of three Bloor Derby meat plates, 10¼in. diam. £280

One of a pair of Bloor Derby sauce tureens, covers and stands, 8½in. wide. £740

One of three Bloor Derby pudding plates, 8in. diam. £500

Bloor Derby soup tureen, cover and stand, 15in. overall. £380

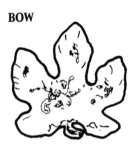

Bow leaf dish formed as a maple leaf with stalk handle. £250

One of a pair of Bow figures of a stag and doe, 4in. high and 3¾in. high, 1754-56. £950

Bow figure of a gold-finch, anchor and dagger period, 5½in. high. £400

.Very rare Bow figure of a cook, 6in. high, about 1755-60.£750

Pair of Bow Italian comedy figures of Harlequin and Columbine, 7¼in. and 7½in. high, about 1765. £380

Bow figure of The Doctor in the white, 6¼in. high, 1755-60. £300

Bow figure of Winter, 5¼in. high, about 1755-60. £170

Rare Bow powder-blue pot and cover, 6in. high, about 1760-62.£200

Rare Bow figure of a toper in the white, 6¼in. high, about 1755-60. £250

Attractive Bow figure of a Turk, 6¼in. high, about 1756-58.   £400

Rare Bow plate of octagonal shape, 8¼in. diam., about 1755-60.   £95

Bow figure of a 'Dismal' hound, 3½in. high, circa 1754-56.   £1,500

Early Bow figure of a shepherdess, 10¾in. high, 1755-58.   £230

Pair of marked Bow figures, 'The New Dancers'.   £625

Bow figure of a nun, 5½in. high, 1755-60.   £150

Rare Bow figure of a woodcutter, 5¾in. high, about 1760-65.   £660

Attractive Bow mug, 5in. high, about 1755-60.   £100

Rare Bow figure of Hearing, 6in. high, about 1755.   £90

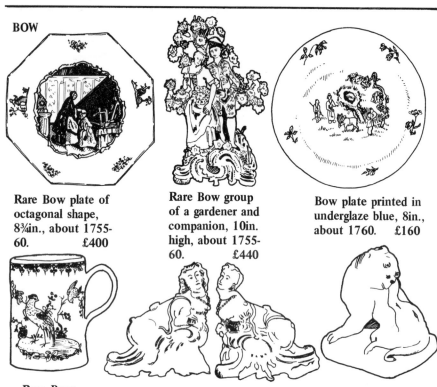

Rare Bow plate of octagonal shape, 8¾in., about 1755-60.   £400

Rare Bow group of a gardener and companion, 10in. high, about 1755-60.   £440

Bow plate printed in underglaze blue, 8in., about 1760.   £160

Rare Bow mug, about 1770, 4¾in. high. £230

Pair of Bow Sphinxes, 5in., about 1750-51.   £140

Rare Bow figure of a pug, 3½in., 1750-55. £300

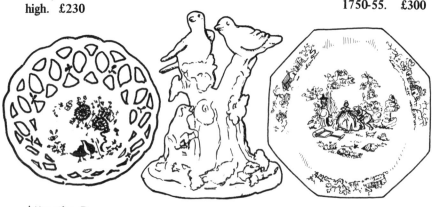

Attractive Bow basket of small size, 5in. diam., about 1760-65.   £280

Rare Bow bird group in the white, 5½in. high, 1755-60. £120

Octagonal Bow deep dish, 9in., about 1756.   £160

One of a pair of commemorative Bristol delft plates, 1760, 9in. diameter. £230

Bristol blue and white delft tankard. £2,200

Bristol or Brislington 'blue-dash' charger showing Adam and Eve, 13½in. diam. £170

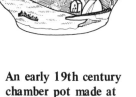

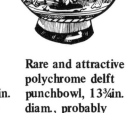

An early 19th century chamber pot made at the Bristol pottery. £66

Rare pair of Bristol figures of Autumn and Winter, 10¾in. high, about 1773-74. £940

Rare and attractive polychrome delft punchbowl, 13¾in. diam., probably Bristol, about 1710. £580

18th century Bristol pear shaped mug with floral decoration. £200

Fine Bristol teapot and cover, 6in. high, about 1775. £360

Rare Champion's Bristol teabowl and saucer, about 1775. £380

BURMANTOFT

Burmantoft vase, about 1885, painted by 'L.K.', 8½in. high.£110

Late Victorian high necked Burmantoft pottery vase. £25

Burmantoft vase, about 1885, painted by 'L.K.', 9¾in. high.£110

CANTON

19th century Canton garden seat, 18¾in. high.   £250

Porcelain body Canton decorated teapot or water-pot.   £28

One of a pair of late 19th century Canton porcelain garden seats, 18½in. high.   £1,900

Large Canton porcelain vase in famille rose enamels, 25½in. high, circa 1840.£500

Pair of Cantonese vases, 13in. high.   £130

One of a pair of late 19th century Canton porcelain vases in famille rose enamels, 22¼in. high. £1,150

One of a pair of
Cantonese vases.
£725

Louis XV ormolu mounted
Canton enamel bowl deco-
rated in gilt, 6in. high.
£1,000

One of a pair
of Cantonese
vases.   £400

Small Cantonese
vase.   £240

Canton porcelain bowl in vivid
famille rose enamels from the
second half of the 19th century,
18¾in. dia.   £350

One of a pair of
Cantonese vases
34½in. high. £2,700

CAPODIMONTE

Extremely rare Capodimonte
Commedia Dell'Arte group of the
Harlequin and two other figures by
Giuseppe Gricci dated around 1750.
£32,000

Rare Capodimonte figure by
Giuseppe Gricci, circa 1745.£16,000

CAUGHLEY

Victorian Caughley jug with floral decoration. £45

Rare Caughley hyacinth pot, 8in. high, about 1780-85. £380

Rare Caughley beaker, 4in. high, about 1785-90. £100

A fine Victorian blue and white Caughley cup and saucer decorated with flowers. £25

Teapot from a late 18th century Caughley tea and coffee service. £200

CHELSEA

Pair of Chelsea leaf dishes, 8in., raised anchor mark, 1750-53. £420

Chelsea double scent bottle, 7.8cm., about 1765. £160

Chelsea bonbonniere in the form of a fruit basket, 5.2cm. wide, circa 1760. £150

Rare Chelsea figure of a peasant, 7½in. high, about 1756. £150

Mid 18th century Chelsea strawberry leaf sauceboat with brown anchor mark. £375

Chelsea coloured acanthus teabowl, 1747-49. £350

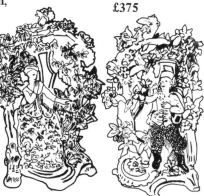

Rare Chelsea figure of a monkey musician, 6in. high, about 1756. £300

Rare pair of Chelsea arbour groups, 8½in. high, 1756-59. £800

Rare Chelsea figure of a monkey 5½in. high, about 1756. £150

Rare Chelsea group of Ganymede and the eagle, 7¼in. high, about 1751. £800

Chelsea figure of a shepherd, 12in. high, about 1765. £360

Rare Chelsea group of Madonna and Child, 8½in. high, about 1755. £1,250

CHELSEA

Chelsea bonbonniere
of a shepherd boy,
2in. high, about
1760.   £200

Unusually decorated
Chelsea dish, raised
anchor mark, 1750-
53.   £420

Chelsea bonbonniere
of large size, 2¼in.
high, about 1760,
gold anchor period.
£190

Rare Chelsea set of the four elements, 8in. to 8½in., gold anchor marks,
about 1760.   £1,000

Chelsea Derby
figure of a young
girl with Cupid
piercing her arm.
£200

Rare Chelsea figure of a
lion, 6in. high, raised
anchor mark, 1749-52.
£210

Chelsea scent bottle
of a fox and a
crow, 3¼in. high,
about 1758-60.£460

Chelsea beaker with
flared rim, 10cm.
high, gold anchor
mark, about 1765.
£120

Pair of Chelsea white
figures of sphinxes,
incised triangle mark.
£1,050

Rare 18th century
Chelsea sauceboat
decorated with sprigs
of flowers.   £425

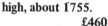

Two rare Chelsea figures modelled
by Joseph Willems, 11½in. and
11¼in. high, about 1758.   £2,500

Rare Chelsea double
scent bottle with
gilt mounts, 3in.
high, about 1755.
£460

Chelsea bon-
bonniere, about
1760, 2¼in.
high.   £400

Chelsea coffee cup and
saucer, gold anchor
mark, 1760-65.   £140

Fine English
porcelain scent
bottle, 3½in.
high, about
1749-54.£1,000

CH'IEN LUNG

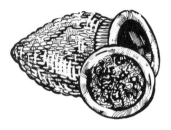

Ch'ien Lung period tankard enamelled in famille rose, 5in. high.   £85

Gourd cricket cage from the Ch'ien Lung period with tortoiseshell lid set in rosewood rim.   £275

Ch'ien Lung blue and white tea caddy complete with lid.   £80

Ch'ien Lung famille rose octagonal plate, 8½in. wide.   £480

A good Ch'ien Lung period porcelain duck tureen.   £3,400

Ch'ien Lung period enamelled teapot stand with floral decoration.   £140

Canton enamel Ch'ien Lung double gourd vase.   £80

Ch'ien Lung period famille rose charger with floral decoration.   £220

Ch'ien Lung period famille rose bottle with floral decoration.   £340

One of a pair of Ch'ien Lung period 'Tobacco Leaf' sauce boats. £140

Ch'ien Lung period famille rose teapot and stand. £390

A good Ch'ien Lung period 'Tobacco Leaf' teapot. £475

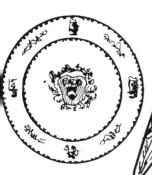

One of a set of fourteen Chinese armorial plates, Ch'ien Lung. £980

One of a pair of Ch'ien Lung period figures of pheasants, 37.2cm. high. £8,900

Ch'ien Lung famille rose plate with floral decoration, 9in. diameter. £120

One of a pair of Canton enamel baluster vases and covers, 55cm. high, Ch'ien Lung sealmark and period. £3,400

Ch'ien Lung period helmet shaped jug. £210

Cantonese famille rose baluster shaped vase, with domestic scenes depicted within panels, 18½in. high. £450

Attractive Chinese export porcelain soup plate, 9in. diameter. £88

Mid 19th century Chinese wine vessel of stoneware with metal inlay. £20

Porcelain Yen-Yen vase, 17¾in. high, K'ang Hsi period. £720

Tou ts'ai wine cup decorated in blue, red, yellow and pale green, with six character mark of Ch'eng Hua. £44,000

Yung Cheng famille rose porcelain plate decorated with blossom, fish and flowers, 8¾in. diameter. £190

19th century Chinese porcelain jardiniere decorated in enamels, 12¼in. high. £260

19th century Chinese porcelain garden seat, 17¾in. high. £340

Kuan-Yao compressed jar, 4¼in. high. £70

Late 18th century Mei Ping blue and white blossom vase, 18in. high. £925

One of a pair of blue and white porcelain bottle vases, Chinese, transitional period, circa 1655, 10¼in. high. **£900**

Chinese porcelain famille rose punch bowl, 10½in. diameter. **£340**

Chinese export tea caddy in blue and white, about 1790, 5½in. high. **£45**

Crouching,Chinese biscuit, leopard, almost 21in. high. **£38,000**

Isnik pottery dish, circa 1600. **£230**

Early 19th century Chinese censer with wood and jade lid. **£70**

Famille rose porcelain plate, 8¾in. diameter, decorated with blossom, insects and plants, late 18th century. **£195**

18th century figure of a Dutch girl in Chinese porcelain, 16in. high. **£4,200**

One of a pair of 19th century Chinese famille jaune barrel garden seats. **£430**

CHINESE

Victorian Chinese design tea canister. £45

One of two Chinese cinnabar boxes and covers, circa 1900. £80

Chinese Buddha. £260

One of a pair of late 17th century famille verte porcelain figures. £420

One of a pair of famille verte brushwashers and water droppers. £600

One of a pair of late Louis XV ormolu mounted Chinese vases, 11in. high. £2,600

Oviform blue and white Chinese vase with lid, circa 1859, 1ft. 2½in. high. £38

Famille verte cylindrical jardiniere, 24in. diam. £470

Mid 17th century Chinese blue and white porcelain vase, 8¼in. high. £230

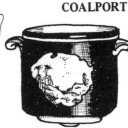

A scarce Coalport cup and saucer with 'bleu de roi' ground. £300

Early 19th century Coalport jardiniere, 6¾in. high. £85

One of a pair of Coalport porcelain jardinieres by Arthur Perry, circa 1900. £480

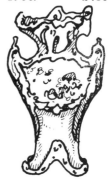

Coalport 'bleu du roi' porcelain vase and cover, signed Chivers, 10in. high. £250

An unusual late 19th century pink ground Coalport tea caddy, 6in. high. £350

Hand painted Coalport vase in rococo style, circa 1840. £175

COPELAND

Caramaninian Copeland and Garrett plate, circa 1840. £28

19th century Copeland cigar box with a fish and netting decoration, 7in. high. £35

Copeland cream jug, circa 1860, 6in. high. £14

DANIEL

Rare H. & R. Daniel armorial dessert service, about 1827, 13 pieces.£700

DELFT

One of a pair of late 19th century Dutch delft vases, 8in. high. £60

London Delft 'Adam and Eve' charger, 13½in. diam., early 18th century. £600

Rare mid 18th century Delft vase painted in blue, 6¾in. high. £200

Dutch delft plaque of oval shape, 16½ x 13¼in. £55

One of a pair of English delft meat chargers, 20in. long. £375

Late 18th century London delft poly-chrome flask, 4¾in. high. £210

English delft posset pot, 3½in., circa 1680-90, either Bristol or Brislington. £160

Early 18th century English delft blue and white dish, 10½in. diam. £45

Early 18th century Lambeth delft bowl decorated with birds and shrubs, 10in. diameter. £260

Dutch delft lozenge plaque, 13in. x 15¼in. £160

Delft double gourd vase. £135

One of a pair of Dutch delft tobacco jars, early 18th century, 22.5cm. high. £450

One of a pair of Delft plates, 1701, 9in. diam. £200

A pair of Dutch delft polychrome oval bowls and covers surmounted by a dappled stag and hinds, 14.5cm. wide. £580

Dutch polychrome Delft charger, 13¾in. diameter. £240

Rare documentary
Derby blue and
white bowl and
cover, 7½in. diam.,
1762. £420

A rare pair of Derby
figures of goldfinches,
4in. and 3½in., about
1760. £220

Rare Derby sporting
mug probably painted
by Cuthbert Lawton,
4½in. high, 1820-30.
£200

Early Derby figure
of a shepherdess,
10¼in. high, 1756-
60. £150

Pair of Victorian Derby urn
shaped vases, 14in. high, with
floral decoration. £150

Royal Crown
Derby pink
ground ewer.
£15

Rare Derby figure of
a young man with an
eagle and a telescope,
patch marks. £250

Rare Derby butter
tub and cover, 5¼in.
long, about 1760,
cracked. £130

Derby figure of 'The
Farmer', 6¾in. high,
about 1765, repaired.
£160

Derby ice pail, cover and liner, 9½in. high, about 1790, in the manner of William Billingsley.   £360

Pair of Derby 'Mansion House' dwarfs, late 18th century, 7in. high.   £380

Derby figure of Leda and the Swan, 10½in. high.   £185

One of a pair of late 19th century Crown Derby vases by Leroy, 8½in. high.   £450

Pair of Derby candlestick figures of 'Liberty and Matrimony', circa 1770.   £550

Derby figure of John Quinn as Falstaff.   £150

Early Derby figure of Diana the huntress, circa 1765, 10½in. high.   £190

Stevenson and Hancock Derby plate with basket weave border.   £250

Rare Derby blue and white coffee pot and cover, 8¾in. high, about 1765-80.   £280

DERBY

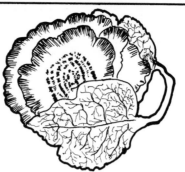

Early Derby group representing Sight, 20.3cm. high, circa 1755. £3,800

One of a pair of early Derby peony dishes, 8¼in., about 1755-60. £580

Large Bloor Derby vase with landscape decoration in gilded borders, 23½in. tall. £375

Early Derby figure of Spring from a set of the Seasons, 4½in. high, about 1758. £210

Fine pair of Derby named landscape plaques, late 18th century, 9in. £6?0

Rare Derby green ground cabaret, painted by George Robertson, circa 1800. £3,400

One of a pair of Derby dishes, 9¾in., about 1820-30. £220

A good Derby cream jug, with floral decoration. £140

Rare Derby blue and white strawberry bowl, cover and stand, about 1760. £260

Rare creamware teapot and cover, 4in. high, probably Derbyshire, about 1770-80. £220

Pair of white 'dry edge' Derby figures of goats, 4in. tall, about 1751. £460

One of a pair of Derby, covered ice pails, 11in. high. £1,100

.One of a pair of plaques, probably Derby, early 19th century, 10¼in. x 8¾in. £520

Pair of Derby figures of Liberty and Matrimony, 11¾in. and 12in. high, about 1770. £350

DOULTON

Self pouring
teapot made by
Doulton, 1886,
9in. high.   £24

Doulton silicon 'leatherware'
jug and matching pair of
mugs, London 1902.   £60

Small, Royal
Doulton figure
of a kingfisher.
£12

DRESDEN

Pair of late Dresden candelabra
figures, 10in. high.   £135

Pair of Dresden two-branch candelabra, A.R. Mark, 17½in. high. £260

One of a pair of
Helena Wolfsohn
Dresden covered
vases.   £340

Mid 19th century Dresden
shell vase.   £190

Dresden figure of a
Buddha with nodding
head and hands, 11½in.
high.   £300

Late 18th century
shoe bonbonniere,
2½in. high.   £70

Pot lid 'Strathfield
Say', with base.
£140

Daniel cream jug,
circa 1835.   £65

Rare porcelain double-handled cup,
cover and stand, 5¾in. high, 1760-70.
£680

Rogers pottery coffee
pot decorated with
Chinese scenes, 12in.
high.   £44

One of a pair of
spirit barrels
moulded with the
Royal Arms and
vines.   £38

Pair of Victorian figures depicting
street traders, 9in. high.   £480

One of a pair of
Coalbrookdale
baluster vases,
10in. high.   £44

ENGLISH

Late Victorian pottery 'Quick Cooker'.   £5

Small English porcelain mug with loop handle, 2½in. high, 1765-70.   £200

English porcelain bowl from the Bodeham service, 6in., 1765-70.   £260

Good and early porcelain creamboat with angular handle, 4¼in. long, 1752-5.   £190

Parian bust of Queen Victoria, signed Noble, 2ft. high.   £250

Late 18th century Yorkshire group of a cow and milkmaid, 7in. high.   £260

English blue-scale porcelain dish, 11½in. long, circa 1770-75.   £220

19th century pot pourri vase and cover, 24in. tall.   £620

Early 19th century porcelain ashet with floral decoration.   £200

Creamboat of flared form and scroll handle, 4¼in. long, 1755-60. £300

Victorian pottery butter dish. £10

Zebra pattern Rogers blue and white charger, circa 1810, marked. £58

English porcelain teapot cover and stand, 6in. high, circa 1770. £190

Doulton vase, 28in. high. £200

Late Victorian bone china milk jug, 5in. high. £6

Hexagonal English porcelain spoon tray, 6¼in. long, circa 1770. £500

Tiled panel of sixteen square tiles, 24in. square overall. £1,700

Late 19th century pottery ewer, 10½in. high. £5

Victorian majolica
sardine dish by George
Jones.   £50

Victorian pottery
vase with floral
decoration, 9in.
high.   £4

Late 19th century blue
and white octagonal
teapot.   £8

English porcelain teabowl, coffee
cup and saucer with pencilled
decoration, circa 1760.   £200

Rare English teacup, coffee cup
and saucer of fluted form, open
crescent marks, about 1770. £400

Dessert dish of London
decoration, 11¾in. diam.,
1770-80.   £150

Rare and early cream
jug, 4in. high, about
1755.   £660

English porcelain dessert
dish of fluted oval form,
10½in. diam., about 1770.
                £680

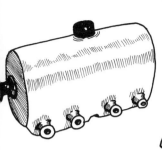

Earthenware nine position pig foster mother. £14

Victorian fairing 'Taking dessert'. £150

Small, late Victorian pottery butter dish by George Jones. £30

Rare English armorial teabowl, coffee cup and saucer by Hancock, circa 1760. £380

English porcelain teacup, coffee cup and saucer, open crescent marks, circa 1770-80. £210

Fine English porcelain dessert dish of fluted oval form, 10½in. diam., circa 1770. £640

English medieval pitcher of globular form, 8½in. high. £220

Attractive English porcelain spoon tray, 5¾in. long, circa 1760-65. £880

Thomas Johnson
novelty ash tray
in swan form,
London 1882.
£130

Dated Bideford bird
bath, 1725, with
pie-crust rim, 15in.
diameter.   £580

Octagonal Victorian
commemorative
plate.   £10

Fine English porcelain
scent bottle, 3½in.
high, about 1749-54.
              £1,000

Rare Plymouth teapot
and cover, 6½in. high,
about 1768-70. £340

Fine Goss figure of
William of Wykeham
on circular base,
8in. high.   £700

Ruskin drip glaze
vase, circa 1930,
9¾in. high. £25

17th century charger
showing William of
Orange.   £980

Large Mason's
ironstone pot
pourri vase and
cover, 26in.
high.   £195

Unusual London enamel inkwell, 1¾in. high, circa 1760. £120

Early 20th century Ridgway's transfer printed plate. £4

Small pot lid with base, showing an Arctic expedition. £130

Rare smearglazed coffee pot and cover of Castleford type, 12½in. high, 1810-15. £260

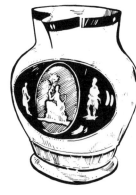

Large Turner biscuit jug, circa 1800, 8¼in. high. £110

19th century moulded blue glaze jug depicting the young Victoria. £75

Martinware oviform vase decorated with tiger lilies and butterflies, about 1890, 40cm. high. £130

English porcelain plate with fluted rim, 7in. diameter, 1765-70. £85

Candle extinguisher with naturally coloured face, 1885. £160

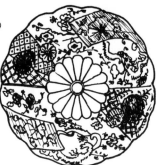

Fine English porcelain dessert dish, 9in. diam., open crescent mark, about 1770. £420

Victorian black glazed pottery water jug. £3

English porcelain deep plate in brocade pattern, 9¼in. diameter, circa 1765. £320

One of a pair of plates with fine fluted rims, 8½in. diameter, about 1770. £420

Rare English porcelain mug by Robert Hancock, 4½in. high, about 1760-65. £480

Rare English porcelain saucer decorated in London, blurred crossed swords and nine marks, 1770-75. £280

Rare English porcelain plate after an Imari original, 9in. diameter, circa 1760-65. £280

19th century Exeter pottery vase, 7in. tall. £4

Fine English circular basket by Robert Hancock, 7¾in. diam., about 1765. £300

Fine basket of circular shape with pierced sides, 6½in. diameter, about 1765.   £220

Blue and white coffee pot. £36

Plate with fluted wavy rim with scrollwork trellis, 7½in. diam., 1770-75.£150

Blue-dash 'Tulip' charger, 3in. high, circa 1700. £500

Blue and white lavatory pan, 'Niagara'.   £55

Porcelain plate with petal shaped rim, two shades of green, 8¾in. diameter, about 1770.   £120

Fine English porcelain fluted dessert dish, 8¾in., diameter, circa 1765.   £190

Fine English porcelain mug of cylindrical form, 5in. high, about 1770.   £800

Interesting English porcelain plate decorated with brocade pattern, 9in. diameter, circa 1765.£440

Sepia print by Robert Hancock on a teabowl and saucer, circa 1760. £170

Rare English porcelain teabowl and saucer in bright enamels, circa 1765. £200

Teacup and saucer in solid turquoise, crossed swords and nine marks, 1770-75. £85

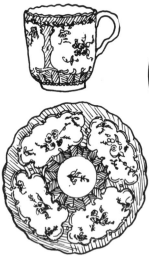

Unusual coffee cup and saucer of fluted form, script W marks, about 1770-75. £200

English teacup and saucer in solid green decoration, about 1770-75. £130

English porcelain tea-cup and saucer painted in famille rose, circa 1765-70. £420

Early 19th century
porcelain cup and
saucer, painted with
flowers.   £10

Porcelain beaker and
saucer in Quail pat-
tern, circa 17__ __.
                 £260

Rare English teabowl
and saucer, open
crescent marks,
about 1770.   £480

Rare teacup and saucer
decorated in London,
crossed swords and
nine marks, about
1770-75.   £210

Rare English porcelain
coffee cup and saucer,
circa 1770, in famille
rose palette.   £190

Teacup and saucer
by Sir Joshua Reynolds,
circa 1770.   £170

Victorian
commemorative
plate.   £22

Rare Astbury teapot
and cover, 4½in. high,
about 1740-50. £280

Round Victorian
commemorative
plate.   £30

Rare Ansbach figure
of a girl, 15.5cm.
high, about 1775.
          £520

Walton group of lambs,
circa 1800.   £36

Signed Absolon
creamware jug,
4½in. high, about
1790.   £100

Late 18th century
Toby jug, probably
Yorkshire, 10½in.
high.   £160

Powder blue and gold
covered tureen and stand
with flower finials. £225

Toby jug of The
Collier, 1770-80,
10in. high. £170

One of a pair of rare
Dublin delft vases,
late 18th century
3¾in.   £500

A large early 18th century
Marseille charger decorated
with a biblical scene. £400

Mid 18th century
Chantilly porcelain
jug with floral
decoration, 16.5cm.
high.   £400

A fine quality late
16th century beard-
ed man jug.   £420

Italian majolica drug
jar.   £60

Italian majolica drug
bottle, 8in. high,
circa 1560, made in
Venice.   £430

Schnelle from
Siegburg, about
1570.   £441

A fine Della Robbia majolica
dish decorated with a border
of stags.   £150

Early 17th century
Montelupo wet drug
jar, 9½in. high. £300

EUROPEAN

Faenza majolica dish decorated with a centaur. £130

Rare Doccia bust of the Roman Emperor Augustus, 1750-60, 51cm. high. £1,700

18th century Castelli plate, 24.2cm. diam. £480

Early 17th century Trapani waisted Albarello, 30.5cm. high. £380

Part of a 292 piece dinner service with the Arms of a Spanish family. £196,000

Vestal virgin by Antonio Corradini. £16,657

17th century Montelupo Albarello. £380

18th century faience vase, 29.5cm. high, probably Scandinavian. £240

17th century Caltagirone jar, 30.7cm. high. £350

'Cousin and Cousine'
a fairing group
mounted on a deco-
rated box.   £200

Royal Dux figure,
9in. long, 6in.
high.   £76

19th century faience
inkwell, 7½in. long.
                  £50

Rare documentary
Castel Durante
drug jar, 35cm.
high, 1562. £2,500

Late 19th century German
porcelain group of lovers,
9½in. high.   £160

A Furstenberg
vase.   £300

17th century
Venetian drug
jar.   £400

Urbino Istoriato
dish by Francesco
Xanto Avelli, 1532.
          £10,000

17th/18th century
North Italian
Albarello.   £360

EUROPEAN

Late 17th century German tin glazed vase, 11½ins. high. £260

Samson cup and saucer decorated in the Newhall style. £10

Berlin porcelain figure, 1837. £75

Boehm of Malvern porcelain group of song thrushes among crab apples, 17in. high. £1,134

Good, Louis XV ormolu mounted porphyry brule parfum, 1ft. 1in. high. £1,100

One of a pair of Louis XV ormolu and porcelain candelabra, 10in. high. £2,200

Louis XVI porcelain 'bleu du roi' porcelain lidded vase, 1ft. high. £450

One of a pair of Louis XV ormolu mounted, biscuit porcelain groups, 1ft. wide, signed Lagneau. £550

One of a pair of Louis XVI ormolu mounted 'bleu du roi' porcelain lidded vases, 1ft. high. £1,400

One of a pair of 19th century classical shaped urns and covers, 26in. high. £750

Late 19th century Continental porcelain cup and saucer. £5

Raeren jug with incised decoration and silver mount, 1580's. £220

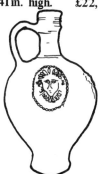

One of a pair of ormolu mounted Berlin porcelain vases, circa 1890, 41in. high. £22,000

Rare Louis XV ormolu, porcelain and lacquer bougeoir d'ecran, 9in. high. £1,800

Late 18th century German porcelain tankard of baluster shape, 30.5cm. £620

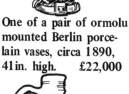

17th century Bellarmine jug with bearded mask in relief. £450

Rare Vincennes white chinoiserie group, circa 1745, 19in. wide. £38,000

One of a pair of Louis XVI ormolu and porphyry candelabra, 1ft.11¾in. high. £2,000

FRANKENTHAL

German porcelain
Frankenthal dog,
15.5cm. high.£850

Rare Frankenthal cabaret teaset, each
piece with panelled landscapes.£2,500

FULHAM

Mid 18th century
Fulham stoneware
mug.   £25

William de Morgan
lustre dish of the
late Fulham period.
                  £100

Rare Fulham
stoneware posset
pot, 17th century,
6¾in. high.   £450

GILES

Rare English teabowl
and saucer decorated
in the workshop of
James Giles, 1770-75.£720

Plate with fluted rim
decorated in the
workshop of James
Giles, 8¾in. diam.,
1765-75.   £200

Unusual teacup and
saucer decorated by
James Giles, crossed
swords and nine
marks, about 1775-
80.   £400

Goss wall pocket
of a cherub.   £85

Goss swan, 4.7in.
long.   £30

Porcelain lithophane
disc, 3½in. diam.,
by Goss.   £300

Goss oven, 3in. high.
£160

Goss mask of a knight.
£160

Goss porcelain model
of Shakespeare's
cottage, complete
with base, 4in. high.
£85

IMARI

Japanese Imari
porcelain vase
and cover, late
17th century,
15½in. high.
£480

Late 17th century Imari
porcelain 'Barber's Bowl',
10¾in. diameter.   £500

18th century Imari
porcelain vase with
ovoid shaped body,
16½in. high.   £440

IMARI

Imari style
jardiniere
and stand.
£700

JAPANESE

Late 18th century Imari
shallow bowl, 21½in. diam.
£1,950

Japanese Imari
floor vase.
£2,400

19th century Japanese
Satsuma ware teapot,
enamelled with flowers.
£3

One of a pair of Kyoto
earthenware vases, late
19th century, Japanese,
7¾in. high.   £220

18th century Arita
fish bowl. £1,250

Late 17th century
Japanese Arita dish,
55.7cm. diam.
£2,600

Japanese export blue
and white teapot and
cover by Makazu.£160

Late 19th century
Japanese porcelain
dish.   £3

A fine teabowl and saucer painted
in the Kakiemon palette, circa
1770.   £190

Late 17th century Kakiemon wine-
pot and cover of ovoid form . £160

Late 17th century
Kakiemon ewer
painted in red, blue
and green enamels.
          £13,000

Late 17th century
Japanese porcelain
bowl, Kakiemon,
24.3cm. diameter
          £42,000

Very fine early Kakiemon
bottle decorated in green
and blue enamel, late 17th
century, 28.6cm. high
          £20,000

K'ANG HSI

Late 19th century
famille verte fish-
tank in K'ang Hsi
style, 18in. diam.
          £540

K'ang Hsi enamelled
vase depicting a female
figure, 11in. high. £450

K'ang Hsi famille
verte plate, 9in.
diameter.   £150

K'ANG HSI

K'ang Hsi period hexagonal bowl with decorative interior band, 8in. diameter. £180

Famille rose dish of the K'ang Hsi period, 12in. diameter. £350

K'ang Hsi period enamelled tea caddy with bird and flower decoration. £200

Good K'ang Hsi period enamel plate with floral decoration. £120

K'ang Hsi period blue and white Yen Yen vase. £340

K'ang Hsi famille verte dish, 17½in. wide. £420

Blue and white K'ang Hsi period vase, 8½in. tall. £120

A famille verte porcelain teapot of the K'ang Hsi period, 4½in. tall. £420

Wu t'sai baluster vase, 10½in. high, early K'ang Hsi. £200

Small K'ang Hsi teabowl with floral decoration. £40

Blue and white double gourd porcelain vase from the K'ang Hsi period, 15¾in. high. £320

One of a pair of blue and white K'ang Hsi trencher salts. £140

One of a pair of Chinese Imari porcelain K'ang Hsi period plates, 9in. diameter. £150

K'ang Hsi period group of two boys, enamelled in colours, 27.5cm. high. £2,500

Chinese china saucer dish, K'ang Hsi period, 9in. diameter. £195

Baluster form porcelain vase of powder blue ground, K'ang Hsi period, 14¼in. high. £280

A large K'ang Hsi dish with tree decoration, 15½in. diameter. £250

One of a pair of famille verte jars and covers of the K'ang Hsi period, 12in. high. £1,050

Lambeth 'Tulip' charger with blue-dash rim, 13¼in. diam., about 1780. £400

Lambeth polychrome delft dish, 13in. diam., about 1720. £300

One of a pair of 18th century Lambeth delft blue and white plates, 8¾in. diam. £60

Commemorative Lambeth wet drug jar of globular form, 7½in., 1671. £280

Late 17th/early 18th century Lambeth ceramic 'pill' slab carrying the coat-of-arms of The Worshipful Society of Apothecaries. £1,200

Rare Lambeth delft posset pot and cover, 8in. high, 1710-30. £360

One of a set of four 18th century Lambeth delft blue and white plates, 9in. diam. £45

Late 17th/early 18th century shield shaped Lambeth ceramic 'pill' slab. £1,300

Rare Lambeth playing card plate, 8¾in. diam., about 1750. £850

Leeds creamware mug, 5in. high, about 1775-80. £110

Leeds creamware teapot and cover, 6in. high, about 1770. £100

Leeds pierced basket outlined in blue. £28

LIVERPOOL

Liverpool baluster jug, black transfer prints, 5¾in. high. £26

Liverpool blue and white meat dish, 14½in. £180

Liverpool creamware jug, decorated in blue, 8in. high. £32

One of a pair of Liverpool delft wall vases, about 1770. £150

Liverpool coffee pot and cover, 9¾in. high, 1772-75, Christian's factory. £440

One of a pair of Liverpool scent bottles, 3in. high, 1755-60. £380

Part of a set of
three Liverpool
tiles with Sadler
prints, 1758-60.
£120

One of two
Liverpool tiles
with Sadler
prints, 1758-
61.   £50

One of two
Liverpool tiles
with Sadler
prints, 1758-
61.   £50

Liverpool bowl printed
in lilac, 6in. diam.,
about 1755-69.   £200

Rare Liverpool
mug printed in
black enamel,
3¾in. high,
about 1768.
          £340

Liverpool punchbowl
of shallow form 9¼in.
diam., about 1775-80.
          £250

Part of a set of
seven Liverpool
tiles printed by
Sadler, 1765-75.
          £260

One of three
Liverpool tiles,
printed in
black, 1758-61.
          £120

One of a set of
four Liverpool
tiles printed by
Sadler, 1758-61.
          £170

One of two
Liverpool tiles
printed in
black, 1758-61.
£95

One of four
Liverpool tiles
printed in
black, 1758-61.
£130

One of three
Liverpool tiles
printed by
Sadler, 1758-
61.   £160

Rare Liverpool bowl,
4¾in., 1795-1800,
printed in lilac. £80

Liverpool mug
of bell shape,
6½in. high,
about 1760-65.
£200

Rare Liverpool vine
leaf pickle dish, 4in.,
about 1755-60.£220

One of a set of
four Liverpool
tiles printed in
black, 1765-75.
£150

One of a pair of
Liverpool plaques,
2½in. high, circa
1780, framed.
£150

One of four
Liverpool tiles
printed in
black by
Sadler, 1758-
61.   £220

LONGTON HALL

Longton Hall plate, 9½in. diam., about 1755. £200

Rare Longton Hall sauce-boat of oval shape, 8in., about 1758. £180

Longton Hall coffee cup, circa 1758-60. £50

Rare Longton Hall figure of a sportswoman, 7in. high, about 1758. £340

George V Coronation plate by Longton. £9.50

Rare Longton Hall group of a lady and gallant, 10¾in. high, 1758-60. £900

LOWESTOFT

Rare 'green-ground' Lowestoft teapot and cover, 6¼in. high, 1780-85. £65

Lowestoft porcelain figures of musicians, circa 1780-90, 17.8cm. high. £1,350

Lowestoft part tea service, 18 pieces, 1775-70. £240

Sunderland lustre-ware cup and saucer. £12

19th century Sunderland lustre jug with pictorial scene, 8½in. high. £45

Large Sunderland lustre-ware bowl depicting Newcastle's High Level Bridge.£52

Elaborate double-spouted kettle by Belleek, the spouts in copper lustre, on a dragon stand. £500

Sunderland lustre-ware pomade jar with circular base. £48

Copper lustre jug, circa 1825, coloured in brown and yellow. £38

Victorian lustre ware goblet with fern decoration, 6in. high. £8

Small early 19th century copper lustre mug depicting a coastal scene. £26

Rare jug of ovoid form, with pink lustre neck, probably Sunderland, about 1815. £320

MEISSEN

Early Meissen armorial plate, 9½in. diam., perfect condition. £600

Meissen figure of 'Feeling' by J. J. Kaendler, about 1765, 27cm. high. £400

19th century Meissen box and cover, 10¼in. wide, 7½in. high. £1,200

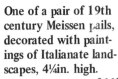

A pair of late Meissen ring dishes, the figures in period costume, each 6in. wide. £320

One of a pair of 19th century Meissen pails, decorated with paintings of Italianate landscapes, 4¼in. high. £660

Meissen tea caddy and cover, 10.5cm. high, about 1740, numeral 19 impressed. £280

Early 19th century Meissen three-branch candelabrum, 13in. high. £250

Meissen comport, magenta, gilt and white. £520

MEISSEN

Meissen part tea
and coffee service,
about 1750. £2,000

Meissen figure of a
jester, possibly by
Reinicke or
Kaendler.   £920

Meissen plate decorated
with sprigs of flowers
and a coat-of-arms. £600

19th century Meissen
pot pourri vase and
cover, of lobed pear
form, 24in. high. £620

Porcelain figures of a lion and
a lioness, by J. J. Kaendler,
12½in. wide.   £15,000

Meissen porcelain
figure, 11in. high.
                £2,000

Late Meissen figure
of Europa and the
Bull.   £220

Meissen tea caddy
and cover, 10.5cm.
high, about 1725.
                £850

Pair of late Meissen ring dishes, 6in. wide.   £240

Cylindrical Meissen
tankard with Augsburg
silver gilt cover, 5¾in.
high.   £6,000

Pair of late Louis XV ormolu and Meissen
porcelain candelabra, 1ft. 4½in. high.
                                      £1,800

Selection from a late Meissen service.   £4,800

MEISSEN

MEISSEN

Mid 18th century Meissen jug and saucer decorated with sprays of flowers in purple.   £500

Mid 18th century Meissen cup and saucer decorated with figures and scenic views.   £400

MING

A Ming quatrefoil vase.   £650

Provincial Ming stone-ware pot with four lugs, 10in. high.   £85

A small late Ming baluster vase.   £245

MINTON

A small pair of mid 19th century Minton cachepots.   £70

A fine Minton cup and saucer decorated with scenes in the Watteau style.   £160

MINTON

A fine Minton majolica game dish, circa 1870, 13½in. long. £250

Mid 19th century pink ground Minton plate with central panel of birds, by J. Wareham. £60

Late 19th century Minton coffee can. £26

A large and important flower encrusted Minton vase. £850

A superb mid 19th century Minton boat shaped vase. £750

Minton vase and cover, 20in. tall. £1,000

Minton pate-sur-pate vase. £775

19th century Minton parian group of a male and female figure. £40

Mid 19th century Minton garden seat, 1ft. 6in. high. £160

148

Mid 19th century
Minton majolica
teapot, 5in. high.
£30

Large Minton Parian
bust of The Duke Of
Wellington.   £60

Minton faience game
pie dish, liner and
cover, 14¼in.   £70

NEWHALL

Rare Newhall tea and coffee service, 1795-1805.£400

Part of a Newhall
tea service, twenty-
eight pieces,
1795-1805. £210

Part of a Newhall tea and
coffee service.   £240

Newhall jug,
circa 1787.
£39

149

ORIENTAL

Oriental figure of a geisha girl with dog. £310

Rear view of Chinese Yung Cheng period saucer dish, one of a pair, circa 1723-36.
£500

Rare Namban figure of a bishop carrying a crozier and rosary, 12in. tall. £300

Pair of large unglazed buff pottery figures, T'ang dynasty, 32in. high.
£4,000

Pair of famille rose garden seats, 20in. high. £1,250

Oriental pottery jar, 11in. high.
£680

Chinese T'ang dynasty pottery horse with dwarf riding. £3,800

Kinkozan earthenware vase, 17in. high, circa 1870. £660

Set of Prattware figures of the seasons, approximately 9in. high, about 1780. £400

Pratt moustache cup and saucer, cup 3in. diameter. £70

Prattware dessert plate, 'The Truant'. £65

ROCKINGHAM

Rockingham miniature teaset, about 1831-42. £250

ROCKINGHAM

Rare Rockingham Toby jug and cover of the 'Snuff Taker', 7½in. high, late 19th century. £95

Rare Rockingham plate, 9½in. diam., 1826-30, printed griffin mark in iron red. £680

Rockingham figure of a small boy, 5in. high, 1826-30. £300

Rockingham pot-pourri vase and cover, 10in. high, about 1831-42. £500

Rockingham solitaire teaset, griffin mark in puce, about 1731-42. £780

Rare Rockingham figure of a milkmaid, 7½in. high, about 1826-30. £200

Rockingham 'named view' potpourri vase and cover, 13¾in. high, 1831-42. £400

Rare Rockingham figure of a Valencian, 7in. high, 1826-30. £440

Martinware saltglazed figure of a bird, signed R. W. Martin & Bros., London & Southall, 1900, 13in. high.£700

Staffordshire saltglazed plate, 9in. diam., 1760-70.   £520

One of a pair of salt-glazed cornucopiae, 10in. long, perhaps Liverpool, about 1745.   £100

Saltglazed 7lb. jar.   £2

Attractive saltglaze teapot and cover, 4in. high, about 1760.   £300

Coloured saltglaze cream jug, 3in. high, about 1760.   £200

Rare saltglaze mug, 2¾in. high, about 1760.   £175

Rare small saltglaze bear mug, 3½in. high, about 1740.   £250

Saltglaze 'scratch-blue' bowl incised and picked out in cobalt, 5¾in. diam., about 1750-60.   £260

SATSUMA

Satsuma jardiniere
and stand, 3ft.
tall.   £380

Pair of Satsuma vases, 19th
century, 7½in. high.   £220

One of a pair of
Satsuma vases,
30in. high. £550

19th century Satsuma
jardiniere decorated
with figure scenes,
26cm. diameter. £35

Late 19th century Satsuma
pottery vase decorated
,with figures, 8½in. high.
                        £10

Japanese Satsuma
plate of good
quality.   £65

SEVRES

One of a pair
of Sevres
vases.   £330

A fine mid 18th century Sevres
cup and saucer with a blue
ground and decorated panels.
                        £160

One of a pair of
16in. tall Sevres
vases.   £1,000

SEVRES

Sevres vase and cover, 38¼in. high. £800

Sevres milk jug with decorated panels within gilded borders, from the last quarter of the 18th century. £250

SEVRES

Mid 18th century Sevres vase. £1,125

SILVER RESIST

Silver resist jug, circa 1810-15, 3½in. high. £220

Silver resist jug, circa 1810, 6½in. high. £95

Silver resist jug, circa 1810-15, 5¼in. high. £440

SLIPWARE

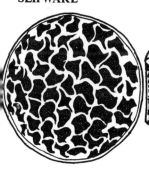

Staffordshire slipware baking dish, freely decorated with a netting pattern. £350

An early Staffordshire slipware cradle, 9in. long. £500

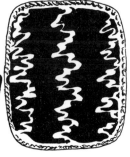

Slipware baking dish with typical notched rim. £175

SPODE

Finely decorated
Spode vase, 5¼in.
high, circa 1810.
£45

Late 18th century Spode baby's
bottle.   £50

Late 18th century
Spode octagonal
shaped jug with
serpent handle,
impressed mark,
7¼in. high. £16

Late 18th century Spode
jug with cover, decorated
in white relief on a blue
ground, 6½in. high,
(small fault).   £21

Rare Spode oviform
vase, 7in. high,
early 19th century.
                    £210

Part of a mid 19th
century Spode 'New
Stone' dessert
service.   £850

Early Spode garniture of three
vases, each on three claw feet,
larger vase 8½in. high, smaller
pair 5in. high.   £360

Garniture of Spode named bird
vases, 6¼ and 4½in. high, 1805.
                            £280

Staffordshire snuff box, 3in. wide, circa 1765.   £140

Rare Staffordshire saltglaze teapot and cover, 8in. high, about 1745.   £340

Staffordshire voyeurs snuff box, 3¼in. wide, circa 1765.   £460

Late 18th century Staffordshire scent bottle with fine decoration.   £220

Pair of Staffordshire greyhound figures, 10in. high.   £110

Victorian Staffordshire figure group of 'The Princess Royal and Fredk. of Prussia.'   £45

Staffordshire group of a lion and a leopard under a tree, enamel colours.   £100

Rare pair of Staffordshire figures of cricketers of about 1865.   £290

Late Staffordshire slipware jug decorated with bands of chequers, circa 1760.   £175

157

Staffordshire pottery figure of Wallace. £58

Staffordshire figure of Queen Victoria, circa 1850.   £45

Staffordshire pottery figure of Queen Victoria.   £58

Staffordshire figure of G. Gordon, 17½in. high.   £68

Rare Staffordshire figure of Mrs Punch on a goat.   £42

16in. tall Staffordshire figure of a 19th century Irishman 'D. O'Connell'.   £215

Mid 18th century Staffordshire salt-glaze stoneware hawk, 22.8cm. high.   £4,200

Rare Staffordshire figure of a Girl In Prayer.   £45

Staffordshire salt-glazed pottery cat, 6½in. high.   £320

Staffordshire figure of the Prince of Wales. £85

Staffordshire figure of a dairy shop sign, 'Milk Sold Here', 14½in. high. £75

Staffordshire figure of Wm. Tell, 18½in. high. £85

Staffordshire group of a lion and a leopard. £100

Staffordshire figure of Jules Perrot, ballet dancer, circa 1842. £60

Staffordshire figure of Prince Albert, circa 1850. £35

Staffordshire pottery figure of a lady. £35

Staffordshire figure of Napoleon I, circa 1848. £55

Staffordshire figure of a vaudeville actor as 'Jim Crow'. £100

STAFFORDSHIRE

Staffordshire snuff
box, 3¼in. wide,
circa 1765, restored.
£100

Staffordshire 'pink lustre'
tea service early 19th
century.   £150

Circular Staffordshire
snuff box, 3in. diam.,
circa 1770.   £220

18th century
Staffordshire
scent bottle.
      £210

Pair of late 19th century Staffordshire
lions with glass eyes.   £30

Staffordshire
oviform nutmeg
grater, 2¼in. high,
circa 1770.   £120

Staffordshire
figure of 'G.
Gordon',
17½in. high.
      £68

Pair of Staffordshire pottery
figures of Victoria and
Albert, 7½in. high.   £360

Staffordshire group of
Emperor Napoleon and
Eugenie, 12in. high.
      £280

Swansea tureen, cover and stand, 7in. diam., 1814-22.   £260

Swansea pottery jug, marked, 5in., sold with tea cups and saucers in lustre.£22

Swansea 'Botanical' dessert dish, 11¼in., about 1820.   £200

VIENNA

19th century Vienna porcelain plaque by F. Lezleh, 16in. diameter.   £475

Vienna porcelain figure of a girl.   £165

Vienna wall plaque, painted by K. Weh, 9½in. diameter.£80

19th century Vienna porcelain plate. £500

Vienna soup tureen and stand with cover, 44.5cm. high overall, circa 1809.   £210

Vienna wall plaque, painted by K. Weh, 9½in. diameter.£90

WEDGWOOD

Small Wedgwood
lustre ware dish.
£135

Rare Wedgwood plate,
9¾in. diam., numeral
221 in sepia, about
1774.   £820

Wedgwood basalt
ware two-handled
urn, shaped base,
7in. high.   £32

Rare Wedgwood
amphora of pear
shape, 13in. high,
late 18th century.
£700

Good Wedgwood and
Bentley black basalt
oval plaque, 7½in.,
about 1773.   £330

18th century Wedgwood
lustre ware vase of square
form.   £380

Wedgwood Fairy
lustre ware bowl.
£400

Wedgwood black
basalt figure of
Cupid with two
love birds at his
feet, 22in. high. £650

Good Wedgwood and
Bentley oval medallion,
about 1770, 4½in. £360

One of a set of twelve Wedgwood Intaglios, late 18th century, 3½in.   £520

Wedgwood green majolica plate, circa 1870, 8½in. diameter.   £7

19th century Wedgwood medallion, 3¼in.   £60

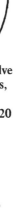

Rare Wedgwood and Bentley vase and cover, 17in. high, about 1770.   £1,300

One of a pair of rare Wedgwood candlesticks modelled as dolphins, late 18th century, 10in. high.   £1,600

Wedgwood majolica ewer dedicated to Bacchus, dated 1870-80, 11in. high.   £250

Wedgwood black jasper bust of Shakespeare. £135

Mid 19th century Wedgwood blue and white jasperware teapot.   £75

Black basalt Wedgwood portrait medallion, 4¾in., about 1777.   £440

WEDGWOOD

Late 18th century Wedgwood plaque of a
Roman procession, 21 x 9½in.   £540

Wedgwood-Whieldon
pineapple teapot and
cover, 5in. high,
1760-65.   £420

Rare Wedgwood and Bentley black
basalt bust of Jonathan Swift,
20in. high.   £680

Part of a thirty-three piece Wedgwood
jasperware tea service.   £110

Rare Wedgwood plaque, late 18th century,
19¾ x 11in.   £520

One of a small
pair of Wedgwood
fairy lustre vases.
£60

WESTERWALD

Early 18th century
Westerwald stone-
ware jug, 10.5cm.
high.   £190

Late 17th century
Westerwald stone-
ware jug, 24cm.
high.   £210

WESTERWALD

Early 18th century
Westerwald stone-
ware jug decorated
in relief, 6¾in. high.
          £260

WHIELDON

Fine teapot and cover
by Astbury-Whieldon,
4¾in. high, about
1750.   £1,050

Whieldon plate, 9in.
diameter, about
1760.   £60

Whieldon teapot
and cover, 4¼in.
high, about 1755.
          £300

Mid 18th century
Whieldon pottery
caddy, 5in. high.
          £450

Whieldon wall vase
depicting a grimacing
mask, circa 1760.
          £150

Very rare Whieldon
tea caddy and cover,
6¾in. high, 1760-
65.   £520

A good, late 18th century model of a squirrel, in the style of Ralph Wood. £300

Rare and massive, Enoch Wood pearlware jug, late 18th century, 17in. high. £400

Late 18th century Ralph Wood pottery figure of a finch, 5in. tall. £3,000

Enoch Wood figure of John Liston as 'Van Dunder', 7in., about 1824. £100

Rare pair of Ralph Wood vases, 8in. high, about 1780. £440

Rare Enoch Wood figure of John Liston, 6¼in., about 1820. £100

Sharp-faced Toby jug by Ralph Wood, about 1770, 9¾in. high. £160

One of a set of six Enoch Wood creamware plates, 10in. diam., about 1790. £420

Attractive, Ralph Wood Toby jug, 9½in. high, 1770-80. £190

Worcester bowl printed in black enamel, 7in. diam., about 1760. £130

Small Chamberlain's Worcester vase encrusted with flowers, 6½in. high. £22

Worcester bowl with signed print by Hancock, 6¼in. diam., about 1760. £70

One of a pair of Royal Worcester vases on a bleu celeste ground, 10in. high. £720

Pair of Royal Worcester ewers, signed C. Baldwyn. £300

Fine Worcester jug printed by Hancock, 7¼in. high, circa 1760. £275

Rare Chamberlain's Worcester figure of one of the Rainer Brothers, 6in. high, about 1830. £110

English powder blue teabowl, coffee cup and saucer, 1765-70. £150

Large Worcester hexagonal vase and cover, decorated in Imari palette, 26in. high. £400

WORCESTER

Worcester punch bowl
with scene of a foxhunt
by Robert Hancock,
11in. diameter, 1760-65.
£240

Worcester mug painted
by James Ross, 6in.
high, about 1760.£260

Rare early Worcester
coffee cup of octa-
gonal form, 1752-54.
£220

Worcester teabowl, coffee cup
and saucer, about 1765.   £90

An attractive Worcester coffee
cup, teabowl and saucer, about
1770.   £410

Attractive Worcester
mug of bell shape, 5in.
high, about 1770.£240

Rare English sucrier
and cover, 5½in. high,
of eloping bride, circa
1758-60.   £420

Worcester 'King of
Prussia' mug, 6in.
high, about 1760.
£190

Fine Worcester mug with portrait of George II, 6¼in. high, about 1760. £300

Rare English porcelain ladle, 5¼in. long, circa 1765-70. £220

First Period Worcester mask jug, transfer decorated and with the word 'cyder'. £190

Fluted Worcester coffee cup, teacup and saucer, attractively painted, about 1770. £310

Attractive Worcester coffee cup, teabowl and saucer, 1755-58. £400

Worcester vase of ovoid shape, 6in. high, about 1758. £200

Rare Worcester bowl and cover, 7½in., about 1780. £280

Early Worcester bottle of hexagonal section, 4¾in. high, about 1755. £1,000

WORCESTER

Worcester cream jug of barrel shape, 2¾in. high, 1755-60. £160

Mid 18th century Worcester partridge sauce tureen. £1,750

Pair of Worcester/ Lunds octagonal beakers in famille verte, 2¼in. high, about 1753. £460

Early Worcester shell sweetmeat dish, 3¼in., about 1751-3. £150

Pair of 20in. high Worcester candle-holders.   £290

Rare Worcester sucrier and cover, 4¾in. high, about 1770.   £560

Early 19th century Worcester or Derby figure of Madame Vestris, 5¾in. high. £80

Part of a Royal Worcester dessert service, printed crown circle, date code for 1901.   £120

Worcester tankard, circa 1770.   £92

A fine early 19th century Worcester pictorial plate.
£100

One of a pair of Worcester double-lipped sauceboats, 8¼in., about 1755. £360

Rare Worcester mug with loop handle, 3¾in. high, about 1755. £240

Royal Worcester pot pourri vase.
£594

Pair of Royal Worcester baluster ewers, painted by Harry Davis, circa 1907, 8¼in. high. £660

First period Worcester coffee pot, painted in famille rose style, 9¾in. high. £350

Early Worcester vase of pear shape, 4¼in. high, about 1755-60.
£400

One of a pair of 'Doctor Wall' first period Worcester porcelain plates, 8¾in. diameter. £300

Royal Worcester baluster vase decorated by Harry Davis, 9½in. high.
£250

WORCESTER

Worcester coffee cup. £35

Flight, Barr and Barr 'named view' basket, 9½in. diameter, 1814-30. £120

Worcester 'Dolphin' ewer creamboat, 4in. high, circa 1760-65. £260

Worcester vase and cover, 17in. tall, 1901. £850

Pair of late 19th century Worcester figures. £170

Royal Worcester Eastern style ovoid vase. £135

One of a pair of Flight, Barr and Barr 'landscape' plates, 8in. diam., 1792-1807. £170

Inkstand by Flight, Barr and Barr, 5½in., full script mark in sepia, 1815-20. £150

One of a pair of Worcester ewers decorated by C. Baldwyn. £300

Rare early Worcester
wine funnel, 5in.,
1752-55.   £3,000

Pair of Royal Worcester
vases painted by Leaman.
                        £275

Worcester bowl with print
by Hancock, 5¼in. diam.,
about 1756.   £75

Worcester figure
of a theatrical
character.   £40

Pair of Royal Worcester urn
vases decorated by W. Powell.
                        £770

Royal Worcester
ovoid vase and
cover.   £105

Worcester teacup and
saucer, pseudo four-
character marks within
double rings, about
1770.   £130

Worcester punch bowl with
foxhunting scene, 11in. diam.,
about 1765.   £210

Late 19th century
white Royal
Worcester jug,
4½in. high.   £8

Worcester 'French-green'
centre dish of lozenge
shape, 10¾in.   £110

Rare and early
coffee cup with
coloured enamel,
about 1755,
Worcester. £140

Worcester vine leaf
dessert dish, 11¼in.,
about 1760-65.
                £400

Part of a Worcester dessert service,
open crescent marks in underglaze
blue, about 1770-75.   £2,000

Early Worcester
coffee cup and
saucer, about
1755-60. £500

Worcester 'Claret
Ground' teapot
and cover, 5¾in.
high, 1770-75.
            £950

Early Worcester leaf
dish, 7½in., about
1755-60.   £620

Worcester mug,
5½in. high, about
1770-75, in peck-
ing parrot pattern.
            £140

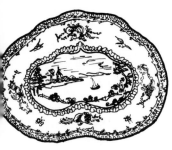

Fine Worcester kidney shaped dish, 10½in., open crescent mark, about 1770. £300

Large Worcester mug, 6in. high, open crescent mark, about 1760-65. £310

One of a set of four Worcester 'French-green' shell-shaped dishes, 8in. £150

Pair of Royal Worcester ewers and similar vase by Harry Davis. £910

Grainger, Lee & Co. part dinner service, 24 pieces, 1812-20.£740

Good Worcester mug, 5¾in. high, open crescent mark, about 1768-75. £210

Rare Worcester coffee cup and saucer, about 1758, workman's mark within double rings. £280

Rare Worcester teapot and cover, 9in. high, about 1770. £320

BRACKET CLOCKS

Bracket clock by Thomas Tompion, London, circa 1700, 40cm. high. £12,500

Large Victorian Gothic revival carved oak bracket clock, 48in. high. £440

Ebony double basket-top alarm bracket clock with 7in. dial, 1ft.5½in. high.£1,900

London,mahogany bracket clock circa 1750, two train pull repeat with calendar. £750

19th century bracket clock in ormolu mounted ebony case. £600

Eight day English fusee bracket clock in ebony case by Anthony Quiguer, London, circa 1687. £3,500

Late 17th century London made striking verge,basket topped,bracket clock.£2,750

Regency rosewood and brass inlaid bracket clock. £245

George III bracket clock engraved Joseph Martineau Snr., London, 19½in. high. £420

176

George II walnut
bracket clock by
Samuel Whichcote
of London.£3,600

Bracket clock by
Henning of
Lymington, 1785.
£350

Bracket clock by
John Ward, circa
1790, 1ft. 8in.
high.   £880

English bracket clock
signed Vulliamy,
London, 16in. high,
in ebonised case.£2,200

English bracket clock by
John Mitchell, circa 1725,
in mahogany case, 19in.
high.   £1,050

19th century maho-
gany bracket clock,
in Turkish style,
27¾in. tall.   £890

An early George III
mahogany bracket clock
by Elicott, London,
1ft. 4in. high.   £1,000

George III mahogany cased
bracket clock on brass
feet.   £780

Victorian bracket clock
with Cambridge and
Westminster chimes.£985

BRACKET CLOCKS

Victorian oak cased bracket clock by Joseph Penlington, Liverpool. £720

Late Victorian mahogany bracket clock signed A. & M. Rowley, London, 25ins. high. £420

Late 17th century walnut bracket clock by Henry Jones, 1ft. 2in. high. £1,500

Early 18th century grande sonnerie bracket clock signed John George Werndle Presburg, 1ft. 6in. high. £550

George III mahogany bracket clock signed Gravell & Tolkien, 1ft. 4½in. high.£1,300

George III mahogany bracket clock by John McDonald, Inverness, 1ft. 5in. high. £2,400

Ebonised basket-top bracket clock by John Barnett, London, 1ft. 1in. high. £3,000

Rosewood bracket clock by Jn. B. Cross, London,19in. high. £655

George III mahogany bracket clock by Thomas Bryant, London, 1ft. 7½in. high. £1,100

George II ebonised bracket clock by John Toppin, London, 1ft. 4½in. high. £1,350

19th century bracket clock by Robert Simpson, London. £1,000

Late George III mahogany bracket clock by Lautier, 10¼in. high. £550

Early 18th century ebonised alarm bracket clock, 1ft. 9½in. high, now with anchor escapement.£2,400

Mahogany cased bracket clock by George Graham. £2,400

George III ebonised chiming bracket clock, dial signed White, London, 1ft. 11½in. high. £1,150

George II mahogany alarm bracket clock by Thomas Hunter, London, 1ft. 3in. high. £1,100

Bracket clock by Joseph Windmills, circa 1695, in ebonised case. £9,100

Early George III ebonised bracket clock by William Creak, London, 1ft. 7in. high.£900

179

BRACKET CLOCKS

19th century Japanese brass striking bracket clock, 165mm. high.
£1,300

Unusual masonic mahogany alarm bracket clock, 1ft. 9in. high.
£400

17th century bracket clock by Daniel le Count, 13½in. tall.
£4,000

Georgian musical bracket clock by R. Roskell, Liverpool, 34½in. tall.
£3,200

George III black japanned musical bracket clock by Wagstaffe, London, 1ft. 9in. high. £2,100

Late 19th century ebonised mantel clock, 28in. high. £520

Mid 19th century English bracket clock. £1,000

George III mahogany bracket clock by W. Wall, Richmond, 1ft. 4½in. high.£780

19th century boulle and ormolu mounted bracket clock. £530

Ebonised chiming bracket clock by Francis Perigal, London, 2ft. 2in. high. £1,600

Early 19th century bracket clock by P. Grimalde. £450

Bracket clock by John Ward, 20in. high, circa 1790. £880

George III mahogany bracket clock by William Cozens of London, 1ft. 3½in. tall. £420

George III pearwood bracket clock, 23in. high, dial signed John Williams.£1,200

Ebony veneered basket top, quarter repeating, bracket clock by Sam. Marchant, London, 14in. high. £2,600

George III mahogany bracket clock by John Robert & Silva, London, 2ft. 2in. high £1,400

Ebonised bracket clock by J. Vulliamy, London, 1ft. 5in. high. £2,700

19th century ebonised bracket clock, 2ft. 1in. high. £470

CARRIAGE CLOCKS

A one-piece carriage clock in brass case, signed Paul Garnier Her de la Marine, Paris, 5½in. high. £600

Repeat alarm carriage clock in a gorge case by Charles Frodsham & Co., Paris, circa 1875. £725

Fine English repeater carriage clock by James McCabe, 6¾in. high. £2,750

A good French repeater carriage clock. £420

Carriage clock in the Japanese manner, 6¾in. high. £700

Grande sonnerie repeating alarm carriage clock. £7,000

An English quarter repeating carriage clock by E. & W. Smith, 8in. high. £1,900

An alarm carriage clock by Hunt & Roskell, London, 6¼in. high. £450

Fine gilt brass cased repeater carriage clock, 7in. high. £340

English gilt metal mantel timepiece, 5in. high. £1,100

19th century French gilt brass carriage clock by J. Soldarno.   £480

Large English repeating carriage clock signed T. E. Payne, Tunbridge Wells.   £1,750

'One-piece' cased carriage alarm clock, 5¼in. high.   £455

Early 19th century travelling clock by Gordon of London, 9in. high.   £720

A small porcelain mounted carriage clock, 11cm. high. £900

English carriage clock by James McCabe, London, 6¾in. high. £2,400

Carriage clock with eight day repeater by Lund and Blockley. £225

Regency timepiece bracket clock by Richard Ganthony, London 1810.£750

CARRIAGE CLOCKS

French brass repeat alarm carriage clock by Leroy et Fils, 7¼in. high.   £850

French brass grande sonnerie repeat alarm carriage clock, 8in. high.   £1,350

19th century French brass carriage clock with alarm.   £145

English carriage clock by Edward Funnell, Brighton, 5in. high.   £1,400

Oval alarm carriage clock signed Henry Capt. Geneve, 5¾in. high.   £650

Enamel mounted carriage clock, 7in. high. £1,050

Good porcelain mounted alarm carriage clock, 6in. high.   £1,250

Carriage clock by Bolviller a Paris, 6½in. high. £580

Gorge cased alarm carriage clock, 5¼in. high.   £650

Quarter striking carriage clock in the Japanese manner, 6¾in. high. **£1,150**

Fine carriage clock, case and key by James McCabe. **£3,600**

French gilt brass carriage clock, 7in. high. **£575**

Grande sonnerie alarm carriage clock signed Chas. Frodsham & Co., 5¾in. high. **£1,100**

Brass gorge cased miniature carriage clock, signed J. J. L. Brevet, 3in. high. **£500**

Miniature oval porcelain mounted carriage time-piece, 3in. high. **£650**

Enamel mounted carriage clock, 6in. high. **£850**

Small enamel mounted carriage timepiece, 3½in. high, in a red travelling case. **£540**

Five minute repeating carriage clock by Henri Jacot, 7in. high. **£790**

Silver and gilded metal clock set, circa 1880. £425

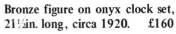

**Ornate garniture de cheminee with
engraved plaque below the clock.
£900**

**Bronze figure on onyx clock set,
21½in. long, circa 1920.   £160**

**Ormolu and bleu du roi Sevres porcelain garniture of mantel clock
and a pair of matching candelabra.   £5,200**

19th century French ormolu and cloisonne clock set. £780

Dark red marble and ormolu
clock set, by L. Barbase, Paris.
£295

French gilt metal and
green onyx clock set.
£520

Late 19th century cloisonne and onyx clock set.   £820

GRANDFATHER CLOCKS

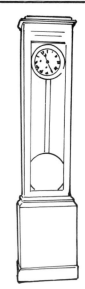

Longcase clock by Richard Colston of London, circa 1700, 7ft.3in. high. £2,000

Fine early Georgian longcase clock, inscribed James Robinson, London, 7ft.7½in. high. £980

Eight day long-case clock by Peter Boner, in marquetry case. £720

Late 19th century walnut longcased clock with brass pendulum. £440

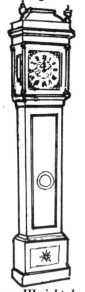

George III eight day longcase clock, signed Geo. Thatcher of Cranbrook, 90in. high. £800

Late 18th century mahogany longcase clock by John Andrews of London, 87in. high. £950

Longcase clock in Cuban mahogany, 8ft.6in. high, by Lawson of Leigh, circa 1787 £1,500

Marquetry and walnut longcase clock by Matthew Bunce, London, circa 1698, 7ft. 6in. high. £2,200

Walnut veneered longcase clock, about 1705, with figuring on the case. £3,200

Mid 17th century striking longcase clock by Edmund Card of London, in floral marquetry case. £2,400

Small mahogany longcase clock of three months duration, height, without finial, 6ft.7in. £1,250

Oak cased grandfather clock by Richard Alexander of Nursteed, circa 1780, 6ft.8in. tall. £285

Late 18th century mahogany longcase clock by Paul Chotard of London, 7ft.10in. high. £1,095

Edwardian mahogany longcase clock signed by Thomas B. Cardwell, Liverpool. £700

Late 17th century marquetry longcase clock by Christopher Gould, London. £3,400

English panelled oak longcase clock with engraved brass face in two sections. £100

189

GRANDFATHER CLOCKS

Mahogany long-case clock by Sam Collier, Eccles, 8ft. 3½in. £500

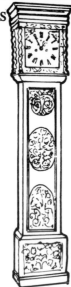

Longcase clock by Joseph Knibb, circa 1685, in a fine marquetry case. £10,750

Inlaid mahogany musical longcase clock, front of the movement signed M. Bradberry, Leyburn, dated 1811. £1,475

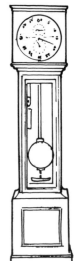

Mahogany longcase regulator with jewelled pallets, 6ft. 4in. high. £1,175

George III eight day inlaid mahogany longcase clock. £280

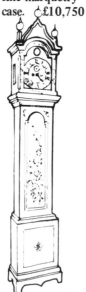

18th century walnut and marquetry longcase clock by John Derve, London, 8ft. 2in. high. £1,500

Longcase clock by Richard Reed, Chelmsford. £530

Early 18th century marquetry longcase clock, inlaid with flowers, scrolls and foliage, 7ft. 9in. high. £2,300

Early 19th century longcase clock signed Robin aux Galeries du Louvre, 6ft. 10in. high. £2,400

George III eight day clock signed Nich. Le Maistre of Dublin, in mahogany case, 86in. high. £610

Fine mahogany longcase clock signed Hadwen of Liverpool, 1760, 9ft. high. £1,080

Walnut long-case clock by John Ebsworth, circa 1690. £1,700

George III long-case clock, signed William and Mary Cooper 1764, 7ft. 5in. high. £450

Green lacquer long-case clock by E. Solomons of Canterbury, circa 1780. £865

Walnut eight day longcase clock, dial inscribed Richd. Grigg, Andover, 6ft. 10¼in. high. £580

Good eight day solid mahogany longcase clock by Wills of Truro, circa 1800. £475

191

GRANDFATHER CLOCKS

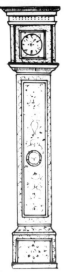

Arabesque mar-
quetry longcase
clock, signed
Asselin, London,
7ft. high. £1,150

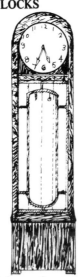

Oak cased grand-
mother clock with
a silver dial and
Westminster chime
£85

Eight day long-
case clock, circa
1675, oak case,
6ft. 3in. high. £2,000

Mahogany long-
case clock, the
break-arch dial
containing moon
work, 7ft. 6in. high,
George III. £2,200

Eight day longcase
clock in lacquer
case, circa 1740,
by William Hall of
Louth, 7ft. 7in.
high. £785

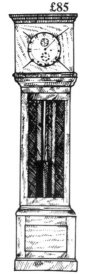

Fine teak regu-
lator, dial signed
V. Kullberg,
London, 5ft. 10in.
high. £2,200

Marquetry longcase
clock, dial signed by
P. Garon, London,
on later bracket
feet, 8ft. high. £2,800

Longcase
clock by John
Fletcher of
Barnsley. £360

Edwardian marquetry longcase clock. £1,500

Early 18th century marquetry longcase clock with eight day movement, by A. Dunlop of London. £2,300

George III mahogany longcase clock, 13in. dial, signed Hindley, York, 8ft. high. £1,100

Rare mahogany calendar regulator with 9in. dial, 6ft. high. £4,200

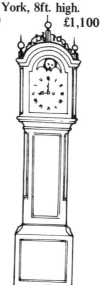

George II walnut clock , figured and crossbanded, by Thos. Moore of Ipswich. £725

18th century eight day longcase clock by Thomas Watts of Lavenham, 89in. high. £620

George III mahogany longcase clock by Asa Hall Raynham, about 1800, 90in. high. £2,125

Ornately carved walnut chiming longcase clock. £2,300

GRANDFATHER CLOCKS

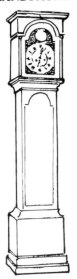

Early 18th century walnut longcase clock engraved Tucker, London.   £1,800

Edwardian inlaid mahogany longcase clock. £2,200

George I burr walnut longcase clock. £2,500

Edwardian longcase clock with three sets of chimes. £2,500

Carved oak longcase clock, 8ft. 2in. tall. £1,450

George I walnut longcase clock by R. Peckover, London. £1,050

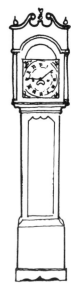

18th century lacquered longcase clock by Robert Baird, Kilmarnock. £780

Eight-day longcase clock in oak case, 7ft. 5½in. high. £545

Burr walnut longcase clock circa 1750, 9ft. 3in. high. £7,000

Late 17th century ebonised longcase clock signed E. Bir, London, 96in. high. £5,400

Edwardian longcase clock with Whittington/ Westminster chimes. £1,150

Carved walnut eight-day longcase clock on eight bells and four gongs.
£3,750

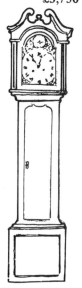

Arabesque marquetry month longcase clock, 11in. dial, 7ft. 1in. tall. £1,550

Mahogany brass inlaid grandfather clock with painted dial. £475

Small oak longcased clock by Washbourn of Gloucester, with 10in. dial, 6ft. 6in. high. £395

Provincial oak longcased clock with brass dial. £590

GRANDFATHER CLOCKS

Musical long-case clock.
£2,800

Edwardian long-case clock, 8ft. 2in. high.£1,450

Late 18th century carved oak longcase clock by J. Jones, Wrexham. £780

Victorian long-case clock with mahogany case.
£1,450

Georgian long-case clock by D. Hubert, London.
£1,500

18th century regulator by T. Church, Norwich.£2,000

Mahogany long-case clock by Wm. Trail of London, 7ft. high.£1,250

17th century marquetry longcase clock.
£1,655

Lantern clock, circa 1690, by Joseph Windmills, London, 16in. high. £1,250

Lantern clock by John Knibb, Oxford, circa 1690, 17½in. high. £4,000

Balance wheel lantern clock by Baker, complete with doors.£925

Small lantern clock signed Sam Wichell, Piccadilly, 9in. high. £1,600

Lantern clock by Windmills, London, 1ft. 4ins. high, with an oak bracket. £2,400

Early 18th century brass lantern clock. £1,080

Brass striking lantern clock, 10½in. high, 20th century. £40

19th century country-made lantern clock, 14in. high. £150

Provincial lantern clock by E. Bilbie, circa 1675, 10in. high. £2,000

MANTEL CLOCKS

19th century boulle and ormolu mounted bracket clock. £530

George III drum clock with brass inlay, circa 1820. £120

Rare late 17th century Hague clock, dial signed P. Visbagh Haghe, 1ft. 1½in. high, circa 1680. £4,000

Early 19th century alarm clock, 11½in. high, Jura. £680

Edwardian inlaid striking mantel clock, circa 1900, 11in. high. £40

19th century French gilt and cast brass lyre clock. £780

Mahogany mantel clock by C. C. Webb, London, 9in. high. £380

19th century Sevres and ormolu clock, 32in. high x 28in. long. £4,250

Striking mantel clock by Breguet in mahogany case, 285mm. high. £4,000

French boulle
mantel clock,
29in. high.£150

19th century gilt metal
Strutt desk clock, 127mm.
overall height.   £200

Victorian brass mantel
clock signed by Z.
Barraclough & Sons,
20in. high.   £300

A French boulle
bracket clock
circa 1850. £600

Early 19th century Louis XIV
style red boulle and ormolu
mounted French striking clock
and bracket, 96cm. high. £950

19th century boulle
mantel clock with
ormolu mounts.
          £590

Mahogany mantel clock
by Donkins, London,
9in. high.   £380

19th century Continental
porcelain mantel clock
in rococo style, 17½in.
high.   £150

Ormolu French striking
clock by Achille Brocot,
circa 1850, 33cm. wide.
          £550

MANTEL CLOCKS

Face of a black lacquered musical longcase clock by Robert Hall of Chichester. £2,200

Early 18th century German Telleruhr, backplate signed Marcus Bohm Augustae, 1ft. 8in. high. £1,500

French ormolu mantel clock by Ferdinand Berthoud a Paris, 2ft. 8in. high. £2,500

Art Nouveau clock signed N. Bochin. £75

Art Deco mantel timepiece in marble case by Maple & Co., Paris, 6¼in. high. £28

Silver plated French clock depicting Louie Fuller, circa 1910. £145

19th century clock with striking movement in a brass and ormolu case. £78

Victorian spelter mantel clock depicting an artist 1ft. 8ins. high. £110

Candle alarm table clock by Pierre Fromery, Berlin, circa 1690, 26cm. high. £17,850

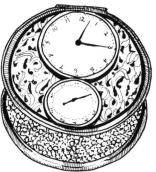

Mid 19th century table clock by Thomas Cole, 6in. high. £1,150

Rare precision clock by Thomas Mudge, in green shagreen case. £62,500

Boulle ormolu mounted mantel clock in Louis XV style. £320

Mid 19th century white onyx and ormolu mounted French striking clock. £425

Eight-day American mantel clock, circa 1880. £11

19th century French mantel clock, 28in. high. £840

19th century ormolu and porcelain mantel clock by Potonie of Paris, 22½in. tall. £900

Frederick Bull electric mantel clock in an arched rosewood case, 23cm. high, circa 1880. £420

19th century clock with striking movement in an ormolu and boulle case. £315

Louis XVI ormolu and white marble mantel clock, 1ft. 2in. high.
£580

18th century gilt metal hexagonal striking table clock by Cabrier of London, 64mm. diam.
£2,600

Gilt metal and porcelain mantel clock, late 19th century.
£480

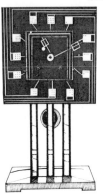

Domino clock by Charles Rennie Mackintosh, circa 1917, 10in. high. £6,500

Ornate Paris made clock and matching bracket.
£725

Rosewood cased eight day mantel chronometer by John Arnold. £1,550

17th century German table clock, 350mm. high.
£3,800

Late 19th century gilt metal desk clock signed Robt. Roskell, London, 235mm. high.
£320

18th century musical bracket clock by John Sanders, London
£2,200

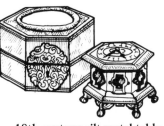

18th century gilt metal table clock with its original travelling case, 4¼in. wide. £3,200

Good, lion mantel clock, enamel dial signed Lepaute a Paris, 1ft. 10½in. high. £4,000

Empire ormolu mantel clock with four inch enamel dial signed Klein a Paris, 1ft. 8in. high. £900

Louis XVI white marble and ormolu timepiece, enamel dial signed Schmit a Paris, 1ft. 3in. high. £650

Early 19th century ormolu mounted Blue John clock, by A.R. Simons of Paris. £9,000

Small Louis XVI white marble and ormolu mantel clock, dial signed Leroy a Paris, 1ft. 2½in. high. £780

22in. tall gilt bronze clock, 19th century, in the form of an Indian building. £220

Automaton clock, Augsburg 1627. £14,500

Early George III gilt-wood cartel timepiece by Edward Hunsdon, 2ft. 11in. high. £720

MANTEL CLOCKS

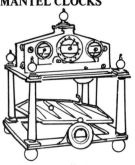

Rolling ball time-
piece by G. M.
Bell, Winchester.
£775

19th century white
marble calendar
mantel clock, 1ft.
4in. high. £1,400

Black marble mantel
clock with bronze and
gilt bronze mounts.
£40

Rare Louis XIV boulle
mantel clock signed
Thuret a Paris, 3ft. 2in.
high. £1,100

Good ormolu and verde
antico marble mantel
clock, 2ft. 3in. high.
£1,100

Early 19th century
French ormolu man-
tel clock, 1ft. 6in.
high. £420

Louis XVI ormolu
clock, dial signed
Imbert L'aine, 1ft.
2½in. high. £550

Small gilt metal mantel
timepiece with enamel
dial, 10in. high. £240

Louis XVI ormolu
mounted white marble
clock, 1ft. 1in. high.
£550

Skeleton clock by Hatfield and Hall, Manchester, 12½in. high. £460

Westminster chiming fusee skeleton clock. £475

Coup perdu skeleton timepiece, 14in. high. £450

Brass chiming skeleton clock with three train movement, 19½in. high. £1,300

19th century skeleton clock by Richardson of Middlesborough, 21in. high. £1,900

Skeleton timepiece by Barrauds, London, 1ft. 3in. high. £550

Skeleton clock by W. P. Evans. £2,400

Skeleton timepiece with brass chapter ring, 10¾in. high. £320

Chiming skeleton clock of Minster type, 1ft. 10in. high. £1,600

WALL CLOCKS

Regency single-train English fusee wall clock. £235

American wall clock with white enamel dial, in walnut case, 74cm. high.£74

London silvered dial mahogany verge wall clock by **Thornton**, circa 1790.   £380

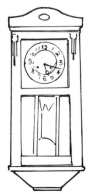

Wall clock with brass face and oak case, 78cm. high.   £36

18th century Friesland Stoelklok, 2ft. 3in. high.   £820

Rare George III master clock by Ablitt, Ipswich, 1.68m.   £700

Rare 17th century Italian night clock in ebony case, 36½ x 22in.   £2,400

Inlaid American eight day clock, circa 1890, 2ft. 4in. high.   £75

Bundy time recorder in oak case, 1.38m. high.£105

Unusual mahogany wall
timepiece by James
McCabe, London, 8½in.
high.   £540

Vienna spring regulator
clock, in oak case, circa
1880, 24in. high.   £70

18th century French
wall clock, 10½in.
high.   £500

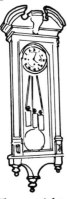

Three weight
Vienna regulator,
circa 1880. £730

Act of Parliament
clock in chinoiserie
case.   £850

Walnut cased Vienna
regulator signed 'W.
Schonberger, Vienna',
49in. high.   £300

Act of Parliament
wall clock with black
japanned trunk door.
                        £320

18th century wall clock
signed W. & J. Kipling,
London, 1ft. 2in. high.£720

Kitchen wall clock by
James Evans, Welshpool,
early 19th. century. £75

Gold and enamel cylinder watch signed T. R. Lund, London, 1830, 43mm. diam. £260

Gold cased pocket chronometer, 1807, 52mm. diameter. £2,300

19th century gold detached lever watch by Morris Tobias, 50mm. diameter. £200

Gold lever watch by F. B. Adams of London, 1835, 43mm. diameter. £210

Silver verge watch by Wm. Tomlinson, circa 1700. £535

17th century gold and enamel watch case, 34mm. diam., with later cylinder movement by Vulliamy, London. £1,400

Gold quarter repeating verge watch by Daniel Quare, circa 1720, 54mm. diameter.£2,400

Gold and enamel verge watch by James Vigne, London 1779, 50mm. diameter. £1,200

18th century metal quarter striking double dialled verge clockwatch, 75mm. diameter. £1,700

Quarter repeating
cylinder watch by F.
Desvarieux of Rouen,
46mm. diam.   £550

Quarter repeating cylinder
watch by Leroy & Fils, Paris,
circa 1820, 51mm. diam.£900

Gold quarter
repeating cylin-
der watch
signed Breguet,
39mm. diam. £850

Gold quarter repeating
cylinder watch by D. F.
Dubois, Paris, circa
1790, 42mm. diam.
            £1,000

Gilt metal oval verge
watch, circa 1600,
70mm. long.   £3,800

Gold and enamel cylinder
watch by Bautte & Co.,
Paris, 19th century, 36mm.
diameter.   £340

Gold half hunting cased
Montre a Tact by Bourdin
a Paris, 43mm. diam.£400

Lever watch by
Barraud & Lunds.
            £3,000

Blued steel keyless
lever calendar watch,
53mm. diam.   £190

Verge watch by Burdet
of London, about 1740,
with silver pair-cases.
£440

Silver pair-cased verge
watch by Worke of
London, mid 18th
century, 51mm. diam.
£230

Repousse gold pair-
cased verge watch.
£1,050

Dutch type verge
watch, by Samson
of London, about
1793.   £210

Swiss calendar repeating
watch by Perrenoud in
a carved gold case.
£1,000

Gold verge watch by
Moon & Son, London,
hallmarked 1812,
46mm. diameter. £230

Gold and enamel verge
watch by Hessen, Paris,
18th century, 48mm.
diameter.   £520

Fine gilt-metal pair-
cased watch signed
Delander, circa 1730.
£420

17th century watch
movement by Henry
Harper, 51mm. diam.
£1,200

Silver plated Swiss watch
by J.G. Vickery, London,
with bulb to light face,
4½in. high.   £78

Late 18th century
silver quarter re-
peating cylinder
watch.   £320

Gold pair-cased pocket
chronometer by Thom.
Earnshaw, 1801, 56mm.
diameter.   £2,000

Gold and enamel skele-
ton verge watch with
white enamel dial, 41mm.
diameter.   £750

Gold minute repeating
keyless lever watch,
hallmarked 1877,
51mm. diameter.
          £2,000

Gold and enamel
verge watch, 52mm.
diameter.   £530

Gold and enamel pair-
cased verge watch by
Raphard, London,
18th century, 48mm.
diameter.   £780

Repousse gold pair-
cased watch by
Ellicot, London,
1733, 49mm. diam.
          £720

Gold and enamel quarter
repeating cylinder watch,
by Francis Perigal,
London, 48mm. diam.,
circa 1780.   £1,250

WATCHES

Gold and enamel cylinder watch, 35mm. diameter, with Geneva bar movements. £240

Silver pair-cased watch, circa 1720, by George Graham. £820

Silver pair cased verge watch by Markwick, London, circa 1710. £580

Early 18th century silver pair-cased verge watch by Richard Westwood, London, 58mm. diameter. £400

Watch by J. Norris, Amsterdam, in enamelled gold case late 17th century, 3.9cm. diameter. £19,000

Silver pair-cased verge watch by Geo. Nicholls, London, circa 1710, 57mm. diameter. £380

Antique French silver gilt open faced pocket watch with an enamelled portrait bordered with pearls. £1,300

Silver pair-cased rack lever watch by Morris Tobias, London, hallmarked 1813, 57mm. diameter. £360

Early 19th century French sedan chair clock, 8in. diam. £250

Georgian verge watch by J. Willer with outer silver pair-cases, about 1770. £170

Early gold souscrip-tion, signed Breguet, 62mm. diameter. £1,050

Silver pair-cased verge clock watch, by John Blundell, Greenwich, 55mm. diameter. £1,400

Silver cased verge watch by G. Gold of London. £200

Gold cylinder watch by L'Epine, early 19th century. £420

Gold cylinder watch by Rentzch of London, hallmarked 1826, 45mm. diameter. £380

Blue enamelled and engine turned pen-dant watch with diamond set border. £600

17th century Dutch gold and enamel watch, 1½in. diam. £19,000

Large French silver open-faced pocket watch with enamelled design and pearl border. £1,300

WATCHES

Gold pair-cased repeating cylinder watch by Joseph Bosley, London, 18th century, 56mm. diam. £1,600

Small silver centre seconds verge watch by Gabriel Holland, Coventry, 1739, 49mm. diam. £920

Late 17th century watch, signed 'Madelainy a Paris', 4.9cm. diam. £20,000

Georgian gold watch and chatelaine, 176⁹, with etui for needles. £2,900

Mid 18th century rare musical striking quarter repeating chaise watch by Joseph Martineau, Snr., London, 145mm. diam. £16,000

Gold and enamel keyless cylinder watch on an enamel pendant, 25mm. diam. £180

Enamelled ring watch with diamonds. £800

Gold quarter repeating cylinder watch, by Ellicott of London, 1766, 49mm. diam. £1,050

18th century paircased pocket watch with engraved dial. £185

Small gold keyless
cylinder watch,
24mm. diam.
£260

Silver pair-cased pocket
watch by Joe Downs of
London, with enamelled
dial.   £50

Clock watch in tortoise-
shell outer case by Justin
Williami, circa 1670.
£960

Gold watch by Courvoisier et Cie,
1820, in oval silver case.   £230

Gilt-metal verge chaise
watch, 19th century,
104mm. diam.   £440

French chatelaine watch
by Leroy made of pate
sur pate.   £1,200

Silver pair-cased verge
watch, hallmarked 1821.
£75

Mid 18th century silver pair-
cased verge watch by Markwick
of London, 73mm. diam.
£1,850

Early 18th century
quarter repeating
watch, signed
William King. £640

215

CLOISONNE

19th century circular, cloisonne enamel bowl with matching lid. 13¼in. diam. £80

Chinese 10in. oval cloisonne jardiniere, 7in. high. £85

20th century cloisonne enamel box, 5in. wide. £48

One of a pair of Chinese cloisonne vases, 31in. high. £1,150

19th century Japanese cloisonne dish, 14in., diam. £55

One of a pair of Japanese cloisonne enamel vases, 36in. high, circa 1900. £980

Late 19th century cloisonne enamel vase of yellow ground, 10in. high. £48

Early 19th century cloisonne enamel incense burner. £250

A good 18th century Chinese cloisonne vase, 11½in., tall. £380

One of a pair of
cloisonne enamel
seated bulls, 9in.,
wide.   £775

Japanese cloisonne enamel
jardiniere, 32cm. diameter.
£140

Late 19th century
small cloisonne
teapot.   £40

Large Japanese
cloisonne enamel
vase, 50in. high.
£2,100

One of a pair of 19th
century ormolu moun-
ted cloisonne enamel
vases.   £250

One of a pair of
cloisonne vases, royal
blue on powder blue,
circa 1860.   £750

One of a pair of
Chinese 12in.
cloisonne enamel
covered vases.
£185

A good late 18th century
cloisonne enamel teapot.
£750

19th century Japanese
cloisonne enamel vase,
7in. high.   £70

COPPER AND BRASS

Victorian cast brass doorstop depicting a horse.   £23

Early 19th century brass lyre-shaped trivet with wooden handle.   £35

19th century brass chamber stick with drip pan.   £10

Early 19th century copper jardiniere, 16in. diam.   £75

Victorian brass fender, 5ft. long.   £60

Victorian brass letter opener in the form of a parrot.   £6

Late 19th century brass crumb scoop with wooden handle.   £7

A Victorian three gallon copper measure, 16in. high.   £50

A large, late 18th century copper kettle with steel handle.   £100

Late 18th century copper kettle complete with stand.   £65

Victorian brass
table gong on an
oak base.   £18

A small 19th century
brass saucepan.   £10

Pair of Victorian
iron and brass
dogs.   £8

Late 18th century
brass pastry
jigger.   £11

Late 18th century pierced
brass footman with shaped
front legs.   £75

Set of three Victorian brass
fire implements.   £30

Rare, late 17th
century brass
firetongs.   £50

One of a pair of
Charles II brass
candlesticks.
            £340

Victorian folding brass
fireguard, 3ft. 6in. wide.
                    £18

19th century
Indian brass
jardiniere.
            £12

COPPER AND BRASS

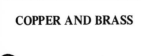

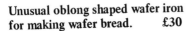

Unusual oblong shaped wafer iron for making wafer bread.   £30

Japanned candle box in black and red.   £6

19th century roasting jack.   £16

One of a pair of ormolu chenets of Louis XV style, 1ft 3in high. £950

Victorian brass hand bell, 12in. high.   £20

Small George III copper boiler, 13½in. overall width.   £75

18th century brass box iron and brass trivet.   £34

Large shapely copper and brass antique kettle.   £30

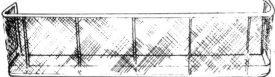

Victorian brass mesh fender, 4ft. 4in. wide, 13in. high.   £25

Mid 18th century copper chamberstick with pierced decoration, 7½in. long. £135

Edward VII
commemorative
horse brass. £24

George III copper bed warming pan, circa
1770, 39in. long.   £52

Mid 19th century
brass hand bell,
7¼in. high.   £10

Brass kettle on stand
with burner, circa
1890, 11in. high. £35

George III lidded
copper tea urn,
18in. high, circa
1800.   £95

Brass cooking
pan.   £10

Late 19th century
brass crumb tray.
£2.50

Cast iron and brass
coffee grinder, 5in.
square.   £35

Decorative ornaments
representing a pair of
peacocks in copper,
silvered and gilt. £150

Victorian polished copper and steel
fender, 4ft. 6in. long.   £40

COPPER AND BRASS

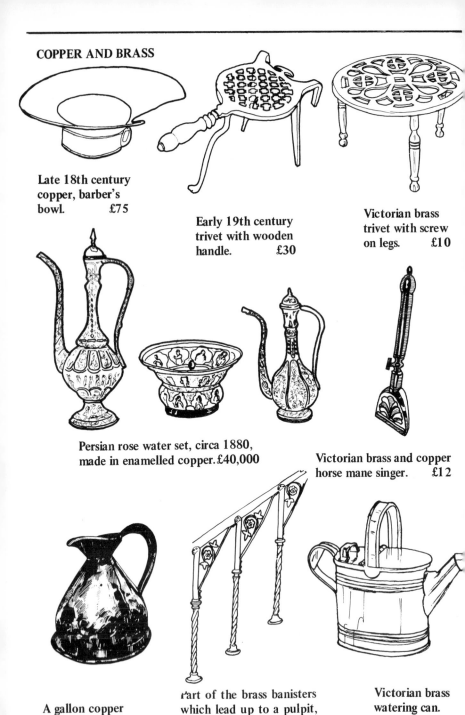

Late 18th century copper, barber's bowl. £75

Early 19th century trivet with wooden handle. £30

Victorian brass trivet with screw on legs. £10

Persian rose water set, circa 1880, made in enamelled copper.£40,000

Victorian brass and copper horse mane singer. £12

A gallon copper measure. £40

Part of the brass banisters which lead up to a pulpit, about 1884. £75

Victorian brass watering can. £8

Early 18th century
copper wine flagon.
£80

Victorian copper
preserving pan.
£32

Victorian copper
jelly mould.   £14

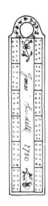

One of a pair of brass
Household Cavalry
cuirasses, 12in. long.
£195

Large copper kettle,
circa 1760.   £85

18th century brass
cribbage board by
James Swadell,
1780, 203mm.
long.   £90

A small Victorian
brass preserving
pan.   £7.50

One of two 17th century
Flemish brass alms dishes.
£810

George III copper
cauldron and lid,
circa 1770, 22in.
wide.   £95

COPPER AND BRASS

Prince of Wales
horse brass.£13

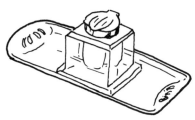

Late 19th century brass
inkstand with glass inkwell.£10

Horse brass in the
shape of a Welsh
harp.   £17

One of a pair of
Directoire ormolu
candlesticks, 11½in.
high.   £450

One of a pair of 17th
century Flemish brass
alms dishes.   £800

One of a pair of late
17th century brass
ecclesiastical candle-
sticks, 2ft. high.£40

One of a pair of ormolu
mounted figure chamber
sticks, 22cm. high. £135

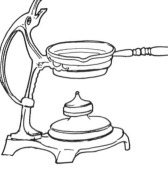

Late 19th century
ornate brass wax
warmer.   £15

One of a pair of
George I brass
candelsticks.£190

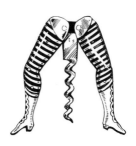

German pocket corkscrew in the form of a can-can dancers legs. £45

Victorian steel corkscrew. £1.50

19th century staghorn corkscrew. £11

A Dowler's type corkscrew. £36

Unusual Dutch silver corkscrew, 4½in. high. £290

Mid 19th century rare bronze corkscrew, possibly French. £1,050

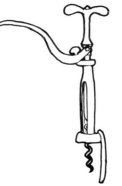

Victorian corkscrew with horn handle and brush, about 1860. £10

Single lever corkscrew by Charles Hull, 1864. £205

Late 19th century plated pocket corkscrew. £3

COSTUME

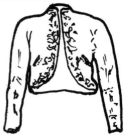

Schiaparelli jacket. £60

Wedding bonnet of ivory georgette, about 1835-40. £24

Tunic of a Georgian Inspector of Yeomanry. £125

An officer's uniform of the King's Hussars. £175

A complete State livery of the noble house of Stourton. £80

A Victorian sergeant's uniform of the 3rd Norfolk Rifle Volunteer Corps. £70

Georgian officer's jacket of the Perthshire Fencibles, circa 1800. £125

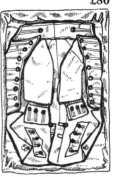

A Georgian officer's scarlet coatee, circa 1810. £200

18th century suit of orange velvet with fine embroidery. £700

17th century Italian
bobbin lace flounce.
£30

Carolean linen
cap.   £165

Victorian Colonel's
tunic of the Middle-
sex Yeomanry.£210

A complete Hussar
officer's uniform.
            £140

Scottish piper's composite
uniform of the Seaforth
Highlanders.   £65

Early Victorian officer's
full dress uniform of the
Prince Albert's Own
Hussars.   £1,050

Hand woven linen
smock frock or
round frock used by
a shepherd.   £75

Late 18th century Chinese
court robe of peach silk.
            £220

Heavily embroidered
Victorian tunic
belonging to Lt. Col.
Stannus.   £210

Kathe Kruse wistful doll signed on foot in purple, 18in. high. £141

Heubach Bunny doll with yellow tinted egg, 5½in. high. £31

French bisque headed doll with kid body and bisque arms, 17in. tall. £175

A rare two-faced doll by Bru. £2,300

Japanese doll by Simon and Halbig. £700

German bisque shoulder headed doll with kid body. £15

Ringmaster from the Schoenhuts Humpty Dumpty circus, with bisque head, 9in. high. £80

French bisque swivel headed doll with composition body and glass eyes, 20in. tall. £250

Italian Lanci felt doll, 1930's. £28

German doll
by Armand
Marseille. £20

China half doll of pale
colouring except for
oranges in the basket,
4in. high.   £38

'Little Nurse' from
the Boer War in ori-
ginal condition,
with fixed blue eyes.
                    £86

An unusual French 'Bon
Bon' doll with bisque
head marked Gebruder
Krauss, 20in high. £118

Heubach boy doll,
circa 1920.   £70

China half doll,
5in. high, with
fine detail, no
marks.   £22

Parian doll with cloth
body, 14in. tall. £250

German bisque
bathing beauty,
7in. tall.   £30

Parian doll with pain-
ted eyes and closed
mouth, 21in. tall.
                    £150

Wooden swivel headed doll with glass eyes, 14in. tall. £75

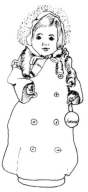

Bisque swivel headed doll with glass eyes, marked Jumeau, 20in. tall. £250

Bisque headed character doll. £600

German bisque shoulder head doll with blue eyes, marked Heubach, 12in. tall. £85

Bisque swivel headed doll with brown eyes, marked Heubach. £85

French bisque Bru doll with paperweight eyes and kid body, 22in. tall. £1,000

Late Victorian wax doll, circa 1900. £60

German thirties type china half doll, 4in. high. £17

Kathe Kruse girl doll with real hair wig, 20in. high. £95

Grandma dolls
house doll,
5¾in. tall. £32

Pedlar doll with papier
mache head and moul-
ded hair, 8in. high,
circa 1840.   £225

Bisque swivel headed
doll with glass eyes
and pierced ears,
marked Steiner. £80

Bisque swivel headed
doll with stationary
paperweight eyes,
marked Jumeau, 18in.
tall.   £200

German bisque swivel
headed doll with com-
position jointed body,
marked Heubach,
18in. tall.   £95

All wood doll with
swivel head and
painted eyes, marked
Schoenhut, 17in.
tall.   £100

German doll,
circa 1890. £15

All bisque 'Nudie' of
fine quality, with
mohair wig, 6in. long.
£41

Bisque dolls
house doll, 5in.
tall.   £34

DOLLS

Bisque headed
character doll by
Simon and Halbig.
£550

Very rare paper doll in box
marked La Poupee Modele
with six dresses and three
headdresses.   £361

A.M. doll, bisque
jointed with
stationary eyes
and mohair wig.
£100

20th century bisque
headed Googly doll
by Simon and Halbig.
£1,600

Trousseau for 19th century
French Bru doll.   £500

19th century
Continental
porcelain headed
doll, 13½in. high.
£120

Bisque headed bebe
doll, in original silk
dress.   £480

'Lord and Lady Clapham',
William and Mary wooden
dolls.   £16,000

19th century
French Bru
doll.   £2,400

232

Late 18th century
Bilston enamel
patch box. £85

Battersea plaque attributed
to Ravenet, 3½in. high,
circa 1755. £300

Oval Battersea portrait
plaque, 3½in. high,
circa 1755. £55

Mid 18th century snuff
box, 3in. wide, possibly
Birmingham. £240

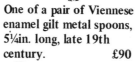

Birmingham patch box,
1¾in. wide, circa 1760-
65. £200

One of a pair of Viennese
enamel gilt metal spoons,
5¼in. long, late 19th
century. £90

Central European
enamelled flask
with pewter mount,
6¼in. high, circa
1750. £400

Bilston finch bonbonniere,
2in. high, circa 1770. £380

Central European
enamelled flask
with pewter mount,
6¼in. high, circa
1750. £190

ENAMEL

Colourful Majorcan vase signed Garcliola Mallorca, with polychrome enamel, 8½in. high, around 1920. £50

Small enamelled gilt vase by Ludvig Lobmeyer of Vienna, about 1870, 5in. high. £280

A small Bilston enamel egg shaped box decorated with flowers. £160

Early Birmingham snuff box, mid 18th century, 2½in. diameter. £170

Bilston scent bottle of baluster form, 3½in. high, circa 1765-70. £100

Rare Battersea portrait plaque after Ravenet, 3½in. high, circa 1755. £220

Cylindrical ivory box inset with a Bilston enamel plaque, about 1780. £50

Bilston cane handle, 2½in. high, circa 1765. £140

Bilston finch bon-bonniere, 2¼in. high, circa 1770, beak chipped. £420

A rectangular,
Birmingham enamel
snuff box painted
with Juno and floral
decoration, 2in. wide.
£85

Art Nouveau gold
and enamel fairy
pendant.   £150

One of a pair of German
enamel plaques, 3½in.
wide, circa 1730.   £650

Rare oval Battersea
portrait plaque, 3½in.
high, circa 1755. £100

Enamelled mosque
lamp decorated in
Islamic taste, circa
1870.   £1,150

Unusual Bilston soap
box, 3in. high, circa
1770.

A small Bilston
enamel case for a
scent bottle. £85

Bilston hare bonbonniere,
3in. wide, circa 1770.
£420

Embossed Bilston
etui, 4¼in. high,
circa 1770.   £260

ETUI

Late 18th century Staffordshire etui complete with thimble, needles and scissors. £400

An etui depicting a girl holding a basket, circa 1756. £110

Chelsea etui of cylindrical form, circa 1756. £180

A rare 'Girl in a Swing' etui with Columbine head top, circa 1754. £700

Etui and scent bottle modelled as a putto. £75

Chelsea etui with harlequin head top, 12.5 in., circa 1760. £170

An etui and scent bottle combined, The Three Graces. £150

Mid 18th century jasper and gold mounted etui. £120

Hand-painted fan on fine silk,
lace and bone, circa 1880, 1ft.
high.   £25

French fan set with mother-
of-pearl panels, circa 1760,
10in.   £950

Fan with collection of forty
signatures of composers,
authors, etc., 1895.   £500

18th century fan, painted after
Lancret and with carved and
pierced ivory sticks.   £55

A black kid fan, painted with
gods and goddesses and flowers
on the reverse, circa 1695. £210

Victorian lace fan with embroidered
flowers.   £12

Victorian ivory fan with pierced
decoration.   £9

Fan with carved ivory sticks,
French, about 1760.   £950

FIRE HEARTHS

George III brass and steel serpentine front grate, 2ft. 2in. wide. £220

Victorian cast iron and brass fireplace with maroon tile surround. £100

Early 19th century Adam style cast iron chimneypiece painted to simulate marble, 5ft. 4in. wide. £200

Pietro Bossi's chimney piece with brass and iron grate. £4,725

Victorian brass and iron firegrate. £100

Regency period brass and steel 'X' frame basket grate. £155

19th century marble fireplace with cherub frieze and original grate. £700

Mid 19th century carved oak fireplace with central mask and columns. £225

Lead example of the firemark of the Worcester Fire Office, 1790.   £800

Shamrock fire and life insurance mark, 1823-25.   £440

Bristol Crown fire mark, lead, 8in. high.   £220

Hants., Sussex and Dorset Security mark.   £400

Porcelain firemark of the Athenaeum Fire Office.   £660

St. Patrick Insurance Company Dublin mark.   £260

Convexed oval firemark of the Phoenix Fire Office, 1782.   £500

Lead firemark of the West of Scotland Insurance Company.   £600

Royal Exchange mark.   £55

239

BEDS AND CRADLES

17th century oak cradle on rockers.
£210

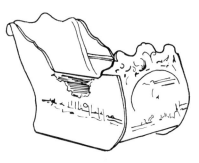

Dutch child's cradle in the form of a sledge, 22in. long. £210

Walnut veneered French bedstead, 45in. wide, circa 1860. £225

Mahogany four-poster bed, circa 1820, 78in. long. £475

Elizabethan oak four-poster bed with panelled headboard. £1,900

Kidney-shaped Empire style child's cradle, circa 1800, 39in. long. £540

18th century French bed, circa 1780, with shaped ends, canopy and bedspread, 8ft. 6in. high.   £800

18th century Italian walnut four-poster bed.   £640

Early 19th century pinewood cradle on rockers, 36in. long.   £45

Late Victorian mahogany half tester bed, complete with original drapes.   £350

19th century Venetian giltwood bed, 78in. wide.   £1,800

Victorian four-poster mahogany bed.   £275

One of a pair of Regency mahogany dwarf bookcases, 25in. wide. £1,900

Late George III mahogany circular revolving library bookcase on turned column and splayed legs, 27½in. diameter. £1,600

One of a pair of portable mahogany bookcases with fine reeded legs and original castors.£2,500

George III mahogany breakfront bookcase, 5ft. wide. £1,700

Dutch marquetry bookcase on shaped chest, 6ft. 3in. high.£1,150

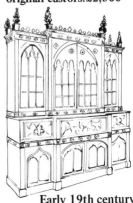

Early 19th century library bookcase. £6,500

Regency rosewood bookcase with brass inlay, 57in. wide. £2,200

Fine 18th century Hepplewhite breakfront bookcase, circa 1780, 7ft.7in. wide. £4,000

One of a pair of early Georgian bookcases.£1,000

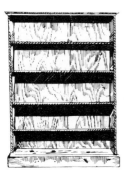

Victorian pinewood
bookshelves, 3ft.
wide.   £35

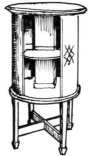

Edwardian mahogany
circular revolving
bookcase, 19¼in. diam.
£78

A tortoiseshell bamboo
bookcase with glazed
doors.   £49

19th century walnut
open bookshelves
with white marble
top.   £125

Late Regency breakfront
rosewood bookcase, 6ft.
6in. wide.   £1,250

Large 19th century Con-
tinental kingwood and
marquetry inlaid book-
case.   £2,500

Regency rosewood
bookcase, circa
1820.   £430

George III satinwood
breakfront library
bookcase.   £4,500

Oak bookcase with
glazed upper half
and carved doors.£395

243

BOOKCASES

Edwardian burr maple bookcase inlaid with ebony and satinwood.
£350

Edwardian mahogany breakfront bookcase, 9ft. long.   £1,300

19th century inlaid mahogany revolving bookcase.   £105

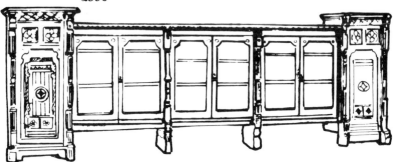

Gillow & Co. inlaid walnut bookcase with cupboards at each end, 1870, 174in. long.   £480

Edwardian mahogany and satinwood marquetry inlaid breakfront library bookcase, 6ft.3in. wide.   £1,850

Early 19th century figured mahogany breakfront bookcase, 100in. wide.   £2,600

Edwardian mahogany breakfront bookcase, 74in. wide.   £4,600

Victorian mahogany
bookcase with glazed
upper section, 4ft.
3in. wide. £280

George II mahogany library
bookcase, 9ft.4in. high.
£2,900

Edwardian Sheraton
mahogany three-section
library bookcase. £850

Mahogany bookcase of
'Strawberry Hill' design,
48in. wide. £740

Late George III period
mahogany breakfront
bookcase. £2,300

Edwardian inlaid
mahogany bookcase,
6ft. long. £2,800

Fine Georgian breakfront
mahogany bookcase, 8ft.
8in. wide. £2,250

Mahogany bookcase,
circa 1790, 39½in.
wide. £1,295

George III breakfront
mahogany library
bookcase. £900

BUREAUX

George I walnut bureau with cross-banding and stringing. £900

George III bureau, circa 1770, 3ft.2in. wide. £395

Yew wood bureau, circa 1750, with moulded and panelled sides, 38in. wide. £800

18th century walnut crossbanded and feather strung bureau. £450

18th century Dutch floral marquetry bureau, 39in. wide. £1,700

Small George I walnut bureau, 2ft. 3in. wide. £1,700

Small Georgian oak bureau of plain design, 2ft.6in. wide. £540

19th century stripped pine bureau on bracket feet, with brass handles, 3ft. wide. £160

18th century oak bureau with wooden handles and bracket feet. £400

18th century Dutch marquetry bureau with floral decoration. £1,650

Queen Anne period burr elm bureau with original handles, 30in. wide. £2,500

Early 19th century mahogany bureau with turned wood handles. £230

Fruitwood bureau in original condition, well fitted interior, 42in. wide, circa 1780. £585

18th century Dutch mahogany bombe bureau with cylinder front and pull-out writing surface, 3ft. 11½in. wide. £850

18th century bureau with parquetry inlay and ebony lines. £900

Fine Georgian mahogany bureau, 36in. wide, circa 1820. £425

Late 18th century Dutch walnut and marquetry bombe bureau. £1,700

18th century fruitwood bureau of unusual grain and colour, 3ft. wide. £450

BUREAUX

Dark mahogany Georgian bureau, interior with ten drawers and pigeon holes, 38in. wide, circa 1830. £485

Late 18th century Dutch marquetry bureau inlaid fitted interior, 38½in. wide. £1,700

A mahogany bureau with well interior and oak linings, circa 1720. £475

George III period mahogany bureau with fitted interior, 91cm. wide. £460

Golden oak bureau with mahogany crossbanding, 40in. wide, circa 1830. £345

Georgian mahogany bureau of good colour, 3ft. wide. £425

Early 19th century mahogany bureau on bracket feet, 3ft. 5in. wide. £300

19th century boulle bureau on cabriole legs. £475

Small Georgian mahogany bureau on bracket feet, 33in. wide. £400

18th century walnut
bureau, 37in. wide.
£620

Fine Dutch marquetry
cylinder bureau.
£4,400

Late 18th century
mahogany bureau
with nicely fitted
interior. £300

George III mahogany
bureau with brass
carrying handles,
39in. wide. £680

Mid 18th century Dutch
marquetry and walnut
bureau, 41½in. wide.
£2,000

Georgian mahogany
bureau, with original
handles, circa 1760,
3ft. wide. £475

19th century Dutch
marquetry bureau in
the Louis XV style.
£1,000

Mid 18th century shaped
front Dutch walnut bureau
on paw feet, 4ft. 4in. wide.
£3,500

Rosewood and mar-
quetry French Bureau
de Dame, circa 1870,
65cm. wide. £395

BUREAUX

19th century Oriental carved teak bureau.
£435

Late 19th century oak bureau on bulbous legs.
£30

Dark mahogany bureau, 42in. wide, circa 1810.
£625

Early 19th century German mahogany cylinder bureau, 3ft. 6in. wide. £600

'Wells Fargo' office cabinet. £1,250

Edwardian oak bureau on turned legs, 2ft. 10in. wide. £75

An Edwardian mahogany inlaid bureau with folding over writing board and three long drawers, 2ft. 6in. wide.
£140

18th century mahogany and satinwood bombe front bureau, 3ft. 6¾in. wide. £940

Early 19th century bureau veneered in curl mahogany.
£550

George III mahogany
bureau bookcase,
41in. wide.   £880

Late George III secretaire
bookcase, 7ft. 6in. high.
£1,600

Queen Anne
walnut bureau
bookcase.
£1,000

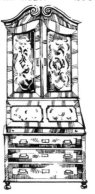

19th century walnut
bureau bookcase. £1,700

18th century bureau cabinet
in three sections, German.
£2,600

George III mahogany
bureau bookcase. £660

Dutch mahogany cylinder
bureau bookcase. £2,450

18th century walnut bureau
cabinet with ivory inlay.
£3,700

Antique oak bureau
bookcase.   £1,050

BUREAU BOOKCASES

19th century marquetry bureau cabinet. £3,000

Queen Anne style oak bureau bookcase on bracket feet. £795

Edwardian mahogany bureau bookcase on cabriole legs. £135

Georgian mahogany bureau bookcase, 3ft. 3in. wide. £950

Victorian bureau bookcase with glazed upper half. £654

Fine 19th century satinwood bureau bookcase of Sheraton design, 2ft.11in. wide. £930

Good George II mahogany bureau cabinet, 3ft.8½in. wide.£1,450

Georgian mahogany bureau bookcase.£820

Exceptional quality Queen Anne bureau bookcase with floral decoration, only 2ft. 7in. wide. £10,000

252

18th century burr maple bureau bookcase on bun feet. £8,000

Rare Queen Anne walnut bureau bookcase. £3,000

Early 18th century maple bureau bookcase with pewter string inlay. £6,200

Edwardian bureau bookcase in mahogany with satinwood banding. £800

18th century South German bureau cabinet in walnut veneer, 1.16m. wide. £6,400

Hepplewhite period bureau bookcase. £675

Chippendale bureau bookcase in figured mahogany, 7ft.7in. high. £2,100

Georgian mahogany bureau cabinet. £900

Small George I burr walnut veneered low waisted bureau cabinet. £4,400

CABINETS

19th century cabinet set with enamel plaques. £22,500

17th century ebony Antwerp cabinet. £2,400

17th century English black and gilt lacquer cabinet on stand, 39in. wide. £1,250

George III mahogany collector's cabinet with bookshelves, 76in. high. £385

Rare 17th century lacquer cabinet painted in gold on black, 38in. wide. £1,850

17th century Flemish cabinet. £1,250

17th century Dutch oak cabinet on bulbous legs. £875

Victorian ebonised cabinet with ormolu decoration and walnut inlay, 3ft. 6in. wide. £285

Edwardian music cabinet with fall front drawers. £35

Mahogany secretaire
cabinet of the Regency
period, 7ft.10in. high. £4,200

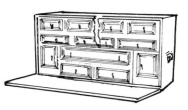

17th century Spanish
walnut vargueno with
iron locks and handles,
45in. wide. £650

Early Queen Anne
burr walnut cabinet
on stand, 70in. high.
£2,900

18th century black
lacquered cabinet
on a carved and
gilded base. £410

Red lacquered cabinet with
chinoiserie decoration , 55in.
wide(in need of restoration)
£590

Fine Oriental hardwood
cabinet, gold panels with
ivory carvings, 48in.
wide. £1,150

Walnut and mahogany
cabinet with leathered
top, 47in. wide, circa
1840. £285

Fine Oriental cabinet
with ivory panels,
46in. wide. £1,350

Late Edo period
Japanese Hasamibako,
64.5cm. wide.£2,900

CABINETS

Mid 18th century carved oak cabinet with gold leaf decoration, 28in. wide. £195

Georgian collector's cabinet with hinged top, by John Toulette, 1830, 21in. £185

Mahogany Edwardian music cabinet, 22in. wide. £175

Oriental carved hardwood display cabinet. £875

Chinese lacquer cabinet on stand, 58cm. wide. £75

Sheraton style cabinet with glazed upper half and boxwood inlay below. £850

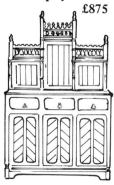

Late 19th century English oak cabinet with pierced gallery, 51in. wide. £110

One of a pair of superb Regency mahogany inlaid cabinets with marble tops. £7,500

18th century South European cabinet. £750

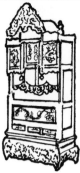

One of a pair of late 18th century mahogany cabinets with shaped marble tops.   £2,250

Oriental chiffonier display cabinet.   £850

Queen Anne walnut cabinet on a chest, circa 1710.   £900

Continental inlaid half glazed cabinet.   £310

Spanish vargueno on stand.   £840

Edwardian mahogany cabinet with marquetry inlay, 64cm. wide. £130

Mahogany Continental cabinet, 50in. wide, circa 1840. £445

Victorian light oak side cabinet, inlaid with ebony, 30in. wide.   £70

Victorian walnut and amboyna side cabinet.   £350

CABINETS

19th century Flemish carved oak cabinet.
£800

Ivory inlaid walnut cabinet on stand.
£2,240

18th century Portuguese ebonised and inlaid cabinet on stand. £9,200

George III mahogany breakfront side cabinet, 6ft. wide. £2,400

17th century Antwerp ebonised and scarlet tortoiseshell cabinet.
£6,200

Spanish walnut vargueno, 18th century, 2ft. 9in. wide.
£1,350

17th century Flemish oak cabinet. £1,400

Late George III mahogany cabinet inset with 18th century Chinese mirror paintings. £6,000

One of a pair of coromandel wood cabinets on pine stands, with chinoiserie decoration. £1,500

Early 19th century Hispano-Moorish cabinet on stand, 33¼in. wide. £1,550

17th century Flemish oak cabinet with fielded panels. £440

George III painted side cabinet, 2ft. 9in. wide, repainted. £1,350

18th century Anglo-Indian bureau cabinet inlaid with engraved ivory, 117.5cm. wide. £36,000

Mid 19th century black lacquer shrine, 2ft. 11in. x 2ft. 8in. £600

Large carved Continental cabinet. £500

Fine Meissen and ebony cabinet, Dresden 1870. £15,500

CANTERBURYS

Victorian burr walnut canterbury with barley twist divisions and a drawer at the base. £85

Early Victorian canterbury 'what-not' in walnut and tulipwood. £168

Regency period rosewood canterbury. £225

Victorian mahogany canterbury in excellent condition. £145

George III mahogany canterbury on slender turned tapered legs. £400

Georgian mahogany four divisional canterbury. £235

Victorian figured walnut canterbury. £200

A fine quality early 19th century mahogany canterbury 'what-not' with book-rest top. £650

Victorian walnut tray top canterbury. £145

One of a set of six Regency mahogany dining chairs.
£920

One of a set of six Georgian mahogany lattice back dining chairs.   £660

One of a set of eight Victorian chairs in dark mahogany. £365

One of a set of five George II mahogany chairs with pierced Gothic splats. £1,400

Queen Anne walnut dining chair, part of a set of twelve singles and two carvers.
£2,000

One of a pair of 18th century dining chairs.
£170

One of a set of eight George III mahogany dining chairs. £1,100

One of a pair of George I walnut dining chairs with shaped pad feet.   £280

One of a set of six William IV dining chairs.   £560

DINING CHAIRS

One of a set of six mahogany dining chairs. £295

One of a set of eight late 17th century style dining chairs, including two arm chairs. £800

Black and gilt lacquer cane seated single chair, circa 1830, 32in. high. £48

One of a set of six mahogany dining chairs with needlework seats. £1,000

One of a set of four Victorian turned leg chairs. £85

One of a set of six Regency mahogany dining chairs. £490

Queen Anne walnut single chair with plain cabriole legs and pad feet. £200

One of a set of six oak and elm 18th century spindle back chairs with rush seats. £520

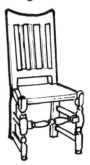

One of a pair of 18th century oak chairs. £135

DINING CHAIRS

One of a set of six Regency mahogany dining chairs. £460

One of a set of ten Hepplewhite period carved mahogany dining chairs.   £2,500

Single 17th century oak chair.   £115

One of a set of six Regency mahogany dining chairs in mint condition.   £695

One of a set of four Hepplewhite period mahogany chairs, circa 1795,   £450

One of a set of four Regency period mahogany chairs, circa 1810.   £375

One of a set of eight early Victorian mahogany dining chairs.   £695

One of a set of four English rosewood side chairs on cabriole legs.   £170

One of a set of six Hepplewhite chairs in mahogany. £700

DINING CHAIRS

Late Victorian Gothic style oak hall chair. £35

One of a set of six George III mahogany dining chairs. £500

One of a set of four plus two small Queen Anne style walnut dining chairs. £300

One of a set of six solid walnut dining chairs, circa 1740. £635

One of a pair of George I walnut side chairs on square cabriole legs. £400

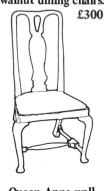

Queen Anne wall chair with central splat. £150

One of a set of six Georgian dining chairs. £850

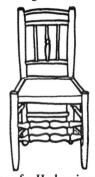

One of a Harlequin set of eleven spindle back chairs, country made. £285

One of a set of six Queen Anne fruitwood dining chairs, with rush seats on cabriole legs. £1,700

One of a pair of
antique hall chairs.
£350

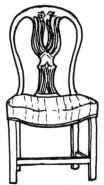

One of a set of ten plus
two Adam style maho-
gany dining chairs. £600

One of a set of six
early 19th century
rosewood dining
chairs.   £270

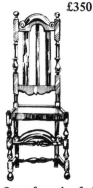

One of a pair of old
oak upright chairs
with scrolled arched
cresting rails.   £280

Queen Anne walnut single
chair with plain shaped
splat back, front cabriole
legs carved with foliage.
£190

One of a set of six
simulated rosewood
chairs, circa 1845. £335

One of a pair of good 19th
century mahogany hall
chairs with painted stag's
head crests.   £100

One of a pair of
Stuart style single
chairs.   £260

One of a set of five
George II walnut
dining chairs. £1,300

DINING CHAIRS

One of a pair of white and green painted chairs of Louis XVI design. £25

A good 17th century Dutch chair with leather upholstery. £520

One of a set of six George III mahogany dining chairs with shield backs. £650

One of a set of four Victorian walnut salon chairs, sold with a similar pair. £200

One of a set of eight Henry II walnut dining chairs. £2,100

One of a set of four Sheraton period sabre-leg chairs in faded mahogany with ebony lines, circa 1780. £395

One of a set of three 19th century satin-birch chairs. £200

One of a set of six Victorian walnut balloon-back chairs. £300

One of a set of six 19th century mahogany dining chairs in Hepplewhite design. £390

19th century elm
stickback chair. £5

One of a pair of
Hepplewhite chairs.
£95

One of a pair of early
19th century ladder-
back chairs with rush
seating. £65

One of a set of seven
Regency beechwood
chairs, with an 'X'
shaped splat. £475

One of a set of six mid
18th century Dutch
walnut chairs. £360

One of a set of fourteen
George III mahogany
dining chairs. £1,400

18th century mahogany
Chippendale chair. £135

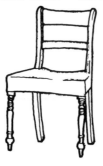

One of a set of six
plus one Georgian
mahogany dining
chairs. £440

One of a set of six
'dropped top rail'
mahogany dining
chairs. £1,600

DINING CHAIRS

One of a set of four
late 19th century
mahogany side chairs.
£150

One of a set of six
Victorian rosewood
chairs on turned
legs.   £325

One of a set of six
Victorian walnut
frame small chairs.
£400

Pair of William
and Mary oak
high-back hall
chairs.   £400

One of a set of eleven
mahogany Chinese
Chippendale chairs.
£5,000

One of a set of
twelve Victorian
mahogany dining
chairs.   £950

Single Victorian
walnut chair,
circa 1850. £28

One of a set of ten early
19th century rosewood
dining chairs.   £640

One of a set of six early
Victorian rosewood
dining chairs.   £670

One of a set of six
Hepplewhite design
shield back chairs.
£1,000

One of a set of three early
19th century Dutch mar-
quetry dining chairs. £290

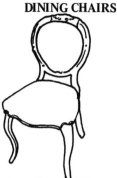

One of a set of four
Victorian walnut
hoop back dining
chairs.   £210

Queen Anne solid
walnut single
chair, circa 1710.
                £85

One of a set of six
Victorian walnut
dining chairs. £475

17th century
walnut chair.
                £75

One of a set of eight
mid Victorian rose-
wood dining chairs,
stamped J.S.   £410

One of a set of six
William IV dining
chairs.   £560

One of a pair of early
William and Mary
black painted beech
chairs.   £650

DINING CHAIRS

Two of a set of five mahogany dining chairs, circa 1830.   £345

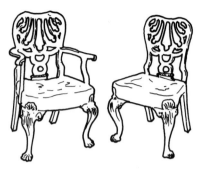

Two of a set of eight mahogany dining chairs, 19th century. £1,600

Part of a set of seven Chippendale style mahogany chairs, 39in. high, circa 1860.   £425

Two of a set of six single and two arm chairs in mahogany, Georgian, circa 1795.   £1,500

Part of a set of eight stick back chairs in golden colour.   £485

Two of a set of six late Victorian chairs.   £380

Two of a set of six dark mahogany dining chairs, circa 1850.   £685

Part of a very fine set of six single and two elbow Sheraton period chairs.   £1,500

Two of a set of twelve Chippendale design mahogany dining chairs.
                            £3,800

Two of a set of eight Hepplewhite style mahogany dining chairs. £900

Part of a set of six Regency mahogany dining chairs.   £720

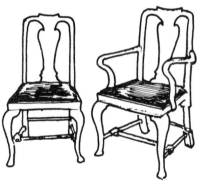

Part of a set of eight 19th century dining chairs on cabriole legs. £1,275

DINING CHAIRS

Two of a set of eight Hepplewhite style mahogany shield back dining chairs.   £900

Two of a fine set of fourteen William IV mahogany chairs, circa 1830.   £3,000

Two of a set of twelve Adam design mahogany dining chairs.   £1,950

Part of a set of eight Chippendale style chairs.   £1,250

Two of a set of twelve Queen Anne style dining chairs.   £2,500

Two of a set of eight 19th century Dutch marquetry dining chairs. £1,500

One of a set of
seven George
III dining chairs.
£800

One of a set of twelve
Chippendale maho-
gany chairs.   £2,600

One of a set of
fourteen William
IV mahogany
dining chairs.£900

George II red
walnut corner
elbow chair.
£175

Edwardian mahogany elbow
chair with boxwood string
inlay and upholstered seat.
£32

George II elm
corner arm
chair with solid
seat.   £74

Walnut renaissance
style 'X' frame
chair.   £210

Late 19th century child's
rocker in mahogany.£360

Large Hepplewhite
style chair made
for the 'Bristol Giant'.
£1,200

ELBOW CHAIRS

One of a set of eight George III mahogany chairs with painted back splats, one carver slightly different. **£900**

One of a set of ten mahogany arm chairs in the Hepplewhite style, with serpentine fronted seats. **£1,250**

One of a set of seven Regency mahogany dining chairs, circa 1810. **£650**

17th century Italian child's oak high chair. **£480**

Georgian cock-fighting chair. **£450**

18th century stick back ash and elm Windsor chair, circa 1779, 41½in. high. **£95**

Charles II beechwood arm chair with phoenix front stretcher. **£320**

Comb back Windsor arm chair. **£130**

One of a set of five reproduction Chippendale style dining chairs. **£205**

One of a set of six dark mahogany chairs with serpentine fronts, circa 1850. £635

One of a set of seven Sheraton period mahogany chairs with serpentine front seats covered in Lees tapestries, circa 1780. £750

One of a set of six Georgian mahogany chairs, two carvers and four singles. £550

Yew wood Windsor chair, circa 1740, with cabriole legs at front. £280

William IV mahogany and caned bobbin-backed corner elbow chair. £42

One of a set of ten mid 18th century Gothic elbow chairs. £4,800

One of two carved and ebonised Oriental chairs. £500

One of a set of seven reproduction Chippendale style chairs. £165

Yew and elm Windsor chair. £170

ELBOW CHAIRS

Early 18th century
walnut arm chair of
superb colour. £950

Mid Victorian open
arm chair.   £160

A nicely proportioned
early 19th century
Mendlesham chair. £250

Watchman's chair in
oak, circa 1800. £400

One of a pair of English
Queen Anne arm chairs
in walnut with needle-
work seat and back.
              £6,800

17th century oak wains-
cot chair, inlaid to panel
back and broad cresting
rail.   £265

Late 18th century
Windsor yew tree
chair.   £125

18th century rush
seated spindle back
arm chair, circa 1760,
39¼in. high.   £75

18th century yew
wood shellback
Windsor chair. £88

Yew wood and burr elm carver, part of a set of two carvers and six singles, circa 1840. £1,100

One of a set of four Windsor armed chairs with bowed stretchers and squab cushion seats. £740

17th century heavily carved oak elbow chair. £260

Restoration period walnut caned arm chair, circa 1680. £145

Lancashire rocking chair. £124

One of a set of four George I mahogany chairs and matching settee. £660

Mahogany arm chair by Gillows, circa 1790. £200

Sheraton mahogany elbow chair, circa 1820. £85

Regency fruitwood arm chair with reeded rail back and leather seat.£25

ELBOW CHAIRS

A Windsor armed chair with bowed stretcher and squab cushion seat. £87

George III yew wood and elm, child's high chair. £200

Victorian Gothic oak hall chair. £60

Early 19th century yew wood Windsor chair with Gothic back. £235

Victorian elm ladder-back carver chair. £38

Edwardian inlaid mahogany corner chair with rush seat. £37

Ash and elm Windsor arm chair with crinoline stretcher, circa 1850. £98

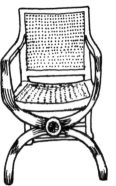

One of a pair of open arm chairs in mahogany. £175

A fine quality, late 18th century mahogany, child's chair. £150

One of a set of four Windsor armed chairs of yew wood and elm on turned legs joined by bowed stretchers.   £580

One of a set of six Provincial quality Sheraton chairs, circa 1790.£700

One of a set of six George III elm Windsor chairs.£820

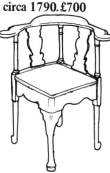

Superb George I walnut corner chair.   £700

18th century Italian carved giltwood processional chair. £90

Mahogany Chippendale elbow chair, circa 1760. £110

Charles II walnut carver chair, sold with two standards, circa 1680. £525

Victorian elm smoker's chair. £15

One of a pair of Queen Anne walnut chairs with oak slats.£275

EASY CHAIRS

19th century cabriole legged prie dieu chair in walnut. £98

One of a pair of Edwardian wicker garden chairs. £320

Silver leaf Carolean high backed chair. £600

Porter's chair in Regency style. £275

Victorian mahogany framed open armed chair £230

One of a pair of carved padouk wood swivel tub chairs. £520

Victorian inlaid walnut buttonback chair. £125

Victorian,lady's, walnut chair. £176

North Italian walnut chair with Moresque ivory inlay. £230

George III wing
chair on turned
legs.   £132

Military officer's
convertible chair-
bed in iron and
brass, circa 1840-
60.   £150

Victorian French style
carved gilt wood chair
upholstered in dark
green dralon.   £195

One of a pair of
heavily carved
oak chairs. £300

18th century Continental
walnut scroll arm easy
chair on cabriole legs.£420

Fine George III
mahogany saddle
wing chair, 81cm.
wide.   £325

Very fine,William
and Mary,walnut
wing chair.£1,400

Small Victorian walnut
nursing chair on turned
legs.   £90

Upholstered and restored
Victorian walnut arm
chair.   £140

EASY CHAIRS

One of a set of twelve Victorian carved oak chairs. £1,100

Chippendale period and design mahogany bergere chair. £800

One of a pair of William IV caned mahogany scoop-back clubroom bergeres. £500

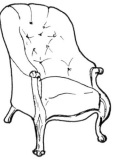

Late 19th century rosewood bergere. £160

One of a pair of rare late 17th century English needlework-covered beechwood armchairs, circa 1685. £2,000

Louis XVI giltwood fauteuil by A. Gailliard. £520

Rare George I giltwood chair on cabriole legs. £450

Victorian papier mache balloon back arm chair. £270

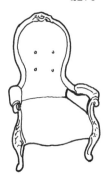

Victorian walnut rococo carved spoon back chair. £240

Queen Anne period, upholstered, walnut wing chair. £1,500

Louis XVI beechwood bergere with shaped back, bow fronted seat and tapering legs. £350

Chippendale period design chimney chair. £350

American library arm chair attributed to Duncan Phyfe, circa 1815. £13, 300

One of a pair of George III mahogany French style arm chairs, with restorations, on cabriole legs. £320

George II walnut wingback arm chair, covered in velvet. £600

Louis XVI bergere with a moulded ribbon carved arched back and bow fronted seat. £350

One of a pair of Victorian walnut framed arm chairs. £380

Louis XV beechwood fauteuil stamped L. Cresson, on cabriole legs. £620

EASY CHAIRS

Edwardian mahogany tub chair with upholstered back and seat.
£26

Victorian walnut balloon back nursing chair.£235

Late 17th century walnut framed open arm chair on turned frame.   £360

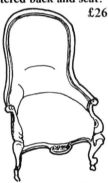

One of a pair of Victorian walnut easy chairs with cabriole legs.£440

One of a set of eight Louis XVI chairs.
£5,000

Louis XVI style carved beech child's chair.£60

Late 19th century mahogany George II style arm chair in leather.   £200

One of a pair of Victorian mahogany balloon back arm chairs.   £800

One of a pair of 18th century library arm chairs in Chippendale style.   £2,200

William and Mary oyster veneered walnut and marquetry chest, 3ft. 5in. wide. **£1,400**

Early 19th century Dutch marquetry bombe shaped chest of drawers, 37in. wide. **£1,000**

Early 17th century Lombard walnut chest, 3ft. 10in. wide, the top drawer converted to a secretaire. **£620**

George III mahogany serpentine fronted chest, 3ft. 10in. wide. **£500**

William and Mary oyster veneered walnut chest of five drawers, 3ft. 2in. wide. **£1,600**

George II mahogany serpentine chest of four drawers, 3ft. 10in. wide. **£1,450**

George II mahogany serpentine fronted chest of drawers, 3ft. 7in. wide. **£600**

Walnut chest of drawers in the William and Mary style, 3ft. 1½in. wide. **£620**

Serpentine mahogany chest in the manner of Thomas Chippendale. **£8,000**

CHESTS

Oak chest of drawers
with original handles,
circa 1780, 3ft.4in.
wide.   £175

Dutch marquetry
and mahogany
chest.   £1,400

Dutch walnut marquetry
bombe chest, 34in. wide.
                £1,475

George II mahogany
serpentine chest,
3ft. 7in. wide. £580

One of a pair of late
Georgian yew wood
veneered chests of
drawers, 19in. wide.
           £1,000

Mahogany chest of
drawers with marble
top, 48in. wide.
                £225

Georgian mahogany chest
of drawers, 37in. wide,
circa 1820.   £195

Queen Anne oak
chest of drawers,
2ft. 10in. wide.
         £185

17th century oak chest
with half bobbin
moulding.   £260

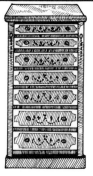

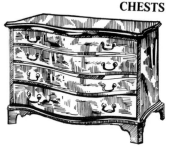

Large mahogany serpentine chest inlaid with ebony, circa 1810, 4ft. wide. £395

Wellington chest by Edwards and Roberts. £600

Serpentine fronted mahogany chest of drawers. £2,100

Walnut Queen Anne chest of drawers with original drop handles, circa 1700, 38in. wide. £450

Early 19th century French rosewood bow fronted chest of drawers with marble top, 24in. wide. £560

Superb George I red walnut chest of drawers, circa 1725, 41in. wide. £685

Mid 18th century walnut, shaped front, chest on bun feet, 32in. wide. £3,000

George I walnut chest, 2ft. 7½in. wide, on bracket feet. £1,250

Charles II oak geometrical moulded chest of drawers, circa 1660, 39in. wide. £750

CHESTS

Regency period
mahogany chest
of drawers, circa
1800.   £220

William and Mary, walnut
veneered chest of drawers
inlaid with geometric
stringing.   £545

Queen Anne, walnut
chest of drawers,
80cm. wide. £1,500

Mahogany chest of
drawers, circa 1840.
          £65

Walnut veneered chest of
drawers on bracket feet,
about 1715, 54in. high.
          £600

Georgian mahogany
chest of four long
drawers on bracket
feet, 34in. wide. £110

Early 18th century
solid walnut bachelor
chest on bracket feet.
          £3,000

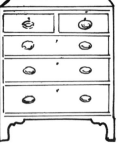

Mahogany veneered
chest of drawers,
ebony strung, 3ft.
wide, circa 1820. £155

19th century straight
front mahogany chest
on bracket feet. £50

Early 19th century
bombe fronted chest.
£480

Charles II walnut
and marquetry chest
of drawers, 37in.
wide.   £920

Mahogany bow-fronted
chest of drawers, 3ft.
wide, circa 1820. £195

18th century marquetry
chest of drawers. £950

William and Mary,figured
walnut,chest of drawers,
38in. high.   £440

Georgian mahogany
chest of drawers,
circa 1820.   £78

Queen Anne walnut
bachelor's chest,
26in. wide. £1,050

French mahogany chest
of drawers with original
ormolu mounts and
handles, 38in. wide,
circa 1850.   £335

Chippendale period chest
of drawers with brushing
slide, circa 1750. £415

CHESTS

18th century walnut marquetry chest.
£1,900

Late 18th century mahogany serpentine chest, 53in. wide.
£2,000

Jacobean oak and mother-of-pearl inlaid chest of drawers. £1,100

Late 18th century Dutch walnut marquetry chest of drawers, 33½in. wide. £1,500

Mid 18th century walnut chest of drawers on bracket feet. £260

Early 18th century walnut Cumberland chest of drawers.
£770

Mahogany bowfront chest of drawers, oak lined, 42in. wide, circa 1820. £165

A superb ormolu mounted cartonnier.
£11,000

Late 19th century walnut chest on a plinth base. £30

Early oak chest of
drawers in original
condition, 38in.
wide, circa 1740.
£245

Georgian mahogany
chest of drawers, 34in.
high.   £700

17th century chest
with drawers in
oak.   £490

Oak chest of drawers
with moulded front,
circa 1690.   £350

Early 18th century
bachelor's chest
with folding top.
£750

Late 18th century
carved oak chest
of drawers, 39in.
wide.   £250

17th century
fruitwood
moulded front
chest of drawers.
£525

Small Georgian
mahogany ser-
pentine fronted
chest. £1,900

Chippendale period chest
of drawers with brushing
slide, 43in. wide. £820

291

CHEST ON CHEST

Very fine Queen Anne walnut tallboy, circa 1705, 39in. wide. £1,700

17th century oak chest in two sections, decorated all over, 38in. wide.   £1,000

Early Georgian walnut tallboy, 183cm. high.   £1,250

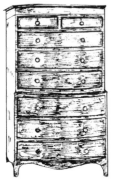

Late 18th century mahogany inlaid tallboy.   £245

Early Georgian walnut tallboy.   £775

Mahogany tallboy with original brasses, 42in. wide, circa 1825.   £365

George I tallboy in walnut and oak, 3ft. 5in. wide.   £820

Early 19th century mahogany tallboy, 3ft. wide.   £850

Queen Anne tallboy on bracket feet, about 1714. £2,750

Queen Anne, walnut, chest on stand, 43in. wide. £1,440

George III oak chest on stand. £300

Early 18th century oak chest on stand, 37½in. wide. £340

Small oak chest on stand with moulded drawer fronts, 52in. high, circa 1780.£265

18th century walnut chest on stand with short cabriole legs. £750

Early 18th century walnut chest on stand. £350

Late William and Mary walnut chest on stand with crossbanded drawers. £3,500

Walnut chest on stand with herringbone inlay to drawers, circa 1780, 55in. high. £565

Early 19th century simulated walnut chest on stand, 2ft. 8in. wide. £455

293

CHIFFONIERS

Mid 19th century
faded mahogany
chiffonier, 35in.
wide.   £105

Small Georgian
mahogany chiffonier,
40in. wide, circa 1830.
                    £175

Unusual chiffonier,
veneered with 'flame'
mahogany, 42in. wide,
circa 1850.   £125

Rosewood chiffonier
with brass grilled doors
and gallery, 42in. wide,
circa 1840.   £245

Solid satinwood chiffonier,
circa 1830, 45in. long.
                    £550

Regency brass inlaid
mahogany chiffonier
with brass grilled
doors.   £400

Early Victorian
chiffonier in
rosewood, 35in.
wide.   £245

Mahogany Regency
chiffonier, 33in.
wide.   £285

Early 19th century
simulated rosewood
chiffonier, 30in. wide.
                £165

Boulle display cabinet, red tortoiseshell, 32in. wide, circa 1840. £275

19th century French kingwood vitrine. £1,200

Dutch walnut and marquetry inlaid display cabinet, 31¼in. wide.£200

Late Georgian mahogany display cabinet, 17in. wide. £240

Louis XV style kingwood display and writing cabinet, circa 1860. £3,600

Veneered mahogany display cabinet in the French style, 27in. wide. £1,300

20th century inlaid satinwood display cabinet. £650

Mid 18th century Dutch colonial calamander wood display cabinet, 7ft. 5in. high. £1,400

18th century Dutch marquetry display cabinet, 36½in. wide. £1,950

CHINA CABINETS

Late 19th century mahogany display cabinet with mirrored back and cabriole legs. £60

One of a pair of walnut and parcel-gilt display cabinets.   £1,412

Edwardian mahogany bow front display cabinet, 1.22m. £260

Edwardian satinwood display cabinet. £665

18th century Dutch marquetry bombe shaped vitrine.
                £4,750

Decorated satinwood two-door vitrine,19th century, 102cm. wide.
                £595

Antique French tulip-wood vitrine in the Louis XV manner, on shaped legs, 4ft. 3½in. wide.   £1,050

Edwardian inlaid mahogany display cabinet.   £340

Edwardian inlaid mahogany china cabinet, 28in. wide.
                £125

Mahogany bijouterie table with glazed top and sides, 61cm. £180

Late 18th century Dutch marquetry display cabinet, 34in. wide. £1,900

Small inlaid mahogany Edwardian display cabinet with dentil cornice, 19½in. long. £185

Mid 18th century Sinhalese display cabinet on stand, 5ft. 3in. wide. £700

Fine example of a 'Louis Revival' Edwardian cabinet. £245

18th century Dutch walnut and marquetry vitrine. £2,950

18th century Dutch marquetry display cabinet, 36½in. wide. £1,950

French kingwood and ormolu display cabinet. £900

Fine Continental walnut display cabinet with arch top, 1.12m. £1,250

297

COMMODES AND POT CUPBOARDS

Victorian mahogany one step commode on short turned legs. £12

18th century oak commode with dummy drawers. £110

Late 18th century mahogany, tambour fronted, night commode, with carrier handles. £130

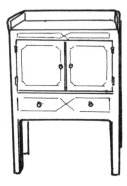

Light mahogany inlaid converted commode, circa 1820. £150

Early 19th century mahogany night commode, 25½in. wide. £145

George IV mahogany bedside commode with fall front, 67cm. £100

William IV mahogany bedside cupboard, panelled door, 44cm. £48

Early 19th century mahogany tray top commode. £115

French provincial oak bedside cupboard with carved door, 43cm. £58

Louis XV kingwood parquetry commode stamped M. Criaerd, 3ft. 4½in. wide. £3,600

Louis XV/XVI marquetry petite commode stamped N. Petit, JME, 1ft. 3in. wide. £4,800

One of a pair of French 19th century parquetry commodes with two drawers and marble tops. £1,336

Mid 19th century ebonised and marquetry commode. £3,000

Louis XV ormolu-mounted kingwood parquetry commode, 4ft. 10in. wide. £4,600

18th century German ormolu-mounted commode of Louis XV design. £2,500

18th century commode in marquetry. £1,750

Louis XV kingwood ormolu mounted commode, 2ft. wide. £2,000

Louis XV kingwood ormolu-mounted marquetry commode with grey and white marble top and two drawers, 2ft. 8in. wide. £2,300

COMMODE CHESTS

A good 19th century marquetry commode with floral decoration. £2,100

Superb late 18th century Dutch marquetry commode.   £2,250

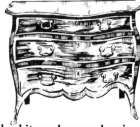

Hepplewhite mahogany dressing commode of bombe form with serpentine front, swept apron and ormolu mounted feet, 3ft. 7in. wide.   £2,900

One of a pair of French commodes by Jacques van Oostenryk, in oak mounted in ormolu, 1.12m. wide.
£26,000

Mid 18th century fruitwood commode with ormolu mounts and curved sides, 34½in. wide.   £1,000

Fine marquetry bombe commode in Louis XV style with serpentine front, 63½in. wide.   £6,000

18th century Austrian walnut commode chest.   £690

Late 18th century Dutch marquetry commode, 36in. wide.   £1,200

COMMODE CHESTS

Louis XV provincial walnut commode, probably made to order. £1,350

18th century Italian ivory inlaid commode chest. £1,600

Small serpentine shaped cupboard commode in kingwood, with ormolu mouldings and mounts. £640

18th century Dutch marquetry commode. £2,250

19th century French kingwood commode. £1,400

Walnut serpentine three-drawer commode, ormolu handles, 35in. wide. £225

Fine 19th century French rosewood commode. £1,885

Louis XV tulipwood and mahogany petite commode, 18¼in. wide, stamped M.E.L. Hermite. £5,600

301

CORNER CUPBOARDS

George III mahogany
bow fronted corner
toilet cupboard, 29in.
high.   £180

Late 18th century
pine corner cupboard
of good colour. £65

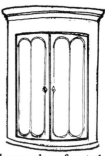

Mahogany bow fronted
and crossbanded Shera-
ton corner cupboard,
circa 1790, 44½in. high.
                    £210

Fine Georgian corner
cabinet in mahogany.
                    £820

Mahogany bow front
corner cupboard,
circa 1790.   £185

18th century pine
corner cupboard
with shaped
interior.   £185

Georgian domed
corner cupboard,
circa 1740. £340

Attractive corner
cabinet, 39in. wide,
circa 1850.   £285

Mahogany Regency
corner cupboard,
36in. wide, circa 1820.
                    £535

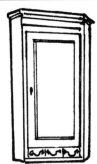

Mahogany corner
cupboard with three
small drawers with
original handles.£245

18th century Dutch
oak corner shelves,
29in. high, circa
1750.   £95

18th century oak
corner cupboard
with original lock
and key.   £140

Late 19th century
pine standing corner
cupboard.   £75

Oak corner cupboard
with mahogany inlays,
33in. wide, circa 1840.
                £115

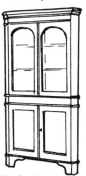

Early 19th century
oak and mahogany
double corner
cupboard.   £295

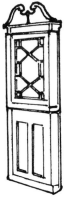

Mid 18th century
double oak corner
cupboard.   £595

Edwardian mahogany
corner cabinet, 40in.
wide.   £175

18th century
corner cupboard,
mahogany. £520

CORNER CUPBOARDS

Victorian pine corner cupboard with panelled door, 1m. high.
£58

Bow fronted mahogany corner cupboard with original brass hinges, circa 1790. £220

Fruitwood corner cupboard, 40in. high. £150

18th century walnut double corner cupboard, 246cm. high. £2,000

George I mahogany corner cupboard, 4ft. wide. £1,900

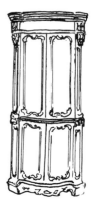

One of a pair of Italian rococo parcel gilt painted corner cupboards, £1,250

Good, George II mahogany corner cupboard in two parts, 4ft. 3in. wide. £650

One of a pair of Louis XV ormolu mounted parquetry encoigurnes by D. Genty, 2ft. 7in. wide. £3,600

George III mahogany bow front corner cupboard, 1.14m. £115

Oak corner cupboard with shell inlay, circa 1800. **£80**

Oak and mahogany double door corner cupboard, circa 1790. **£165**

18th century oak corner cupboard with arched panelled door, 40in. high. **£105**

George III oak double corner cupboard, 3ft. 3in. wide. **£420**

18th century Dutch marquetry corner cupboard. **£3,750**

George III mahogany corner cupboard, 1.06m. **£155**

Mahogany corner cupboard with boxwood inlay, 1.03m. **£95**

Louis XV kingwood hanging encoigurne with three shaped shelves, 1ft. 3in. wide. **£320**

Bow fronted oak corner cupboard, circa 1750. **£210**

CREDENZAS

Victorian serpentine front burr walnut and ebonised credenza, 6ft. 6½in. wide.   £1,220

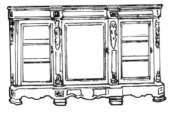

French ebonised and red boulle side cabinet, probably 19th century.
£780

19th century rosewood breakfront credenza.   £460

19th century French ebonised cabinet inlaid with hardstone and boullework.
£650

Victorian walnut and marquetry credenza with bronze mounts.£2,500

Victorian walnut and marquetry inlay credenza.   £500

Mid 19th century walnut credenza with marquetry designs.   £1,275

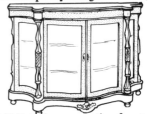

Mid Victorian serpentine fronted credenza with glazed doors, 166cm. wide.   £595

French walnut food
hutch, circa 1780.
£325

Small Victorian pine
bedside cupboard.
£25

Victorian carved oak
hanging cupboard.
£20

Georgian oak livery
cupboard, 4ft. wide.
£360

George III country
made oak cupboard,
6ft. high.   £200

17th century oak
parlour cupboard.
£800

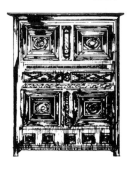

17th century French
provincial carved oak
cupboard.   £500

Late 17th century
oak bread cup-
board.   £365

17th century carved oak
court cupboard with
panelled doors, 4ft. 3in.
wide.   £900

CUPBOARDS

Small size early
18th century oak
tridarn.   £820

17th century oak
court cupboard,
61in. wide. £700

Late 17th century
Welsh oak tridarn.
                    £600

17th century oak
tridarn, 51in. wide.
                £900

18th century French
provincial oak buffet,
210cm. long. £1,050

17th century oak
court cupboard, 4ft.
6in. wide.   £980

Fine 18th century
oak Breton cupboard,
59in. wide.   £1,050

Jacobean oak court cupboard.
                                £2,000

17th century South
German walnut and
inlaid side cupboard.
                    £1,400

A good Bavarian carved
walnut cupboard, 7ft.
wide.   £2,200

Victorian 17th century
style corner court
cupboard.   £160

20th century reproduction
oak court cupboard with
leaded glass doors.   £90

A finely carved 17th
century Dutch oak
cupboard.   £7,000

18th century Dutch
mahogany linen
press, 66in. wide.
           £920

17th century court cup-
board in medium coloured
oak with carved date 1636,
5ft.9in. wide.   £575

Gothic oak court
cupboard with
finely carved panels.
           £2,500

Early 18th century carved
oak court cupboard. £660

Late Victorian carved
oak buffet.   £95

CUPBOARDS

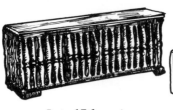

18th century Continental carved walnut bread cupboard with spindled front. £620

Late 17th century yew wood bread cupboard. £725

17th century needlework casket with the arms of John Evelyn. £1,000

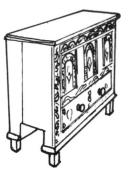

Oak coffer with lunette carvings and arcaded panels, circa 1700. £375

19th century French carved oak cupboard on a stand, 48in. wide. £600

17th century small oak court cupboard, 2ft. 11in. wide. £2,700

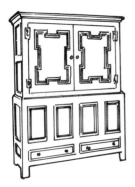

Late 17th century oak press. £520

17th century oak hanging cupboard with iron furnishings. £530

An early 17th century panelled oak cupboard. £925

Victorian walnut davenport, amboyna and boxwood line inlay.   £250

Victorian walnut davenport with inlaid top and front.   £250

Late George III mahogany Davenport attributed to Gillows, 1ft. 8in. wide.
£380

Regency rosewood swivel top davenport.   £350

Attractive George III mahogany davenport.
£490

Regency rosewood davenport surmounted by a brass gallery, 17in. wide.   £350

Victorian walnut davenport with spring-operated super-structure and brass gallery, 22in. wide.   £380

Victorian walnut davenport with cabriole leg supports.
£325

Victorian walnut davenport, 21½in. wide.   £400

DRESSERS

Queen Anne oak dresser of nine drawers with central cupboard. £740

George III oak dresser on cabriole legs, with three drawers.   £570

Small Charles II oak dresser with two turned legs at front, 41in. wide.   £1,150

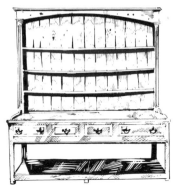

**Early 19th century dresser and rack in honey coloured oak, 64in. long.
£560**

George III stripped pine dresser with four drawers and pot board, 6ft. 9in. wide.   £395

Small 19th century stripped pine dresser with drawers and cupboards, 3ft.3in. wide.   £190

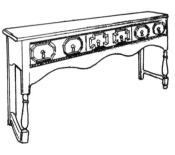

Late Georgian Welsh oak dresser, 72in. wide.   £900

George II oak dresser, 67in. wide.   £670

Oak dresser base, 66in. long, circa 1840.   £345

17th century oak dresser base with three moulded panelled drawers. **£900**

Late 17th century oak dresser with turned front legs. **£740**

Late 17th century oak dresser base. **£900**

Victorian pine dresser of good honey colour, 50in. wide. **£190**

Antique solid walnut dresser with lift up top on ogee bracket feet, 59in. wide. **£650**

18th century oak dresser with shelves. **£1,575**

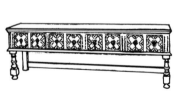

18th century cottage dresser. **£650**

Unusually long Charles II oak dresser, 17th century, 108in. wide. **£3,500**

Open potboard dresser, 6ft. high. **£225**

DRESSERS

18th century oak dresser. £840

Early 18th century oak dresser base, 4ft. 6¼in. wide. £1,725

18th century oak dresser, 66in. wide. £1,280

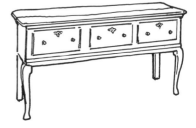

Jacobean oak dresser of three drawers, with pot board, 73in. wide. £1,100

Early 18th century oak dresser with cabriole leg front supports, 69in. wide. £590

Early 18th century small oak dresser with brass knobs, 53in. £1,600

Mid 18th century oak dresser, circa 1750, 69in. wide. £1,450

Good quality late Victorian pine dresser. £100

Victorian Jacobean style dresser, 4ft. 7in. wide. £145

17th century oak and mahogany crossbanded Welsh dresser. £1,600

18th century oak Welsh dresser, 75½in. x 80in. high. £725

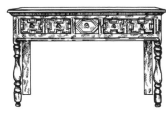

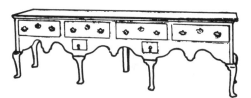

Early 19th century reproduction oak dresser with split bead decoration. £330

A good early 18th century oak dresser, the drawers crossbanded with walnut, 9ft. wide. £2,700

Handsome Welsh dresser on cabriole legs. £720

18th century French provincial oak dresser. £1,250

18th century oak clock dresser, dial signed Nathaniel Olding, Wincanton, 96in. wide. £1,100

DRESSING TABLES

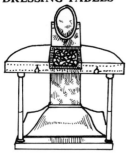

Dressing table by Emile-Jacques Ruhlmann, circa 1920, 43½in. wide. £6,655

Queen Anne walnut side or dressing table, 2ft. 8in. wide. £1,700

Rare Sheraton period mahogany 'D' table, 36in. wide, circa 1780. £575

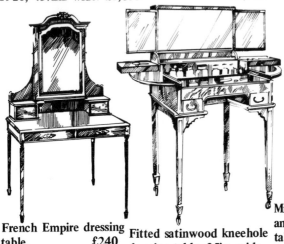

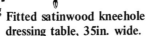

French Empire dressing table. £240

Fitted satinwood kneehole dressing table, 35in. wide. £780

Mid 19th century walnut and ormolu mounted toilet table, signed Tahn of Paris, 53cm. wide. £395

Georgian mahogany dressing table with rising mirror, 42in. wide, circa 1820. £255

George I walnut side or dressing table, 2ft. 8in. wide. £1,450

Superb, ladies fully fitted satinwood dressing table, 90cm. wide. £580

George I walnut secretaire chest. £540

Dutch walnut secretaire on bracket feet. £1,200

18th century fall-front escritoire, lacquered. £370

Louis XVI style kingwood and satinwood inlaid escritoire. £1,350

Louis XVI secretaire a abattant by F.G. Teune. £2,200

Early 19th century Italian walnut and marquetry escritoire, 34¾in. wide. £640

19th century walnut escritoire inlaid with enamel, on cupboard base, 3ft. 4in. wide. £3,600

Walnut veneered Bieddermyer escritoire, 40in. wide, circa 1860. £385

Rare mid 18th century German kingwood secretaire a abattant, 3ft. 5½in. wide. £6,000

317

KNEEHOLE DESKS

Ormolu mounted boulle kneehole desk, 43½in. wide.   £1,050

George III mahogany architect's desk with rising top, 40in. wide.   £600

A nicely proportioned Queen Anne walnut kneehole desk with original brass handles.   £1,200.

Regency mahogany pedestal kneehole desk, 4ft. wide.   £385

Oak kneehole desk of nine drawers and centre cupboard, 33in. wide, circa 1820.   £245

A George III mahogany kneehole desk on platform base.   £850

George IV mahogany kneehole desk, top inset with leather, 3ft.5½in. wide.£280

Partner's double sided oak desk with leather top, circa 1860, 31in. high.   £395

Rare 18th century fruitwood kneehole desk of fine golden colour, 2ft. 11in. wide.   £975

Early 19th century ivory inlaid kneehole desk, 3ft.5in. wide.   £7,900

George III pine kneehole desk with cockbeaded drawers, 3ft.4in. wide.   £320

Continental kneehole desk in parquetry applied walnut, circa 1680, with hinged top, 43in. wide.   £2,500

Chippendale kneehole desk, circa 1770, 3ft. 9in. wide.   £535

Late 18th century kneehole desk in mahogany.   £900

Oak partner's desk with panelled sides, green leather top, nine drawers either side.   Top size 6ft. by 4ft.   £585

Mahogany kneehole desk with leathered slide, 38in. wide.   £680

Small Georgian mahogany kneehole desk, circa 1735.   £650

Mid 19th century mahogany banker's desk.   £130

KNEEHOLE DESKS

Edwardian reproduction satin-wood kneehole pedestal desk. £880

Handsome George III partners desk in mahogany, 4ft. wide, circa 1790.   £1,285

Victorian mahogany cylinder front pedestal desk of nine drawers, 4ft. 6in. wide.   £200

Oak kneehole desk with bow doors and six drawers, circa 1850. £265

Fine 19th century japanned pedestal desk, 3ft. 10in. long.   £420

Mid Victorian carved oak partner's desk , 6ft. 1in. long.   £525

George I burr walnut kneehole desk, 30¼in. wide.   £1,750

Late George II padoukwood kneehole writing table, 4ft. wide.   £800

Queen Anne walnut lowboy with quarter-veneered crossbanded top, 2ft. 6in. wide. £800

Walnut veneered lowboy, 30in. wide, on cabriole legs. £1,050

Queen Anne walnut and crossbanded lowboy with glass top, 30in. wide. £360

Small 18th century oak lowboy with brass drop handles. £350

A fine George I oak lowboy on square cut legs. £280

Early Victorian walnut lowboy with claw and ball cabriole legs, 30in. wide. £200

Early 18th century walnut veneered lowboy on cabriole legs. £1,100

George III walnut and fruitwood lowboy, 30in. £230

321

SCREENS

Empire style pierced brass fire screen, 26½in. high. £550

Early Victorian, mahogany framed, octagonal firescreen. £45

Late Victorian hardwood screen with applied ivory decoration. £220

Victorian carved hardwood Chinese screen with floral decoration. £240

Early 20th century beechwood firescreen with needlework panel. £15

A good late Victorian carved coromandel wood screen with lacquered decoration of birds and foliage. £700

Victorian walnut framed firescreen with embroidered panel. £45

Mid 19th century French giltwood screen with painted panels. £325

Victorian mahogany screen with adjustable slide. £25

Late 18th century mahogany framed firescreen with embroidered silk panel. £80

A fine two-fold Shibayama table screen. £360

Late Victorian rosewood polescreen with needlework panel. £35

Victorian embossed leather three fold screen. £115

Late 18th century Chinese seven fold lacquer screen, 7ft. high. £2,700

Victorian three fold scrap screen, 5ft. 6in. high. £115

Victorian carved walnut and gilt fire screen, 5ft. 5in. £190

Late 19th century embossed four panel bird screen, 8ft. 4in. wide. £350

19th century Oriental silk panelled four fold screen, 5ft. high. £85

SCREENS

Four-fold painted screen, 5ft. 6in. high. £480

Pole screen in rosewood and walnut with tapestry, circa 1850. £90

Kengoku grained lacquer two-fold screen, late 19th century. £7,000

Louis XVI giltwood screen with eight panels. £3,400

18th century Chinese draught screen, 1.88m. high. £2,200

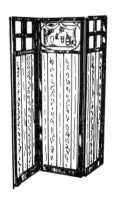

19th century French screen. £75

Late 18th century gilt-wood firescreen with needlework panel. £110

French gilt frame two sectional draught screen. £56

Small mahogany chest of drawers with secretaire drawer, 34in. wide, circa circa 1800. £285

Regency secretaire chest in flame mahogany, circa 1820. £285

Good mahogany secretaire of the Sheraton period, interior with concave drawers and inlay, 43in. high, circa 1800. £445

Late George III secretaire bookcase, 7ft. 6in. high. £1,600

Early 19th century American mahogany writing cabinet, 4ft. 2in. wide. £700

Victorian mahogany secretaire bookcase in superb condition. £880

Louis XV period French secretaire a abattant on oak. £5,200

An Edwardian satinwood secretaire bookcase, 92cm. wide. £580

George III mahogany secretaire chest, 42in. wide. £2,000

SECRETAIRES

Early 18th century burr walnut secretaire cabinet. £7,500

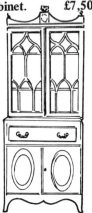

Late 18th century rosewood secretaire bookcase. £850

Early 19th century satinwood secretaire bookcase. £850

George III secretaire bookcase with Gothic glazing bars. £625

Small Louis XV kingwood secretaire a abattant with brown marble top, 2ft. 1in. wide. £5,500

Fine breakfront bookcase with fitted secretaire drawer. £1,500

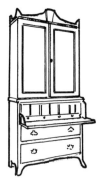

George III country oak secretaire bookcase, circa 1790, 3ft. 6½in. wide. £465

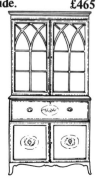

George III mahogany secretaire bookcase on splayed feet, 4ft. wide. £1,600

George III mahogany secretaire bookcase. £540

George III maho-
gany secretaire
bookcase. £610

Hepplewhite mahogany
secretaire inlaid with
rosewood and satin-
wood.   £1,800

18th century walnut
secretaire cabinet with
barley twist columns.
                    £620

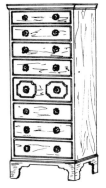

George III mahogany
secretaire tallboy, 2ft.
5in. wide.   £600

Late George II maho-
gany secretaire cabinet
attributed to Thomas
Chippendale, 96in.
high.   £2,800

Georgian secretaire,
4ft. 2in. wide by
7ft. 10in. high.£750

Early Victorian
mahogany secretaire
bookcase.   £640

Early 19th century chiffonier
with secretaire drawer and brass
gallery, 4ft. wide.   £395

Late Georgian maho-
gany secretaire book-
case, 42½in. wide.£700

SETTEES AND COUCHES

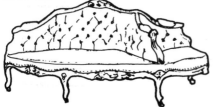

English gilt, plaster and wood settee of shaped oval form, divided into four sections, about 1830.   £900

19th century ebonised beech day bed on sabre legs with brass castors.   £260

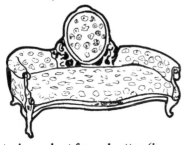

Victorian walnut framed settee (in need of upholstery).   £290

Chippendale period mahogany framed settee, 5ft. 2in. long. £400

Chair back four seat settee, 6ft. 6in. long.   £380

Part of a seven-piece walnut framed suite of drawing room furniture.   £1,200

Early 19th century couch of classical form, 6ft. long. £525

Excellent curved pine settle, circa 1840, 4ft. wide.   £195

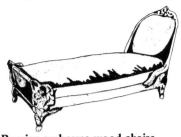

Russian amboyna wood chaise
longue with gilt enrichments. £5,500

A carved oak hall settle, 56in. long.
£260

Victorian carved mahogany, buttonback settee on cabriole legs. £180

19th century oak monk's bench,
the back hinged to convert to a
table. £150

SETTEES AND COUCHES

Unusual Victorian tubular brass-
framed settee. £620

Late 19th century inlaid mahogany
couch on cabriole legs. £120

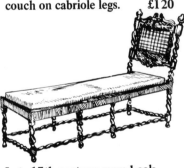

Late 17th century carved oak
day bed. £300

18th century oak triple chair back
settee, 62in. wide. £230

329

SETTEES AND COUCHES

17th century oak box settle. £1,450

19th century carved oak settle, 1.23m. wide. £240

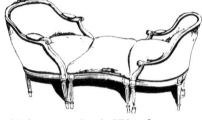

19th century Louis XV style duchesse in three parts. £600

Rare, early 19th century Danish neo-classic settee, 8ft. 4in. wide. £520

Fine Queen Anne period red walnut settee, circa 1710, 48in. wide.£1,250

Late 19th century rosewood settee, 5ft. 7in. long. £440

Louis XVI gilt canape with petal-moulded frame, 4ft. 5in. wide. £620

Upholstered swing seat, 90in. tall, circa 1880, made in India. £900

Louis XV beechwood canape on moulded cabriole legs, 5ft. 1in. wide. £450

Victorian walnut framed sociable settee. £320

A good Victorian double ended rosewood settee on cabriole legs. £475

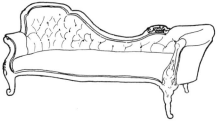

Regency walnut framed chaise longue. £500

Late 19th century mother-of-pearl inlaid hardwood settee, circa 1880, 6ft. 7in. long. £580

Late 19th century beech settee stained to resemble mahogany. £85

Walnut frame settee of George II design with rectangular back and feet, 46in. high. £330

Victorian rosewood framed chaise longue on turned legs. £160

SHELVES

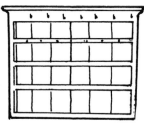

18th century oak pewter plate rack with shaped top, 57in. long, circa 1790. £125

George III, turned mahogany hanging bookshelves, 33in. wide.   £128

Fine Welsh delft plate rack, circa 1750.   £195

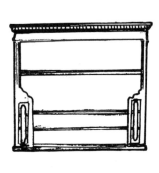

Queen Anne oak hanging delft or pewter plate rack , circa 1720.   £225

Georgian mahogany bookshelves, 35in. wide, circa 1825.
£185

Regency mahogany hanging bookshelves, circa 1820, 26½in. wide.   £95

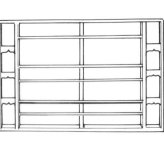

Dutch triangular hanging shelves with carved top, circa 1820, 31½in. wide.
£125

18th century oak plate rack, 55in. wide.   £210

Victorian stripped pine glazed hanging cabinet 2ft. 6in. wide.   £44

Late Victorian Jacobean style carved oak sideboard. £90

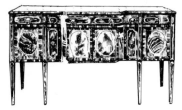

Late 18th century Sheraton mahogany sideboard with inlaid ovals. £4,000

George III mahogany bow-fronted sideboard crossbanded in satinwood, 5ft. 6in. long. £1,300

Late George III mahogany sideboard with scrolled superstructure, 6ft. 2in. wide. £620

Regency mahogany bow-fronted sideboard, 6ft. 5in. long. £600

An Edwardian mahogany breakfront sideboard, with boxwood inlay, 6ft. wide. £140

Early 19th century bow-fronted sideboard, 45in. long. £125

Large carved oak sideboard, 19th century, Flemish, 8ft. 2in. long. £2,050

SIDEBOARDS

Georgian mahogany sideboard with tulipwood banding, 54in. long.
£1,200

Small Georgian mahogany sideboard, 36in. wide, circa 1830. £165

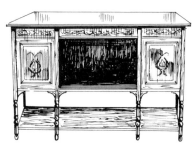

Edwardian inlaid rosewood sideboard with undertier. £120

Mahogany George III sideboard inlaid with ebony, 7ft. wide, circa 1810. £550

Reproduction Georgian mahogany bow-fronted sideboard, 1.22m. wide. £80

Sheraton breakfront mahogany serving table with line inlay. £500

Sheraton style sideboard in mahogany with marquetry reserves, 72in. high. £550

Victorian stripped pine sideboard of good colour. £170

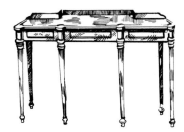

George III satinwood breakfronted serving table, 71in. wide. £750

Sheraton mahogany half-round sideboard with glass top, 72in. wide.
£440

Late Georgian mahogany bow-fronted sideboard, 49in. wide. £270

Late 19th century oak sideboard in the Gothic style, 59in. high. £220

Early 19th century mahogany sideboard with crossbanded drawers and boxwood string inlay. £750

Small Sheraton sideboard, 18th century, in faded mahogany, circa 1790, 50in. long. £685

Early 19th century mahogany pedestal sideboard with lion's mask handles. £275

Fine Sheraton period bow-fronted mahogany sideboard with good patination. £550

Sheraton sideboard of superb colour, 5ft. 6in. long. £1,450

George III mahogany serpentine sideboard, 4ft. 6in. wide. £2,200

19th century D-shaped mahogany sideboard inlaid with box and ebony stringing, 59in. x 24in. £650

German mahogany bow fronted sideboard, crossbanded in satinwood. £1,300

German concave sideboard in figured mahogany, 54in. wide. £275

George III mahogany bow fronted sideboard, 78in. wide. £700

Attractively figured Sheraton serpentine fronted sideboard. £2,200

George III mahogany bow fronted sideboard, 4ft. 7in. wide. £1,150

George III mahogany bow fronted sideboard, 5ft. wide.   £1,200

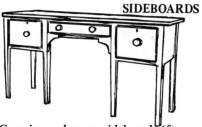

Georgian mahogany sideboard, 6ft. wide.   £290

Small mahogany sideboard with drawers, cellaret and sliding trays, 48in. wide, circa 1850.   £125

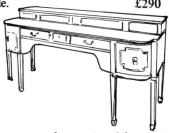

Regency mahogany breakfront sideboard with ebony inlay, 7ft. 6in. wide.   £440

Small mahogany Georgian sideboard 55in. wide, circa 1825.   £165

Victorian walnut marquetry inlaid sideboard with mirror back, 5ft. 4in. wide.   £1,700

Antique demi-lune sideboard. £725

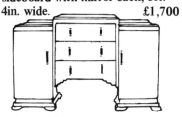

Art Deco sideboard in amboyna wood, 5ft. 2in. long.   £35

STANDS

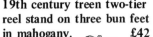

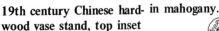

19th century treen two-tier reel stand on three bun feet in mahogany. £42

19th century Chinese hardwood vase stand, top inset with marble, 36in. high. £74

Oriental hexagonal hardwood stand with inset marble top. £30

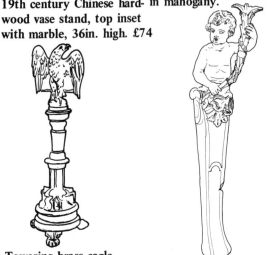

Towering brass eagle lectern, 70in. high, 1904. £500

Rare portrait stand used by photographers. £600

One of a pair of Napoleon III bronze, gilt-bronze and marble torcheres, 6ft. 2½in. high. £5,500

William IV mahogany music stand on shaped platform base. £285

Victorian bamboo magazine stand with lacquered decoration £95

One of a pair of Chinese rosewood and mother-of-pearl inlaid urn stands, 41in. high. £360

One of a pair of
Japanese vase stands,
24in. high. £2,300

19th century black lacquer
and gilt jardiniere.   £160

Victorian mahogany
music stand, 11in.
wide.   £130

Victorian mahogany hat-
and-coat stand.   £90

One of a pair of Italian
tapering pedestals, with
pietra dura panels. 37in.
high, circa 1860-70. £1,550

Victorian carved oak
hallstand, 7ft. high.
                £705

Victorian mahogany music
stand on cabriole legs. £75

Late 19th century
jardiniere, possibly
Continental.   £80

19th century Chinese hardwood vase stand with marble
top, 36in. high.   £66

STEPS

Set of oak Gothic library steps, 1850, 13in. wide. £60

Early 19th century mahogany library steps. £200

Regency mahogany bed steps with tooled leather step treads, circa 1820. £125

George III oak and satinwood library steps, 7ft. 8in. high. £2,450

Set of George III folding library steps, 7ft. 5½in. high, open. £320

George III mahogany library steps. £250

A set of early Victorian mahogany library steps which convert to a small arm elbow chair. £275

Unusual pair of mahogany bed steps, circa 1815. £480

Small late 17th century elm stool with an oval top.   £25

English yew tree joint stool, circa 1640, 23in. high, with good turnings and fine patination. £200

Edwardian mahogany piano stool.   £5

Victorian wind-up piano stool, upholstered in Dralon.   £38

A superb mid 19th century brass X frame stool, 2ft. 5in. wide.   £1,250

Victorian wind-up piano stool, upholstered in Dralon.   £40

One of a pair of fine Queen Anne stools, . 17½in. high. £3,500

Elm stool or stand with six legs and shaped undertier.   £26

Early Victorian rosewood stool with original needle-work seat, 24in. x 24in. £80

STOOLS

Edwardian mahogany stool on tapered legs with spade feet. £22

Late George II mahogany stool, 1ft. 10½in. wide. £500

George I walnut and parcel gilt stool with floral tapestry, 22in. £70

One of a pair of stools attributed to William Kent, of carved giltwood, 1.4m. wide. £5,500

One of a pair of early 17th century joined stools, maker's mark I.N. £950

18th century rectangular elm stool of good colour. £26

Good Victorian rosewood revolving piano stool. £25

One of a pair of George II mahogany stools, 1ft. 10in. wide. £425

Edwardian mahogany piano stool with an upholstered seat and cabriole legs. £18

One of a pair of Regency x-framed stools in simulated rosewood and parcel gilt. £1,500

Chippendale mahogany stool, circa 1760, 18½in. high. £1,450

19th century country made elm stool with turned legs. £7. 50p.

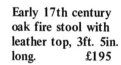

Victorian walnut cabriole leg dressing table stool. £45

Wind-up music stool in simulated rosewood, of American origin. £85

Early 17th century oak fire stool with leather top, 3ft. 5in. long. £195

Elizabethan joined stool with arcaded frieze and turned legs, 20in. high. £475

Mid 17th century oak stool, 1ft. 5in. wide.£375

Rare Wedgewood spinette stool, 18in. high. £480

Part of a Dutch salon suite, comprising a settee
and six dining chairs. £1,650

A superb quality mid-Victorian period suite, comprising settee, grandfather
chair and grandmother chair, inlaid with ebony and amboyna wood. £700

  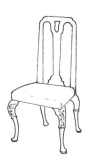

Near matching suite of Queen Anne furniture consisting of eight
chairs and walnut settee. £5,800

Part of a late 19th century high Victorian mahogany drawing room
suite of seven pieces.   £350

Part of a Victorian eight-piece suite in rosewood covered
with green leather.   £1,650

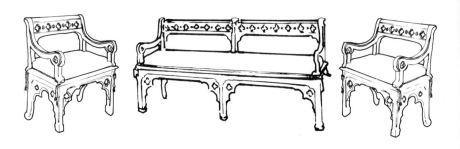

Part of a suite of Victorian Gothic revival seat furniture,
about 1845.   £1,150

CARD AND TEA TABLES

Early 19th century
tea table.   £135

George II mahogany
games table banded
in kingwood.   £420

Mahogany card table
on platform base,
29in. high, circa 1810.
£330

Edwardian Sheraton
revival mahogany
envelope top folding
card table.   £120

Rare Dutch marquetry
games table, two drawers,
circa 1790, 34in. diam.
£575

Italian mahogany and
tulipwood card table,
3ft. 2½in. wide. £480

Fine mahogany tea
table, crossbanded
top and front,
29in. high, circa
1800.   £375

Folding inlaid satin-
wood card table,
baize lined, circa
1800.   £150

Fine Regency rosewood
tea table on four con-
cave shaped legs, 2ft.
11½in. wide.   £780

Edwardian mahogany
envelope card table.
£70

George III tea table in
mahogany, on turned
legs.   £135

Regency card
table on splay
feet.   £185

Victorian burr walnut
fold-over tea table.
£325

One of a pair of satin-
wood card tables,
circa 1785.   £2,750

Regency swivel top tea
table on quadruple
base, circa 1830. £155

18th century laburnum
wood card table with
concertina action. £1,500

Regency mahogany
card table with
unusual front legs.
£250

19th century red boulle
card table mounted
with face mask ormolu
mounts, 95cm. wide.
£595

347

CARD AND TEA TABLES

Compact rosewood card table, circa 1860.   £215

George IV brass inlaid rosewood card table, 3ft. wide.   £750

Victorian burr walnut folding top card table on cabriole legs. £190

One of a pair of George III mahogany card tables, 3ft. wide. £1,450

19th century red boulle fold-over swivel top card table.   £310

Regency tea table on quadruple support.   £175

19th century mahogany fold-over top card table.   £280

George I walnut card table, 2ft. 10½in. wide, top replaced.   £500

Hepplewhite mahogany tea table, 33in. diam., circa 1790. £175

19th century Dutch marquetry card table, 2ft. 8in. high. £280

Early Victorian bird's eye maple tea table. £225

18th century mahogany inlaid tea table, 73cm. high. £425

19th century fold-over top card table. £1,050

William IV rosewood tea table on circular base, 92cm. wide. £210

George II mahogany tea table with ball and claw front legs, 31in. wide. £385

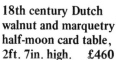
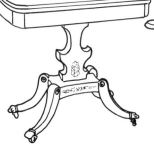

18th century Dutch walnut and marquetry half-moon card table, 2ft. 7in. high. £460

One of a pair of George IV rosewood card tables, 3ft. wide. £1,350

18th century inlaid walnut centre table with circular recesses for gaming counters. £3,900

CONSOL TABLES

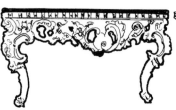

One of a pair of George II painted consol tables, 3ft. 5½in. wide. £1,100

Part of a French consol table, 6ft. 6in. wide. £195

Victorian cast iron consol table with marble top. £70

Early 18th century German carved oak consol table. £1,550

One of a pair of Empire ormolu-mounted bronze and mahogany consols, 1ft. 6in. wide. £1,700

Louis XVI ormolu mounted mahogany consol desserte, one of a pair. £2,300

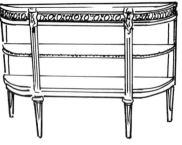

Regency brass inlaid consol table with marble top, 31in. wide. £275

Louis XVI consol desserte in kingwood veneer with marble top. £1,500

Early 19th century rosewood pier table with gilt decoration. £500

George IV mahogany breakfast table, 4ft. 5in. diameter. £600

Victorian walnut oval breakfast table on a quadruple base. £240

Regency brass inlaid rosewood table, 49½in. diameter. £650

Victorian circular walnut table, 52in. diameter. £580

English William IV circular rosewood dining table. £520

George IV circular mahogany breakfast table, 3ft. 5in. diameter. £440

Regency mahogany breakfast table, 5ft. 1in. x 4ft. 1in. £650

Early Victorian Continental salon table, 39in. diameter, with marble top. £445

19th century mahogany dining table with three spare leaves. £3,900

DINING TABLES

19th century oak dining table with carved frieze. £770

Fine Regency mahogany library table, 49in. diam., circa 1820. £750

Walnut Victorian centre table, 4ft. 3in. diameter. £820

17th century Flemish oak draw leaf table on bulbous legs. £900

Victorian circular inlaid rosewood dining table with scroll feet. £760

One of a pair of 18th century satinwood tables inlaid with bog wood. £1,750

Fine Victorian table with walnut veneers, top 52 x 35in. £675

Early 19th century mahogany pillar dining table. £275

Late Regency rosewood circular table, 127cm. diam. £500

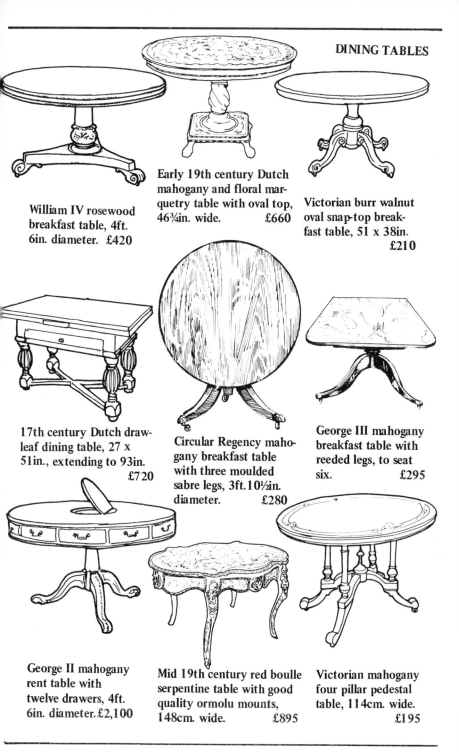

William IV rosewood breakfast table, 4ft. 6in. diameter. £420

Early 19th century Dutch mahogany and floral marquetry table with oval top, 46¾in. wide. £660

Victorian burr walnut oval snap-top breakfast table, 51 x 38in. £210

17th century Dutch drawleaf dining table, 27 x 51in., extending to 93in. £720

Circular Regency mahogany breakfast table with three moulded sabre legs, 3ft.10½in. diameter. £280

George III mahogany breakfast table with reeded legs, to seat six. £295

George II mahogany rent table with twelve drawers, 4ft. 6in. diameter. £2,100

Mid 19th century red boulle serpentine table with good quality ormolu mounts, 148cm. wide. £895

Victorian mahogany four pillar pedestal table, 114cm. wide. £195

DROPLEAF TABLES

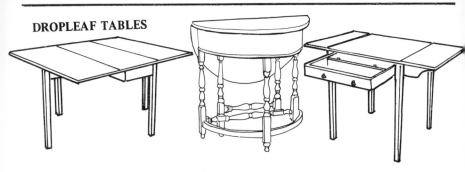

Early 18th century
oak cottage dining
table on square
tapering legs. £150

17th century oak
well table on
turned legs. £750

Mid 18th century
drop-leaf writing
table, 3ft. 6in.
wide.   £420

Rare yew wood envelope
table with flap supported
by a loper, circa 1730.
                    £690

Early George II mahogany
drop-leaf table with oval
top, 3ft. high.   £425

Country made oak
drop-leaf table, circa
1820.   £52

Mid 17th century oak
drop leaf table. £450

Early 19th century maho-
gany breakfast table on
quadruple sabre leg base.
                    £150

Oval drop-leaf table
in red walnut, 39in.
x 10in.   £288

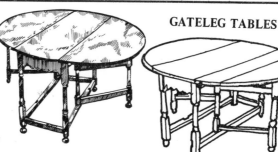
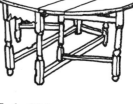

Victorian carved oak gateleg table on barley twist supports. £50

Oak gateleg table on turned legs. £500

Early 18th century oak gateleg table, 4ft. 5in. long. £330

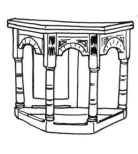
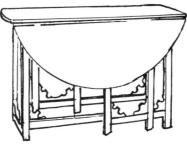

Mid 17th century oak credence table with carved frieze. £680

17th century Spanish walnut gateleg table with oval top, 4ft. 2in. wide. £550

Rare 17th century oak gateleg table with plain gate supports, 27½in. high. £545

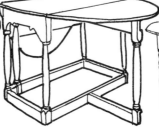
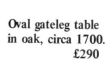

Large early 18th century gateleg table. £750

Early and unusual gateleg table in dark oak, 27in. high, circa 1730. £285

Oval gateleg table in oak, circa 1700. £290

LARGE TABLES

17th century Florentine walnut
refectory table, 7ft. 6in. long. £2,150

Carved rosewood library table. £440

Regency mahogany extending dining
table.   £1,000

Original George IV two pillar dining
table, circa 1820.   £1,450

Fine mahogany dining table with
lattice underframing, George IV,
circa 1825, 7ft. 6in. x 4ft. 5in.£580

18th century elm tavern table with
attractive patina.   £760

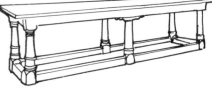

20th century reproduction pine
refectory table, 8ft. long. £185

17th century oak table with long
provenance.   £1,750

356

17th century South German refectory table in oak, 84in. long.   £1,750

Early 18th century Continental walnut dining table on shaped legs, 6ft. long.   £825

Solid mahogany dining table which makes two breakfast tables, circa 1830.   £485

Late George III figured mahogany twin pedestal dining table, turned columns and splayed supports. £1,000

Reproduction oak table in 17th century style.   £325

Austrian centre table of ash with oval ends. 5ft. 3in. wide, circa 1840.   £140

Mahogany dining table with cross-banded top, circa 1830.   £265

George III mahogany three pedestal dining table, 51 x 152in. extended.   £1,100

357

OCCASIONAL TABLES

George III oak tripod table with tip-up top on cannon barrel column.   £57

Victorian burr walnut salon occasional table.   £75

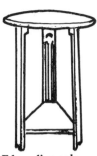

Edwardian oak occasional table. £12

Napoleon III kingwood display table with glazed oval top, 2ft.½in. wide.   £180

Edwardian satinwood marquetry two-tier table with shaped gallery and urn finials, 2ft.4in. high.   £160

Mid Victorian papier mache occasional table, top painted with a Highland scene, 1ft.9in. wide.   £120

George III mahogany circular supper table, 29½in. diameter.£220

Jacobean walnut oblong table, with moulded edge,of five spirally moulded legs with cross stretchers and bun feet, 3ft.6in. long.   £620

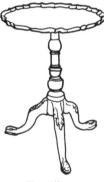

George II scallop and pie crust edge tripod table in finely figured mahogany.£210

French ormolu
marquetry table.
£300

One of a pair of 19th
century octagonal top,
occasional tables in
mahogany with marble
tops, 12in. wide. £180

18th century walnut
chateau wine tasting
table with folding
top.   £110

Centre table with
marble top on
tapering legs, 52cm.
diameter.   £450

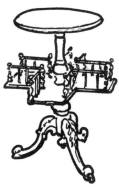

Victorian walnut dumb
waiter on tripod cabriole
legs, 18½in. wide. £180

19th century French
walnut and kingwood
occasional table, 29 x
19in.   £440

Mahogany tripod table
of Chippendale design
with top and base sup-
port carved, 30in. high. £115

Late 17th century
Spanish walnut
table.   £880

18th century pinewood
cricket table with stretchers.
£35

359

OCCASIONAL TABLES

19th century oriental bamboo and black lacquer centre table, 23in. wide. £185

Unusual Regency brass inlaid simulated rosewood mirror top table. £205

One of a set of four late 19th century rosewood occasional tables. £180

Fine 19th century Dutch marquetry centre table. £1,200

Louis XV transitional circular ormolu mounted table a ouvrage stamped RVLC JME, 1ft. 2½in. diameter. £4,000

Regency rosewood occasional table, with inlaid cut brass, 36 x 20½in. £1,100

18th century fruitwood cricket table with undershelf. £95

Indian ivory and ebony miniature chess table, 10½in. high. £140

Regency carved centre table with marble top, 2ft. 8in. diam., circa 1815. £395

OCCASIONAL TABLES

Victorian walnut tripod table with circular top, 21in. wide. £55

An unusual mid 19th century Gothic oak centre table with drawer. £190

Yew wood hexagon table with glass top, 29in. high, circa 1850. £265

18th century Oriental padouk centre table, 52½ x 23in. £420

Louis XVI tulipwood small table with white marble top, 1ft. 3in. wide. £900

Quartetto of early 19th century black lacquered tea tables. £157

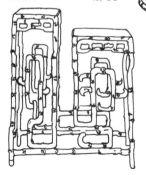

Mahogany tripod table with piecrust top on claw and ball feet, 29in. high. £140

Late 19th century rosewood etagere with two tops. £360

Marquetry table of Madeiran woods, circa 1851. £280

OCCASIONAL TABLES

Late George II mahogany tripod table, 2ft. high. £750

Late 18th century Dutch marquetry centre table, 84cm. long. £310

Victorian elm tilt-top table. £54

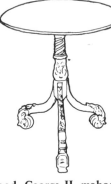

George III mahogany tripod table with tilting top, 31in. diam. £450

A Continental walnut circular table with tip-up action, the top satinwood inlaid, 2ft. 6in. diam. £120

Good, George II, mahogany tripod table with circular top, 1ft. 11in. diam. £600

Louis XVI style, oval giltwood table with inset marble top, 70cm. £240

George II mahogany tripod table, 2ft. 6in. high. £1,300

Oval satinwood occasional table with square tapering legs, 58cm. high. £88

Sheraton period mahogany Pembroke table with rosewood crossbands, 29in. wide. **£400**

Late 18th century mahogany Pembroke table with shell inlay. **£220**

Late George III satinwood Pembroke table, 2ft. 5in. open. **£660**

Mahogany Pembroke table, with one drawer, circa 1830. **£125**

Sheraton period mahogany Pembroke table. **£385**

Victorian walnut Pembroke table, top inlaid with chess board, 67cm. **£150**

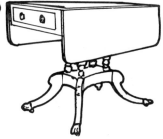

Sheraton period satinwood and tulipwood crossbanded Pembroke table, 37in. wide. **£480**

Fine George III mahogany inlaid oval Pembroke table in Adam style, 41in. wide. **£360**

Mahogany Pembroke table on platform base, 36in. wide, circa 1810. **£365**

SIDE TABLES

  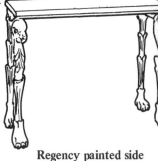

Mahogany three drawer side table with cross-banded and matched feathered veneered top, circa 1770.　£185

English oak side table, 3ft. wide, late 17th century.　£220

Regency painted side table with marble top, 3ft.10in. x 1ft.6in.　£580

  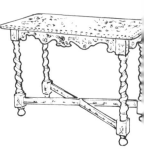

Thomas Hope gilt pier table with black marble slab.　£8,000

George I walnut side table on cabriole legs and pad feet, 3ft.3½in. wide. £780

17th century Dutch mother-of-pearl and lacquered side table, 48in. wide. £2,400

 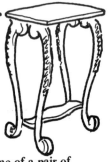 

Oak side table with one drawer, 29in. long, circa 1690.　£240

One of a pair of Regency simulated rosewood side tables with marble tops.£850

Regency rosewood pier table in the manner of Thomas Hope, 46½in. wide.　£440

Sheraton free standing side table in satinwood, circa 1800.   £595

George III mahogany side table on square tapering legs, 34in. high.   £230

Pearwood side table with drawer, circa 1830.   £30

Early 18th century walnut side table of two drawers, on cabriole legs. £650

One of a pair of late 18th century satin-wood and marquetry tables, 1.18m. wide.   £2,400

Elm side table with original handles, circa 1790.   £170

One of a pair of rose-wood side tables with remarkable figuring of the wood, 55in. wide, circa 1840. £335

Victorian walnut side table, circa 1890.   £65

Late Victorian walnut side table with under-shelf.   £34

SIDE TABLES

George II Irish mahogany side table, 4ft. 10in. wide. £750

Louis XV marquetry table d'accoucher, 2ft. 2½in. wide.£800

Late 18th century Dutch marquetry side table. £1,200

A Directoire mahogany side table inlaid with brass and ebony lines, 1ft. 10½in. wide. £800

Small 17th century oak side table in excellent condition. £400

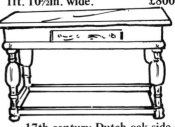

17th century Dutch oak side table. £800

Rare Louis XIV boulle side table, 4ft. 10in. wide. £4,200

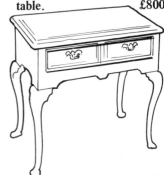

George I walnut and elm side table, 2ft. 6½ x 1ft. 7in. £1,150

Good Regency brass inlaid rosewood sofa table, 3ft. 2in. wide. £1,400

Georgian mahogany and parcel gilt sofa table, 65in. wide. £380

Sheraton satinwood sofa table cross-banded with rosewood and inlaid with boxwood and ebony stringing, circa 1800. £1,250

Georgian mahogany sofa table.£280

Mahogany sofa table of useful size, top 30 x 36in., with two drawers, circa 1850. £295

Regency sofa table, 5 x 2ft, in figured rosewood. £1,600

Very fine rosewood sofa table with writing slide, circa 1810. £875

Mahogany sofa table, circa 1840. £295

SOFA TABLES

18th century mahogany sofa table, crossbanded with rosewood. £1,150

Regency rosewood sofa table with split top. £1,950

Regency rosewood sofa table. £800

A small sofa table in mahogany with ebony inlay, circa 1840. £165

Regency mahogany sofa table. £580

Regency rosewood sofa table. £1,600

Regency mahogany sofa table on pedestal supports on brass castors, 152 x 59cm. £400

Regency rosewood sofa table, 39in. wide. £520

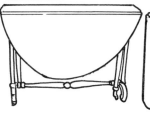

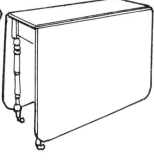

Victorian mahogany Sutherland table, 1m. wide. **£95**

Solid mahogany Sutherland table on turned legs, circa 1840. **£115**

Walnut veneered Victorian Sutherland table. **£157**

TEAPOYS

A delicate, early 19th century, rosewood teapoy complete with caddies. **£380**

Georgian period teapoy in mahogany, 20in. wide, circa 1825. **£165**

Regency mahogany teapoy with ebony inlay, 29½in. high, circa 1810. **£385**

Victorian mahogany teapoy on a shaped platform base with scroll feet. **£105**

Early 19th century rosewood teapoy on platform base with vase feet. **£115**

George III satinwood teapoy on splay feet with brass cup castors. **£250**

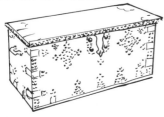

17th century oak coffer of Spanish influence, 46in. wide. £240

18th century German oak marriage trunk, 56in. long, dated 1767.£380

Late 17th century Dutch iron strong box, 27½in. high. £550

17th century oak coffer, panel lid, 49in. long. £190

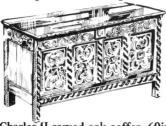

Charles II carved oak coffer, 60in. wide. £310

17th century oak blanket chest, 40½in. wide. £170

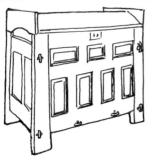

Rare early joined oak kist in original condition, 52in. long, circa 1700. £645

Carved oak coffer, circa 1680, 41in. wide. £240

Late Tudor oak chest.   £760

17th century oak chest with carved panels.   £185

Late 17th century oak marriage chest with original lock and key, panelled and carved.   £375

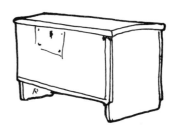

Small 17th century oak plank coffer.   £175

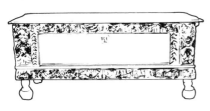

Rare early oak coffer, probably 15th century.   £850

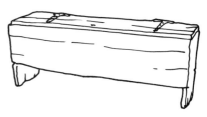

16th century oak plank coffer with iron hinges.   £570

16th century oak coffer with carved portraits in the panels. £720

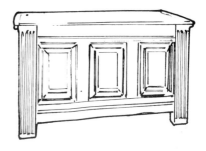

18th century oak chest with linen-fold decoration, 47in. long.   £320

TRUNKS AND COFFERS

Late 17th century oak chest. £210

Singhalese teak chest.   £400

Early 18th century carved oak coffer.
£268

Early 17th century small oak coffer,
29½ x 18½in.   £550

Oriental hardwood bridal chest with
brass furnishings.   £185

Armada chest.   £950

One of a pair of 18th century
painted sea chests.   £850

A rare Northern France coffer front.
£720

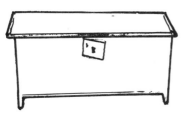

18th century oak chest. £80

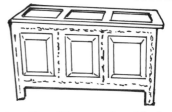

Oak coffer with parquetry stringing, circa 1710. £280

'Armada' iron chest, 33¼ x 19 x 19in. on wooden base. £640

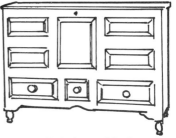

Oak panelled chest with three drawers, circa 1700. £320

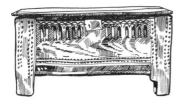

Late 15th/early 16th century oak plank chest. £280

17th century Spanish iron chest, 31 in. wide, with floral painted panels. £700

Dutch style bound oak coffer. £155

17th century oak chest with Romanesque panels. £720

TRUNKS & COFFERS

17th century carved oak coffer with lozenge panels. £295

Oriental carved camphorwood chest, 94cm. long. £110

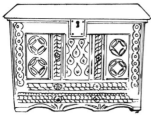

Fine quality late 16th century oak coffer. £950

17th century Continental iron-bound oak chest on stand. £620

17th century Nuremburg iron chest, 30in. wide. £900

17th century three-panel coffer of pegged construction. £425

Small example of an Armada chest. £700

Mid 16th century Italian walnut cassone, 1ft. 9in. wide. £1,600

Late 18th century Dutch mahogany armoire with a pierced cresting and cornice, 5ft. 2in. wide. £700

Carved Flemish armoire with panelled doors. £1,100

A Dutch mahogany wardrobe with an arched moulded cornice, 5ft. 9in. wide. £1,600

French oak armoire, 18th century, with carved frieze and door panels. £1,000

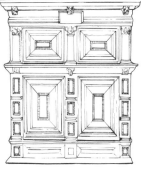

Mid 17th century Flemish ebony and rosewood cupboard, 5ft. 10in. wide. £2,500

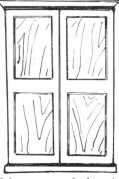

Mahogany wardrobe with two panelled doors, 1.35m. wide. £45

Mid 17th century Dutch oak armoire, 4ft. 10in. wide. £1,950

George III mahogany wardrobe on ogee feet, 4ft. 3in. wide. £140

Late 18th century carved oak armoire. £1,000

WARDROBES AND ARMOIRES

18th century carved oak Normandy armoire, 66in. wide. £950

A large, good quality, Victorian pine wardrobe. £85

Victorian carved oak hall wardrobe. £105

A small 17th century German carved oak linen press. £4,500

Mid 18th century Dutch mahogany armoire with serpentine front and three long drawers, 6ft. 6in. wide. £1,900

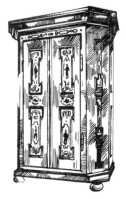

South German armoire. £1,600

Georgian period mahogany wardrobe, 48in. wide, circa 1820. £285

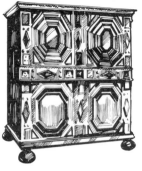

Early 17th century North German fruitwood and oak armoire. £1,600

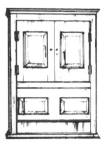

Early 18th century oak press with fielded panel doors, 4ft. 3in. wide. £315

19th century Dutch
mahogany and
marquetry wardrobe.
£910

Mahogany gentleman's
wardrobe, circa 1820,
48in. wide.   £185

18th century oak
Normandy armoire,
56in. wide.   £650

German armoire with
carved and panelled
doors.   £1,750

Late 18th century
Dutch marquetry
wardrobe, 69in.
wide.   £1,650

17th century Dutch
rosewood and ebony
armoire with heavy
cornice, 7ft. 7in.
wide.   £1,700

18th century French
armoire in oak veneered
with tortoiseshell, 1.47m.
wide.   £10,000

17th century
Burgundian
walnut armoire.
£1,300

Plum Pudding mahogany
gentleman's wardrobe,
54in. wide, circa 1850.£165

WASH STANDS

Georgian enclosed wash stand in mahogany, 3ft. high. £210

Victorian painted pine washstand with two drawers. £45

Victorian stripped pine washstand with a tiled splashback. £30

Rare Georgian corner wash stand decorated in green and gold Chinese lacquer. £175

George III mahogany campaign wash stand/ writing desk, 28in. wide. £400

Mahogany Sheraton corner wash stand, circa 1790, 25in. wide. £145

19th century mahogany, square basin stand, with hinged cover, a drawer below and undershelf. £55

Victorian marble top wash stand. £20

George III mahogany wash stand, 24in. wide. £380

Victorian rosewood three-tier whatnot, 1.09m. high. £130

Victorian walnut two-tier stand with drawer in base, 25in. wide. £65

George III mahogany whatnot with brass castors, 52½in. high. £240

One of a pair of mahogany whatnots in original condition, 58in. high, circa 1820. £695

Late 18th century mahogany whatnot with turned supports. £230

Fine square Georgian mahogany whatnot. £265

Dainty rosewood whatnot with twist supports and fretted panels, 26in. wide, circa 1840. £195

Regency period mahogany etagere with fine ormolu mounts. £250

Early 19th century stripped pine whatnot. £145

379

WINE COOLERS

George III mahogany wine cooler with brass bound body, 2ft. 4in. high. £380

Early 18th century Sinhalese hardwood and ebony wine cooler, 2ft. 7in. wide. £360

Late 18th century Dutch marquetry oval wine cooler, 1ft. 8½in. wide. £650

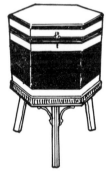

Regency mahogany open wine cooler, 28in. wide. £220

George II brass bound cellarette. £1,450

Early 18th century Sinhalese hardwood wine cooler, 2ft. 8½in. wide. £270

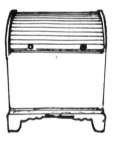

Early 19th century mahogany wine cooler of sarcophagus shape with paw feet. £200

Georgian dome shaped tambour shuttered wine cooler. £550

George II mahogany brass bound jardiniere on square legs. £650

19th century French boulle chess table with engraved cut pewter inlays, 23in. wide. £95

Small Regency rosewood games table on quadruple sabre legs, 2ft. 9in. high. £450

Antique French ebonised gaming table with brass ornamentation and marquetry, 36in. wide. £440

Regency mahogany work table, 21½in. £310

William IV mahogany sewing table, 24in. wide. £175

French circular marquetry games table with reversible top. £270

Unusual Charles X rosewood sewing table on down-curved legs, 1ft. 2in. diameter. £450

Late Regency walnut and rosewood work table inlaid with brass, copper and mother-of-pearl, 21in. wide. £260

Miniature turned fruitwood games table with 9in. diameter, top, 30in. high, circa 1790. £135

WORKBOXES AND GAMES TABLES

A superb early 19th century rosewood games table on turned and reeded legs. £4,250

Early 19th century combined games and sewing table in rosewood. £260

Unusual late 17th century games table. £1,800

Walnut games table with a hinged rectangular top and elaborately turned legs, 2ft. 5½in. wide. £450

Superb 17th century South German games table complete with games. £4,200

Fine early Victorian black lacquered papier mache worktable, 20in. wide. £460

Good quality early Victorian sewing table with drop flaps and a U-shaped centre support. £150

Late 18th century satinwood work table with painted decoration. £725

Early 19th century Chinese export lacquer work cabinet on paw feet. £1,000

Regency games table with sliding middle panel.   £225

Sheraton period tulipwood tricoteuse of French influence, 27in. x 16in.   £950

Regency period worktable with boxwood string inlay.   £460

Fine quality Victorian papier mache worktable with fitted interior. £210

Good, George III, parquetry sewing and writing table, 1ft. 11in. wide. £500

One of a pair of walnut games tables, 19th century, 3ft. wide.   £1,250

Victorian burr walnut and marquetry work-table, 22in. high. £520

19th century Biedermeier ebonised and parcel gilt globe worktable, 96cm. high.   £1,300

A Victorian papier mache, mother-of-pearl inlaid and painted octagonal shaped worktable, on shaped tripod feet.   £145

Lady's writing table in walnut and other woods with brass inlays, 32in. wide, circa 1870.   £585

Rare small writing table signed de Joseph (Baumhauer). £116,144

Good Georgian mahogany writing table with original handles and green leather top. Top size 36 x 23in., circa 1800.   £195

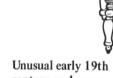

French kingwood and tulip-wood writing table with ormolu mounts, 1.12m. wide.   £6,250

Small Edwardian satinwood cylinder writing desk on tapering square feet, 1ft.10in. wide.   £350

Unusual early 19th century mahogany tutor's desk.   £395

Mahogany writing desk of 18th century design, 33½in. wide.   £280

19th century French style bureau de dame with bombe fall front, 24in. wide. £550

Edwardian mahogany Carlton House writing desk.   £490

Victorian mahogany
Carlton House writing
desk, banded with
beechwood and ebony,
3ft.7in. wide.   £460

Rosewood reading
table with drawer
and candle slides,
circa 1850.   £235

Victorian carved oak
desk on square tapering
legs.   £75

Edwardian lady's break-
front writing desk, 3ft.
6in. wide.   £550

Regency period
mahogany shaped-
top writing/reading
table, 30in. wide.
                £400

18th century walnut
writing desk with
crossbanding and
feather stringing. £450

Louis XIV floral
marquetry bureau-
plat.   £9,600

French style
mahogany writing
desk, 26in. wide.
                £500

French mahogany writing
table of about 1880, 44in.
wide.   £660

WRITING TABLES

19th century boulle
writing table. £1,700

Mid Victorian walnut
bonheur-du-jour,
91cm. high.   £350

19th century French
rosewood and par-
quetry bonheur-du-
jour, 25in. wide. £470

Louis XIV boulle
bureau mazarin.
£4,200

Sheraton period
bonheur-du-jour in
satinwood on square
tapering legs, with
cross stretchers, 2ft.
wide.   £980

Useful mahogany
table with centre
turn over panel,
42in. wide, circa
1820.   £295

Black lacquered
bonheur-du-jour
with ormolu
mounts.   £210

19th century French
writing table inset with
Sevres plaques and
having fine ormolu
mounts.   £1,500

Mid 19th century burr
walnut bonheur de
jour with boxwood
inlay.   £650

Mahogany writing table with green leather top, 38in. wide.   £235

An Edwardian, lady's writing desk on tapered legs.   £135

Regency burr yew library table with green leather top, 47in. long.   £325

George III mahogany bonheur du-jour on fine square tapering legs.   £450

George III satinwood bonheur-du-jour on square tapering legs, 2ft. 3in. wide. £1,400

Elegant library table with concave front, reeded legs and leather top, 53in. wide, circa 1850.   £365

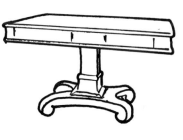

Library table with finely marked rose-wood veneers, 58in. long, circa 1840.   £335

Edwardian Sheraton revival inlaid maho-gany folding desk, 24in. wide.   £105

Attractive rosewood two-drawer library table, circa 1820, 27in. wide.   £295

WRITING TABLES

Louis XVI boulle small bureau plat with moulded brass border, 3ft. 5in. wide. £3,800

Italian writing table, mid 19th century, on tapered legs. £1,700

William IV mahogany writing table with gold leather top, 42 x 23in. £135

Edwardian Carlton House desk with inset leather top, 48in. £900

19th century ebonised writing table with brass inlay. £365

Late 19th century inlaid mahogany Carlton House table. £1,100

Louis XVI marquetry writing table on square tapering legs, 1ft. 4in. wide. £1,500

18th century, mahogany, architect's table with adjustable top and turned legs. £275

French marquetry bonheur-du-jour, 19th century. £1,085

Early 18th century
North Italian walnut
writing table.   £875

Substantial mahogany
writing desk with
leather top, circa 1870.
£265

Louis XVI mahogany
bureau plat with
panelled frieze, 4ft.
3in. wide.   £3,600

Louis XV ormolu mounted
tulipwood bureau plat, top
inset with tooled leather,
3ft. 10in. wide.   £5,800

Victorian desk,
circa 1870.£95

Early 19th century mahogany
writing table on turned and
fluted legs.   £100

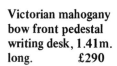

Victorian mahogany
bow front pedestal
writing desk, 1.41m.
long.   £290

Louis XVI writing
table in satinwood
and mahogany with
brass bandings, 2ft.
wide.   £750

Early 19th century
Louis XV style
bureau plat, 5ft.
2in. long.   £875

BEAKERS AND TUMBLERS

19th century
engraved fox-
hunting tumbler,
3½in. high.   £70

Venetian calcedonio beaker
of bell shape with small
foot, the marbled brown,
blue and green glass flecked
with adventurine, 18th
century.   £120

19th century
engraved fox-
hunting tumbler,
4in. high.   £80

18th century
enamelled
German beaker,
7in. high. £580

German enamelled and
dated beaker, 5¾in. high,
1711.   £625

Bohemian flared
beaker in white
glass, 12cm. high.
                    £720

Victorian cranberry
glass tumbler.   £6

Silesian footed
beaker engraved in
Tiefschnitt, 5½in.
high, circa 1730.
                    £500

Victorian purple
slag glass tumbler.
                    £7

Engraved Bohemian tumbler, 5in. high, circa 1700.   £210

Bohemian amber flash beaker, engraved around four oval panels, 5½in. high. £26

Fine engraved commemorative tumbler, 3¾in. high, circa 1807.   £600

18th century Bohemian cut and engraved glass tumbler, 4¼in. high.   £55

Pale green Roman glass vessel in the form of a bucket, 13.7cm. high.   £16,000

Naval tumbler engraved with anchors, 4½in. high, circa 1800.   £70

BELLS

Late 16th century silver mounted latticinio bell, 5½in. high. £2,100

Victorian cranberry glass bell, 12in. high.   £45

Latticinio bell mounted in silver gilt, circa 1600, 9½in. high. £1,500

BOTTLES

Victorian satin glass bottle, 7½in. high. £75

18th century green glass bottle, circa 1726. £175

19th century Nailsea bottle, 8in. high. £60

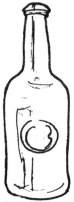

Early 19th century green sealed bottle, 12in. tall. £22

Sealed wine bottle inscribed John Luke 1721, 9in. high. £320

Single bottle of vintage port, 1863. £36

Small, 18th century, iridescent bottle of mallet form. £35

A pair of small Bristol blue coloured sauce bottles with lozenge stoppers, 6 in. £50

Victorian green glass poison bottle, 7in. tall. £2

Victorian, baby's feeding bottle. £4

Late Victorian green glass bottle, 10in. tall. £4

19th century clear glass chemist's bottle. £2

George III green wine bottle, 13in. tall. £14

One of a set of six etched and cut glass spirit bottles, circa 1840. £375

Dutch spirit bottle, 6in. tall. £80

Early 20th century blue syphon bottle. £7.50

One of a pair of Georgian silver and glass condiment bottles, 1808, 7in. high. £44

Netherlandish blue glass bottle. £620

BOWLS

Early 16th century Venetian bowl enamelled in red and white, 6¼in. diameter. **£900**

Good Irish canoe fruit bowl, 14in. wide, circa 1810. **£350**

A small pressed blue glass Victorian dressing table bowl and cover, 3in. diam. **£5**

Victorian white slag glass bowl with thistle decoration. **£10**

Victorian purple carnival glass bowl with a wavy edge. **£10**

Bohemian 'Schwarzlot' covered bowl by Ignaz Preissler, 6¾in. high, circa 1725. **£6,500**

19th century French glass bowl with enamelled decoration, 8in. wide. **£30**

Edwardian pressed glass sugar bowl. **£3**

Victorian glass mortar with lip. **£5**

Achaemenid bowl,
5th century B.C.
£62,000

5th century B.C. Iranian
pale green glass bowl,
6¾in. diameter. £62,000

Ravenscroft large
glass bowl, 15½in.
diameter, circa
1674/82. £3,700

Garniture of cut glass covered jars with
Dutch silver mounts. £260

Edwardian moulded
glass bowl with
plated rim. £7

Bristol finger bowl
marked I. Jacobs,
Bristol. £150

Victorian ruby glass
bowl, 6in. diam.
£12

19th century Lalique glass
bowl of clear and opaque
white glass, 10in. diam.
£45

CANDLESTICKS

Victorian ruby glass
candlestick.   £8

Pair of 20th century
moulded glass candle-
sticks.   £5

Art Deco red and
clear glass candle-
stick.   £12

A rare taperstick, the
nozzle set on inverted
baluster air twist stem,
6½ in.   £370

One of a pair of
glass and gilt metal
candelabra.   £400

Richardson opal glass
candlestick, circa 1850.
                    £62

Victorian multi-
coloured glass
candlestick. £7.50

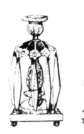

Pair of ormolu and crystal
lustre sidepieces, circa
1830.   £140

Late 19th century
glass candlestick,
10in. high.   £7

Victorian cut glass candlestick. £4.50

Pair of Tiffany bronze and glass candlesticks, 14½in. high. £1,500

Edwardian moulded glass candlestick. £2

19th century Nailsea glass candlestick. £40

One of a pair of Regency plaster, marble and glass candlesticks. £275

19th century purple slag glass candlestick. £12

Late 18th century candlestick with flat cut stem. £30

Pair of Regency period cut glass candlesticks with drops. £260

Victorian cut glass candlestick. £14

DECANTERS

Late 19th century
engraved decanter.
£16

Early 19th century
ship's decanter. £60

Early 19th century
plain glass decanter.
£30

Victorian etched
glass decanter.
£10

19th century
cut glass
decanter. £34

George III cut
glass decanter.
£35

Lalique glass decanter
12in. high.   £200

Victorian moulded
glass decanter.   £9

Late 18th century
mallet-shaped
decanter.   £100

Victorian etched
glass decanter.
£5

Victorian, green,
Mary Gregory
decanter.   £40

Late 18th century
Burgundy engraved
decanter.   £50

19th century Irish glass decanter.
£110

Early 19th century bulbous decanter.
£34

Late 18th century tapered and engraved decanter. £60

Heavy, early 19th century cut glass decanter. £65

Late 18th century Irish decanter.
£60

18th century marriage decanter with cut spire stopper. £220

19th century stirrup glass decanter. £15

Late 18th century plain club-shaped decanter. £40

Late Victorian etched glass decanter. £8

Early 19th century Baccaret decanter with silver gilt cap. £100

Early 19th century ship's decanter with bull's eye stopper. £125

Early 19th century diamond cut decanter. £75

DECANTERS

Small, Bristol blue glass decanter, circa 1800. **£40**

Mid 19th century heavy quality ships decanter. **£75**

Late 18th century engraved decanter 'Port'. **£60**

Early 19th century club-shaped decanter with bull's eye stopper. **£75**

One of a pair of rare Apsley Pellatt incrusted decanters, 10in. high, circa 1820. **£500**

George III decanter with cut stopper. **£15**

Georgian cruet bottle, circa 1810. **£24**

Early 19th century plain glass decanter. **£22**

Early 19th century barrel-shaped decanter. **£30**

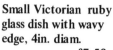

Small Victorian ruby glass dish with wavy edge, 4in. diam. £7.50

Empire period turquoise verne opaline mounted tazza. £270

Victorian coloured glass dish with wavy edge. £8

Early 18th century English sweetmeat dish. £225

Venetian filigree tazza, circa 1600, 6¾in. diam. £2,400

Early English sweetmeat dish. £240

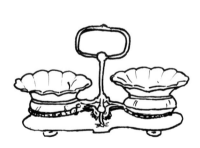

Bobbin-knopped sweetmeat dish with double ogee bowl, 5¼in. high, circa 1740. £200

Victorian ruby glass double bon bon dish in a plated stand. £32

Victorian cranberry glass jam dish in a plated stand. £18

FLASKS

Flat circular shaped scent flacon, circa 1830, with gold stopper.   £190

Early 18th century French blue glass scent flacon with silver mounts, 3¾in. high.   £140

Milchglas Central-European flask with pewter mount, 5in. high, circa 1750.   £120

Rare coldpainted Venetian ring flask, 11¼in. high, 16th century.   £400

Late Victorian pressed glass scent flask.   £5

17th century German silver gilt scent flacon, 3½in. high.   £260

19th century Nailsea flask.   £35

Mid 18th century Bohemian chinoiserie scent flask.   £1,000

Victorian cranberry glass flask.   £17

Victorian dark blue slag glass jug, 5in. high.   £7

Victorian Bohemian glass jug with red ground, 7in. high. £90

Victorian ruby glass water jug, 10in. high. £17

Late Victorian cranberry glass jug with frilled handle.   £25

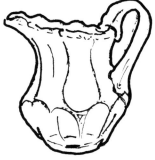

Cut glass cream jug, circa 1830.   £30

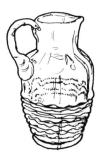

Victorian cranberry glass jug with ridged decoration, 6½in. high. £22

Victorian ruby glass jug with applied white glass flowers, 10in. high.   £20

French glass ale jug, circa 1790.   £55

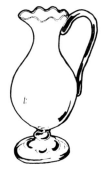

Victorian frosted and cut glass ewer, 14in. high.   £50

JUGS

Mary Gregory glass jug, 8 in. high. £24

Victorian white slag glass jug with thistle decoration. £10

Late Victorian ruby glass carafe, 10in. high. £35

Victorian purple slag glass jug with ribbed decoration. £8

Catalan Latticinio ewer of the 17th/18th century, 7in. high. £850

Mid 19th century Bristol clear glass jug. £45

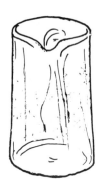

Late Victorian plain glass water jug, 10in. high. £4

Victorian cranberry glass jug, 7½in. high. £18

Victorian amber glass water jug. £15

One of a pair of
ruby glass double
lustres, about 1880.
£320

One of a pair of Victorian
pink opaque glass lustres,
complete with drops. £50

One of a pair of ruby
glass lustres with floral
decoration and cut
glass drops.   £110

MISCELLANEOUS

Victorian cut glass
pickle jar.   £1.50

Victorian oil lamp
shade of pink glass.
£4

Victorian glass ship
under a glass dome.
£80

17th century German
glass called a
'Scherzgefass'.   £320

Victorian engraved glass
biscuit jar on a plated
and engraved stand with
bun feet.   £18

Edwardian plain glass
caster with a plated
lid.   £5

MISCELLANEOUS

One of a set of
six black and
white glass
buttons. £2.50

19th century apothecary
box complete with bottles.
£65

Victorian clear glass
jelly mould, 6in.
wide.   £3

18th century Mughal
India vessel, the base
of a hookah.   £700

One of a pair of
Lalique glass
figures. £1,700

Glass match striker
with silver container,
Mappin Bros., 1896.
£25

One of a pair of
St. Louis fruit
door handles, 2in.
£800

Bristol blue glass
and silver plate
lidded drum,
circa 1860. £58

19th century
chemist's clear
glass shop sign,
circa 1850, 26in.
high.   £78

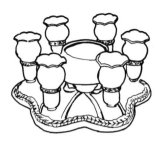

Victorian purple slag glass tea caddy of sarcophagus form. £40

19th century ruby glass circular box and cover, 4in. £28

Coffee and cream glass centrepiece by Webb , 10¼in. diameter. £260

Small, Victorian, glass shoe match holder. £10

L'oiseau du Feu by Lalique moulded in relief with a bird woman in exotic headdress. £1,200

Imperial German glass beerstein with soft metal mounts. £35

Mid 18th century Milchglas cane handle, 3¾in. high. £190

Part of a sixty-five piece gilt glass service. £290

One of a pair of step-cut Georgian cruet bottles, 1815. £40

PAPERWEIGHTS

Clichy pansy flower weight with leaves of pale purple and lemon. £710

Baccarat portrait weight of Queen Victoria, 3½in. £320

Baccarat sulphide weight with portrait of St. Antoine, 2¾in. £150

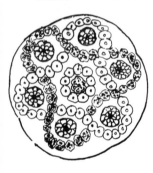

Baccarat colour-ground patterned millefiori weight, 3in. £440

Rare Baccarat flat bouquet weight, 3in. £800

Baccarat dog rose weight with five heart shaped petals, star cut base, 2¾in. £300

St. Louis 'crown' glass paperweight. £675

Victorian glass paperweight depicting a view of Scarborough. £9

Good Clichy patterned millefiori weight, 3in. £680

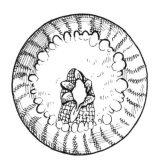

St. Louis amber-
flash flat bouquet
weight, about 1848.
£130

Baccarat red clematis
weight, encircled by
green and white canes,
2½in.   £320

Unusual inscribed St.
Louis weight of close
millefiori type, 3in.
£210

Rare Baccarat primrose
weight with five rounded
orange petals and star-
dust stamens, 2½in.£720

Clichy swirl weight
with pink and white
pastrymould cane,
3¼in.   £310

Good Baccarat
concentric
mushroom weight,
3in.   £400

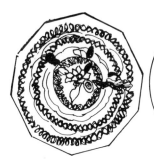

St. Louis faceted
upright bouquet
weight, 3in. £400

St. Louis fruit weight
on a swirling white
ground, 2in.   £310

Baccarat clematis
weight with two
rows of white
petals, 2¾in.£340

PIPES

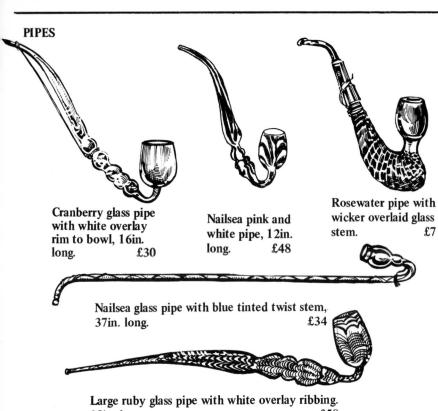

Cranberry glass pipe with white overlay rim to bowl, 16in. long. £30

Nailsea pink and white pipe, 12in. long. £48

Rosewater pipe with wicker overlaid glass stem. £7

Nailsea glass pipe with blue tinted twist stem, 37in. long. £34

Large ruby glass pipe with white overlay ribbing. 28in. long. £58

Nailsea glass pipe with mauve tinted twist stem, 46in. long. £34

PLATES

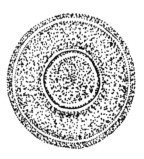

Victorian plate commemorating Gladstone. £5

19th century light blue slag glass plate with basket weave edge. £8

Late Victorian frosted pressed glass plate, 8in. diameter. £2

Lalique figure 'Suzanne au Bain', 9in. high.   £200

Lalique plaque sold with a similar piece.   £2,200

Art glass plaque by George Woodall.   £4,200

Cameo glass plaque by George Woodhall, circa 1885.   £11,500

PORTRAIT MEDALLIONS

Tassie glass paste medallion of A. Coventry M.D. of Edinburgh 1794, 3½in., framed.   £120

A John Henning glass paste portrait medallion, 3¼in., signed Henning F., framed and glazed.   £70

A Tassie glass paste portrait medallion on frosted glass over blue paper, 4¾in.£110

SCENT BOTTLES

Victorian ruby glass
scent bottle with
silver top.   £14

Cut crystal perfume
bottle with silver
top, 1898, 5in. high.
                £28

Victorian Bristol blue
scent bottle with
embossed silver top.
                £16

Victorian green and
clear glass scent
bottle.   £16

Mid 19th century
Bohemian glass
scent bottle.   £40

Late 19th century blue
glass scent bottle with
silver top.   £20

20th century cut
glass scent bottle.
        £5

Victorian vinaigrette
cum scent bottle by
S. Mordan & Co.
                £150

Mid 19th century
painted glass
scent bottle. £12

20th century
moulded glass
scent bottle. £2

Silver mounted cut
glass perfume spray,
1899, 5in. high. £25

Art Deco coloured
glass scent bottle.
£12

Victorian blue and
white overlay scent
bottle.   £35

Heart shaped scent
bottle on chain,
Chester 1888. £45

Victorian engraved
glass scent bottle
with silver top. £25

Victorian silver mounted
ruby glass scent bottle
with vinaigrette end. £50

One of a pair of
opaline scent
bottles, circa
1880, 8½in. high. £38

Gold mounted Venetian
scent bottle, 7cm. high,
mid 19th century. £120

SNUFF BOTTLES

Carved chalcedony
snuff bottle with
a russet inclusion.
£200

Red overlay
glass bottle
for snuff.£150

19th century Chinese
glass snuff bottle,
carved at the shoulders
and with a coral stop-
per.   £150

Rare enamelled
glass snuff
bottle by Ku
Yueh Hsuan.
£4,600

Blanc de chine snuffbottle
carved with the Immortals,
2¾in. high.   £141

Red glass snuff
bottle.   £30

Cylindrical porce-
lain snuff bottle.
£65

Interior painted
snuff bottle by
Ten Yu-t'ien,
dated 1907.£230

Late 19th century
interior painted
glass snuff bottle.
£18

19th century stained glass window of a Saint. £25

Large, 20th century, stained glass window depicting a ship in full sail. £30

Early 20th century stained glass window depicting a peacock, 22in. high. £28

TANKARDS AND CUPS

Cut glass mug, circa 1820. £34

Early 20th century green and clear glass cup with silver rim. £6

Glass tankard with initials B.H., W.S., circa 1825. £45

Humorous German engraved tankard, 4¾in. high, circa 1810. £200

Victorian cranberry glass custard cup. £6

Mid 18th century Central-European enamelled tankard in milchglas, 4½in. high. £320

VASES

One of a pair of Victorian opal glass vases, 4ins. high.   £8

Late Victorian light blue slag glass basket.   £8

Victorian orange carnival glass vase.   £6

Victorian ruby glass eperne with flared rim.   £40

Late 19th century vase attributed to Joshua Hodgetts, Stourbridge, white on amethyst glass, 27.5cm. high.   £4,000

Late 19th century iridescent glass vase with applied decoration, 6½in. high. £14

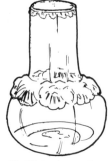

Small, Victorian, ruby glass vase with applied decoration, 4½in. high.   £12

Signed Sabino vase, circa 1920, with fish motif, 8in. high.   £55

Victorian opaline glass vase with flared rim.   £10

Late 19th century Roman style glass vase with spiral decoration.   £70

Lalique two-handled vase, 1ft.1½in. wide.   £190

Small, Victorian, satin glass vase with gilt floral decoration.   £20

Gold and yellow iridescent vase by Louis C. Tiffany, 38cm. high, circa 1900.   £2,000

Late 17th century German vase mounted in copper and gilt, 8½in. high.   £380

Rare Venetian diamond-engraved vase, late 17th century, 11in. high.   £1,400

Late 19th century iridescent vase with applied decoration, 5½in. high.   £12

Glass vase by Emile Galle, with an applied decoration of a glass rose, around 1900.   £4,600

One of four Swiss 19th century baluster vases in glass with silver gilt mounts, 3½in. high, by Bossard, Lausanne.£480

VASES

Late Victorian iridescent opaque glass vase, 6in. high. £10

Victorian pressed glass flower vase, 6in. high. £2

One of a pair of 18th century German apothecary jars, 7¼in. high. £850

One of a pair of Victorian opal glass vases, 10ins. high. £35

Late 19th century green and white glass vase, 10in. high. £18

Pate-de-cristal vase by Francois Decorchemont in deep blue glass, 25.5cm. high, circa 1910. £3,000

Victorian fruit and flower eperne with flared rim. £40

Deep amber glass serpent vase by Rene Lalique, 24ins. high. £850

Victorian white slag glass spill holder. £8

Victorian overlay glass with portrait medallion, 14in. high. £100

Edwardian ruby glass vase in a plated mount, 9in. high. £12

One of a set of five 18th century German milchglas apothecary jars. £800

One of a pair of green tinted vases and covers by James Giles, 16in. high, circa 1765. £4,500

Tiffany flower vase of milky tone, 44cm. high. £1,350

German passglas, 1725, 24cm. high. £2,400

4th century pear-shaped jar with indented base, 6in. high. £1,700

Pair of Art Nouveau blue cameo vases, 10in. high. £65

Stourbridge ovoid vase enamelled on a crackle ground, 10in. high. £50

WINE GLASSES

Jacobite firing glass with short trumpet bowl, circa 1770, 5¾in. high. £150

19th century armorial rummer, 7½in. high. £110

Unusual Dutch engraved goblet, 7in. high, circa 1740. £200

Engraved Newcastle wine glass with conical foot, 7½in. high, circa 1765. £240

German engraved goblet on square base, 5in. high, circa 1815. £85

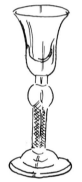

Wine glass with bell bowl, and domed foot, 6½in. high, circa 1735. £170

Mixed-twist wine glass, 6½in. high, circa 1750. £125

Emerald green goblet or ale glass, 6in. high. £300

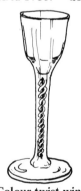

Colour-twist wine glass, 6in. high, circa 1760. £250

One of a pair of
hunting rummers,
early 19th century,
5½in. high.   £175

Goblet by William
Beilby, 8in. tall,
with twist stem.
£9,240

One of a pair of
dated rummers,
5in. high, 1795.
£110

Engraved goblet with
bucket bowl, 6¾in.
high, circa 1760.£190

Unusual Sunderland
Bridge goblet, 6¾in.
high, 1859.   £170

18th century
drinking glass.
£32

Colour-twist wine glass
with bell bowl, 6in.
high, circa 1760. £300

Colour twist wine
glass with bell
bowl, 7in. high,
circa 1760.   £260

Colour twist wine
glass, 6in. high,
circa 1760. £180

WINE GLASSES

18th century armorial goblet by William Beilby, 8in. high. £8,400

Large fox hunting rummer, 19th century, 8½in. high. £100

Multi-knopped air-twist wine glass, 7in. high, circa 1750. £430

18th century drinking glass. £70

One of a pair of St. Louis goblets of blue glass with gilded Islamic design, about 1845-50. £150

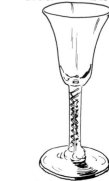

One of a pair of colour-twist wine glasses, 6½in. high, circa 1760. £650

Mid 18th century engraved German goblet, 7¾in. high. £300

Rare Jacobite portrait firing glass, 3½in. high, circa 1750. £950

Dutch engraved glass goblet, 8in. high, circa 1740. £480

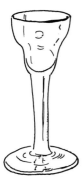

Green tinted wine
glass with double
ogee bowl, 6in.
high, circa 1750.£220

Glass rummer,
circa 1800.£15

Engraved facet-stem
goblet, 7in. high,
circa 1780.   £230

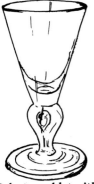

Baluster goblet with
large funnel bowl,
8¼in. high, circa 1695.
                £230

Early 19th century
engraved Williamite
glass, 6½in. high.
                £210

Engraved Newcastle
wine glass with
conical foot, 7½in.
high, circa 1765.£240

Nuremberg Hausmalerei
Schwarzlot goblet deco-
rated by J. L. Faber, circa
1700, 7¾in. high.£11,000

Bohemian miniature
glass roemer, 3½in.
high, 1688.   £340

18th century
drinking glass.
                £55

423

WINE GLASSES

Dutch engraved goblet, 6½in. high, circa 1740. £175

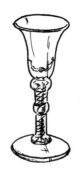

Tartan twist wine glass, 6in. high, circa 1760. £180

Rare Lynn wine glass with ogee bowl, 5½in. high. £130

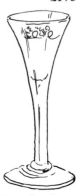

Wine glass by Beilby, 6¾in. high, circa 1765. £360

One of a set of five Sunderland Bridge rummers, 4¾in. high, early 19th century. £275

Dutch engraved composite stem goblet, 7½in. high, circa 1740. £130

Opaque twist wine glass, circa 1770. £42

U-bowl ale glass with arch decoration, circa 1850. £8

One of a set of six flutes with tall trumpet bowls, 7¾in. high, circa 1760. £280

Very rare Beilby
wine glass, about
1770, 5¼in. high.
£600

Composite stem
wine glass, 6¼in.
high, circa 1760. £90

Unusual wine
glass, 5¼in.
high, circa 1760. £110

Very rare wine
glass with trumpet
bowl on bobbin
stem, 7¾in. high,
circa 1730. £460

Large baluster
goblet, 8¾in.
high, circa 1710. £240

Engraved ale glass
with ogee bowl,
7½in. high, circa
1760. £110

Unusual engraved
ale glass, 7in. high,
circa 1760. £85

Jacobite wine
glass, 6in. high,
circa 1750. £200

18th century
drinking glass.
£50

WINE GLASSES

Baluster goblet with funnel bowl.   £230

Engraved ratafia glass with tall straight sided bowl, 7¼in. high, circa 1770. £160

Colour twist wine glass, 5¾in. high, circa 1760.   £200

Dutch engraved wine glass, 6½in. high, circa 1730.   £210

Cordial glass with small ogee bowl, 6¾in., high, circa 1760.   £150

Rare Jacobite colour twist wine glass, 6½in. high, circa 1760.   £250

Red and green twist wine glass, 6¾in. high, circa 1760.£330

Baluster wine glass, 6½in. high, circa 1730.   £300

Wine glass with bell bowl, 6½in. high, circa 1760.   £210

Qajar gold and
enamel Qalian
bowl, 6.7cm.
£22,000

18th century gold
brooch with ruby
eyes.   £45

George III gold
vinaigrette set
with a gold citrine.
£625

Victorian diamond
set and enamel
oval gold locket.
£400

Rare Victorian cameo of
horses in 15 carat gold
frame, circa 1810. £400

18 carat gold
presentation flask
given to General
Buller.   £1,150

9 carat gold
cigarette box,
3¾oz.   £275

Pair of ornaments,
signed 'Hashimoto
Isshi' show autumn
flowers in gold.
£520

A Friedrich Fyrwald
18 carat gold snuff
box, lid and base
turned with concen-
tric circles, 3½in.
wide, Stockholm,
about 1798.   £320

GRAMOPHONES

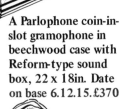

French Pathe Horn gramophone, circa 1910-1920, with 11in. turntable.
£200

Edison standard phonograph. £430

A Parlophone coin-in-slot gramophone in beechwood case with Reform-type sound box, 22 x 18in. Date on base 6.12.15. £370

Gramophone and Type-writer Ltd. double spring Monarch gramophone, 1ft.10in., English, circa 1904. £200

Gramophone Company Limited trade mark gramophone, 7in. turntable, English 1902. £370

Gramophone Co. inter-mediate Monarch gramo-phone with 10in. turntable, English, dated Jan. 1917. £220

An Apollo gramophone with 9in. turntable, English, circa 1910. £260

Duophone table con-sole gramophone with twin sound boxes, English, circa 1924. £150

Gramophone Co. Junior Monarch gramophone, 1ft.6in., English, circa 1910. £220

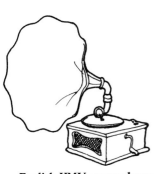

English HMV gramophone with Lumiere pleated paper diaphragm, in an oak box with hinged lid, circa 1925. £340

English Maxitone portable gramophone, circa 1925-35, 10in. turntable. £75

Columbia model AA graphophone with two-minute gearing, American, circa 1902-1904. £120

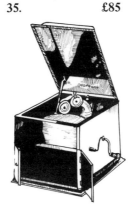

Gramophone Co. horn gramophone with Zonophone sound box, English, circa 1904. £150

French Pathe portable gramophone with 28cm. turntable, circa 1925-35. £85

Edison Bell discaphone gramophone, English, circa 1910-1920. £150

French Pathe Horn gramophone, circa 1910-1915. £340

HMV model 460 gramophone with 12in. turntable, Lumiere pleated paper diaphragm, English, circa 1924.£270

EMG mark 1XB gramophone with papier mache horn, 1ft. 9in., English, circa 1930. £240

INSTRUMENTS

Silver Butterfield type dial.   £420

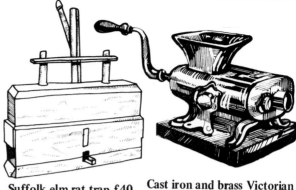

Suffolk elm rat trap. £40

Cast iron and brass Victorian mincer by Burgess and Key, 13 x 6in.   £38

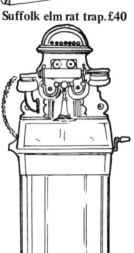

Early 20th century English wall telephone, 2ft. 4in. high.   £190

Victorian egg timer made for Victoria's jubilee.   £10

Victorian Tunbridge ware cribbage board.   £12

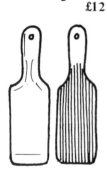

Butter pats for shaping.   £2

17th century Germanic or Central European padlock.   £80

Octagonal incised slate sundial, 10½in. across, with cast bronze gnomon.   £78

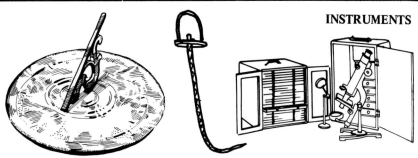

17th century brass
sundial by Henry
Wynne, London,
16¾in. diameter.
£350

Rare East Anglian
haybond twister
made from wood.
£6

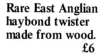

Fine John Benjamin
Dancer brass binocular
microscope, 1861.
£540

Beck tropical
box form
stereoscope.
£130

19th century
terrestrial globe,
24in. diameter.
£950

Fine cased marine
chronometer by
Arnold and Dent.
£925

An English amplion radio
speaker in domed wooden
case.   £28

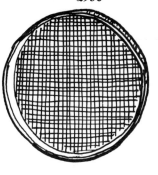

Mid 19th century
coachman's sieve
for sieving oats. £5

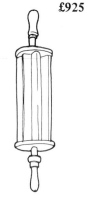

Butter worker
used on a
sloping tray. £5

INSTRUMENTS

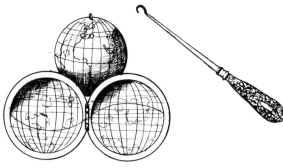

A J.P. Culls, Toms & Sutton 'Cary type' pocket microscope, signed on the pillar, which is screwed to a mahogany case, 20cm. wide, circa 1820. £160

Black sharkskin covered pocket globe by Newton showing a celestial map. £400

Edwardian button hook with a decorative silver handle. £5

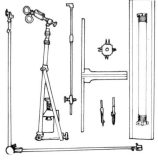

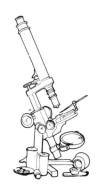

Early 20th century brass monocular microscope by W. Watson & Sons, in a rosewood case, 36cm. high. £80

Late 19th century set of Stanley drawing instruments, in fitted wooden case. £100

Compound microscope, probably by Pillischer of Bond Street, circa 1860. £95

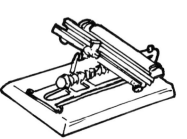

Celestial globe by Newton, 1850, 12in. diameter. £240

A rare 'Invincible' typewriter, no. 498, 12in. long. £180

Huntsman's cut steel pocket tool kit with eight folding tools, circa 1820. £47

19th century
steel calipers.
£18

Beechwood and brass
plough plane by J.
Mosele, Bloomsbury,
London.   £19

Early 20th century Negretti
and Zamba two-day chrono-
meter in a double hinged
mahogany case with brass
handles at the sides.   £430

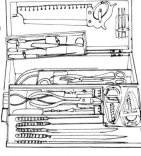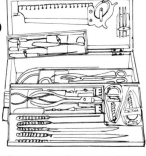

One of two brass bound mahogany cases of medical instruments, late 19th century, 43cm.
wide.   £380

Brass pantograph by
W. & S. Jones,
London.   £60

Monocular brass
microscope 'W.J.
Salmon', 16in.
high, circa 1850. £145

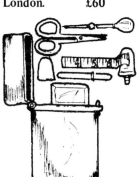

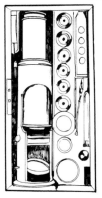

Lady's sewing case
in brilliant blue
papier mache, circa
1840, 3¾in. high.
£65

A brass 'Martin type' monocular microscope, the barrel inscribed J. Crichton,
112 Leadenhall St., London,
circa 1840.   £150

George III Scottish
bannock toaster,
27½in. long overall,
Edinburgh 1819.
£220

433

INSTRUMENTS

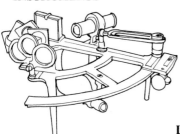

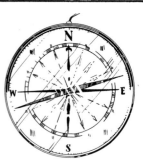

Early 20th century Butler's brass sextant with two sets of filters. £110

Large, wheelwright's dividers, circa 1820. £26

Mahogany 19th century compass. £35

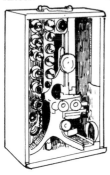

A Swift & Sons brass binocular microscope, 42cm., English, late 19th century. £290

Magnificent microscope made by Alexis Magny, circa 1750, for Madame de Pompadour. £41,518

Victorian cased set of scales complete with weights, 11½in., high. £60

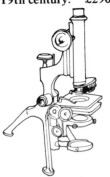

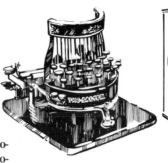

A Swift & Sons brass monocular microscope in a mahogany case, with two boxes of slides, English, early 20th century. £150

Mid 1890's Salter typewriter. £200

A microscope made by Powell & Lealand. £460

434

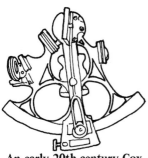

INSTRUMENTS

An early 20th century Cox and Coombs oxidised brass sextant with two sets of filters. £190

Early 19th century pair of brass Gunners calipers, 176mm. long, in original shaped case. £280

Naval officer's sextant 'A. Willings & Co.', circa 1840. £175

Late 19th century English brass binocular microscope by Henry Crouch, contained in a mahogany carrying case. £210

Early 19th century two-day marine chronometer by Parkinson & Frodsham, London, 4¾in. diam. £490

Mahogany cased brass pantograph by 'Cole, London', 25¾in. long, circa 1780. £148

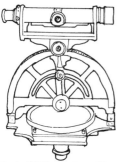

Late 19th century Troughton & Simms brass altizimuth theodolite in a mahogany case. £220

Brass sundial, dated 1743, 8¾in. diam. £58

Mahogany brass and glass Wimshurst experimental electric machine, circa 1880. £265

435

INSTRUMENTS

English, late 19th century stereoscopic viewer in a walnut case with an eyepiece at the front, 50cm. high. £85

Henry Crouch brass monocular microscope, late 19th century. £95

A silver bottle stand on wooden base, 13¾in. high overall. £240

19th century butcher's bone saw, 23in. long. £34

19th century English mahogany jockey's scales, the rectangular support on turned baluster shaped legs. £460

Fine, fisherman's salmon gaff, 16½in. long, circa 1840. £35

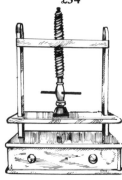

Victorian wooden book press. £50

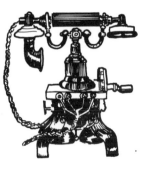

Ericsson table telephone, circa 1900, 1ft. high. £140

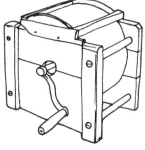

Table type box churn, late 19th century. £8

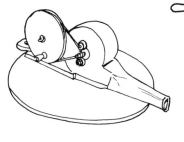

18th century oak and brass bellows, 17in. wide. £65

Haycutting knife for use on ricks. £5

Later keyboard type model of a typewriter. £25

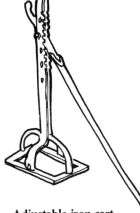

Adjustable iron cart jack, 19th century. £8

Columbia printing press, with distinctive golden eagle crest. £240

English 'Wheel of Life' zoetrope with pierced cylindrical drum, 36cm. high and thirty-three cartoon strips, circa 1860. £210

Fine cased chronometer by Charles Frodsham. £650

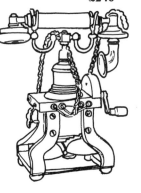

Ericsson table telephone, 1ft. high, circa 1900. £110

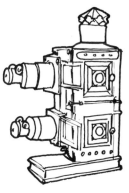

Bi-unial magic lantern, late Victorian mahogany and brass. £275

INSTRUMENTS

19th century metronome in a figured walnut case, by R. Cocks & Co., London, 9½in. high. £48

Boxwood cased pocket sundial and compass, circa 1860, 2in. diameter. £37

Wooded lemon squeezer with rounded place for half lemon. £3

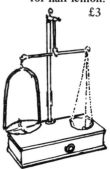

Horn straightener and trainer, late 19th century. £3

One of a pair of late Georgian terrestrial and celestial globes by Cary, with compasses on the stand bases. £1,050

Attractive balance made by Avery, circa 1850-60. £30

American rare and interesting radio in the form of a Coca-Cola bottle, 24in. high, circa 1930. £180

Victorian jockey's scales. £400

French Thomson-Houston brass telephone, 1ft. high, circa 1920. £45

Small Kilburn stereo-
scopic Daguerreo type
and fitted viewing
case.   £320

Fine Universal sundial
by Watkins and Hill.
                         £350

Kilburn stereoscopic
Daguerreo type por-
trait in collapsible
viewing case, circa
1855-60.   £120

Brass and cast iron
beam scales, circa
1860, 2ft. 9in.
high.   £185

A rare American
National microphone
dancer, 1ft. 1in. high,
circa 1935.   £125

Brass Cary type micro-
scope, 19th century,
length of box 200mm.
                         £310

Terrestrial globe on
mahogany turned
stand, 15in. high,
1877.   £135

English Celestian radio
speaker in mahogany
cabinet.   £18

A 'Baby Daisy'
vacuum cleaner.
                    £35

INSTRUMENTS

Small brass sextant by Cary, early 19th century, 130mm. radius. £620

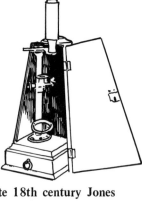

Late 19th century French Leroy two-day marine chronometer, 7in. high. £560

Late 18th century Jones improved type microscope. £580

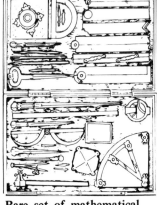

Rare set of mathematical instruments by Dominicus Lusuerg, Rome, 1701. £13,000

Late 19th century, J.W. Ray & Co., brass ship's telegraph, 3ft. 2in. high. £150

Early 19th century French 'Taxiphote' stereoscopic viewer, 1ft. 7in. high. £160

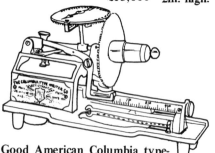

Good American Columbia typewriter, 11in. wide, circa 1890. £280

Late 19th century Padbury's patent 'Indispensable' music leaf turner, 9in. wide. £80

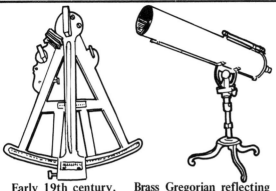

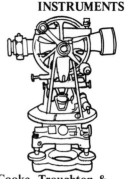

Early 19th century, H. Hemsley, ebony octant with ivory scale, 10in. radius. £180

Brass Gregorian reflecting telescope by James Short, 1763, 24in. long. £950

Cooke, Troughton & Simms, brass altizimuth theodolite, late 19th century, 1ft. high. £130

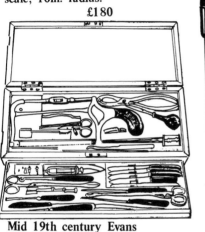

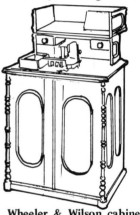

Mid 19th century Evans & Wormull veterinary surgeon's instrument set, 1ft. 6in. wide. £190

Hand held telescope, Hammersley London, 17¼in. closed, 24in. extended, circa 1840. £59

Wheeler & Wilson cabinet treadle sewing machine, 3ft. wide, circa 1862. £95

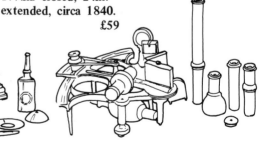

Good, American Lambert typewriter, circa 1900. £160

Late 19th century Andrew Christie, brass sextant, 6in. radius. £160

Wooden mouse trap.
£2

Circular silver pocket almanac
by Loos, 1805, 44mm. diam.
£260

Victorian tortoiseshell
handled lorgnette. £50

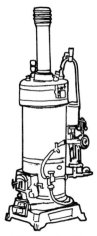

Fine Bing vertical boiler
and steam engine, 1ft.
4¼in. high, circa 1930's.
£300

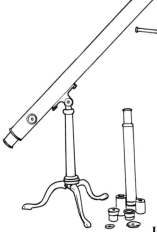

Early 19th century, 2-inch,
Gilbert & Co., refracting
telescope on stand. £280

Late 19th century, 4-inch,
Callaghan & Co., brass
refracting telescope. £380

19th century butcher's
cleaver. £17

Cary brass monocular
microscope, circa 1830.
£240

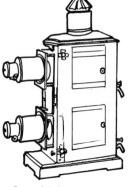

Late 19th century,
E.G. Wood, double
lantern, 2ft. 5in. high.
£260

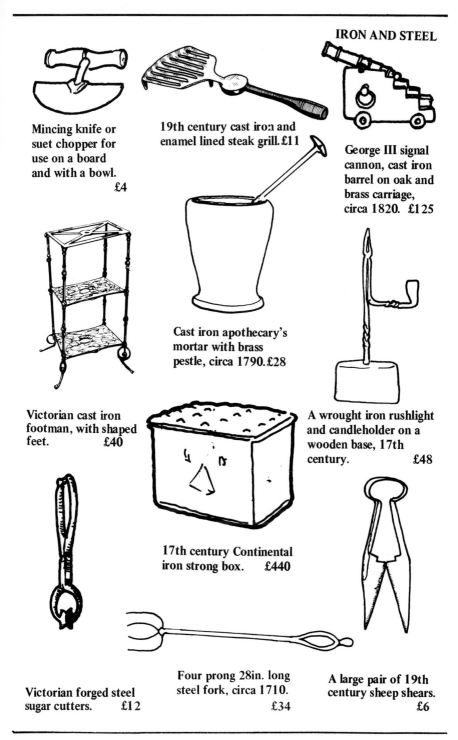

Mincing knife or suet chopper for use on a board and with a bowl. £4

19th century cast iron and enamel lined steak grill. £11

George III signal cannon, cast iron barrel on oak and brass carriage, circa 1820. £125

Cast iron apothecary's mortar with brass pestle, circa 1790. £28

Victorian cast iron footman, with shaped feet. £40

A wrought iron rushlight and candleholder on a wooden base, 17th century. £48

17th century Continental iron strong box. £440

Victorian forged steel sugar cutters. £12

Four prong 28in. long steel fork, circa 1710. £34

A large pair of 19th century sheep shears. £6

IRON AND STEEL

Mincing knife or suet chopper for use on a board. £4

Victorian flat iron complete with pierced iron stand. £9

18th century iron steak griddle, circa 1720. £37

Wrought iron sugar cutters. £9

A 19th century Indo-Persian steel model of a human headed bird, with damascened gold decoration, 14 5/8in. high. £220

One of a pair of 19th century Indo-Iranian steel candlesticks with gold inlay, 11¾in. high. £1,700

Brass and steel penny lavatory lock, circa 1870. £48

Victorian cast iron cooking pot with a medallion on the side. £15

Large Victorian cast iron pestle and mortar. £24

Oblong ivory toothpick case, late 18th century, 3½in. wide.   £85

Late 18th century ivory Corpus Christi, 6¼in. high.   £80

Oriental ivory head on wooden stand, circa 1900, 5¾in. high. £50

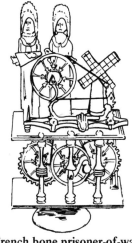

Model of a sea nymph rising from the waves.   £280

French bone prisoner-of-war model, early 19th century, 5¾in. high.   £140

Victorian ivory paper knife with carved handle depicting foliage.   £40

Japanese ivory figure of a mask carver by Ishikawa Komei, circa 1900, 9¼in. high.   £2,500

19th century German carved ivory stein, 14in. high.   £830

Rhinoceros horn Libation cup.   £110

IVORY

Regency ivory and tortoiseshell spy-glass, 5¼in. extended. £48

Naturalistically carved ivory banana. £260

19th century ivory figures of Henry IV of France and Elizabeth I of England, Dieppe. £1,700

19th century African Owo bowl and cover of carved ivory, 21.5cm. high. £22,000

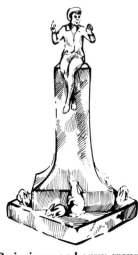

Preiss ivory and onyx group depicting woodland friends, 5½in. high, signed, circa 1930. £180

A carved ivory figure of Hotei, Japanese, circa 1900, 5in. high. £300

Mid 19th century ivory wrist rest, Chinese. £185

Ebony and ivory elephant, 1920, 7in. high. £8

Japanese ivory figure of a girl and a baby, signed Shugyoku, circa 1900. £1,250

Japanese tinted ivory group. £420

English oblong ivory toothpick case, with interior mirror, 3½in. wide, late 18th century. £110

Continental silver gilt, onyx and rock crystal and ivory group playing poker, 15½in. high. £4,200

Interesting 19th century German gilt-mounted ivory tankard, 10½in. tall. £390

An ivory fowl, 16.5cm. high. £250

Late 19th century Japanese ivory figure. £160

Ivory carving of a girl lighting a tobacco pipe, Japanese, early 20th century, 10½in. high. £420

Large German jewelled and ivory group of a camel led by a blackamoor, 16½in. wide. £6,000

Masayasu shibayama ivory tusk vase, circa 1900. £580

IVORY

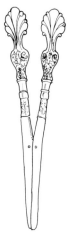

German ivory and copper gilt tankard, 18th century. £780

Mid 19th century ivory head for a walking stick. £80

Ivory glove stretchers with silver handles, 1905. £10

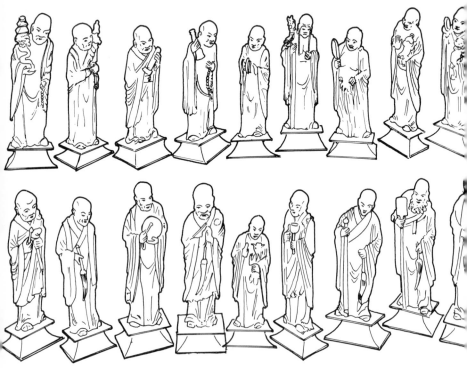

Fine ivory set of the eighteen Lohan, 7in. high, Chinese, circa 1900. £680

Small 19th century jade medallion depicting two fish. £45

Chinese jade dragon and lizard belt buckle. £312

18th century Chinese celadon jade bowl, 23.5cm. wide. £6,500

One of a pair of soapstone Chinese Temple Dogs of Fo on carved bases, circa 1860, 7in. high. £35

A Moghul moss-green jade stand, 31cm. x 28cm. £4,200

18th century carved jade mythical beast, 2in. high. £120

Hardstone and jadeite screen on carved hardwood stand, Chinese, circa 1900. £270

Superb jade carving of mythological figures rising from the sea. £1,405

Translucent jade table screen, 9in. x 6¾in. £2,500

JEWELLERY

Heart shaped brooch with diamonds and pearls.   £100

Chinese necklace of finely pierced hollow coral prayer beads, interspersed with silver gilt beads.   £385

Fine two-headed cameo in gold frame, circa 1810.   £400

Victorian silver brooch with embossed decoration, 1¼in. long.   £10

Pair of Scottish hard-stone earrings.   £50

Diamond set double clip brooch. £1,150

Diamond set 'half moon' crescent brooch, circa 1870.   £1,950

Garnet, chrysoberyl and gold brooch, circa 1850.   £725

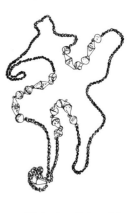

Victorian 9ct. gold fancy necklet. £150

Late Victorian silver brooch set with agate.   £50

Victorian opal and diamond crescent brooch.   £375

Georgian gold and garnet hair brooch, circa 1810.   £70

19th century pendant set with rose diamonds, rubies and pearls. £460

19th century peach-stone necklace, carved with flowers and with a coral bead. £25

Victorian gold and half pearl hair brooch. £285

Diamond set gold bracelet with floral and foliate scrolls. £620

Victorian gold and garnet leaf brooch. £320

Thirty stone diamond and ruby set gold bracelet. £1,100

Victorian citrine, emerald and pearl brooch. £415

Victorian cameo brooch with shell carving in pinchback mount, 3in. wide. £75

Victorian carved ivory brooch. £10

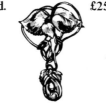

Antique diamond eleven stone pendant cross. £4,000

French gold pectoral by Rene Lalique, circa 1900, 18 x 12cm. £22,100

Pair of enamel, garnet and gold bachelor's buttons by Giuliano, in original case. £360

JEWELLERY

Unusual glass ring with gold mount, circa 1870.   £240

Diamond set gold half bangle.   £650

Victorian silver baby rattle, Birmingham 1846, by Yapp and Woodward.   £110

Diamond and black enamel gold antique brooch, French, circa 1860.   £1,200

Victorian carved ivory necklace. £12

One of a pair of Victorian hair earrings.   £22

Pendant by Alphonse Mucha and Georges Fouquet.   £26,380

Antique cameo ring.   £85

Diamond and emerald set gold ring in the Art Nouveau style.   £150

Georgian sapphire and diamond cluster ring.   £375

Victorian shell cameo brooch mounted in gold. £55

Racing brooch, in diamonds. £120

Art Deco cornelian and marcasite brooch on silver backing. £10

One of a pair of Georgian filigree gold and citrine earrings. £675

Victorian silver gilt locket, 9ct. gold chain.£80

Gold and chalcedony set watch key, early 19th century, 62mm. long. £350

19th century Scottish 'dirk' brooch surmounted with a cairngorm. £7

Victorian gold cast brooch. £28

Victorian diamond tiara.£1,800

Gold cameo in the Art Nouveau style mounted as a ring. £150

LAMPS

Lalique lamp in frosted glass, 1920's, 10½in. high. £520

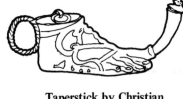

Taperstick by Christian Hammer in the form of a sandalled foot, Stockholm 1857, 5¼in. long. £100

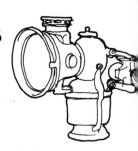

A. J. Lucas acetylene bicycle lamp, 18cm. high. £28

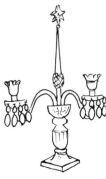

One of a pair of Regency glass candelabra. £350

Tiffany Studio wisteria lamp. £16,000

French plaster lamp on fluted column, 2.15m. high overall. £210

Queen Anne engraved wall sconce, 6½in., high. £135

Miller & Co. brass lamp, 9in. high. £12

Late 6th century A.D. stoneware lamp with green glaze. £34,000

454

Black-painted metal Lucas bicycle lamp, 5in. high. £9

Miller & Co. brass edlite lamp with green and red glass bull's eyes at the sides, 13cm. high. £50

20th century painted glass hanging shade. £10

Venetian Saracenic brass lantern, 9in. high, 16/17th century. £480

Lamp as a lady dressed in black and silver with ivorine face and hands, 10in. high, 1920's. £98

Large sanctuary lamp by T. Thomason, pierced and worked with Gothic foliage, 74in. high. £780

Victorian opaline and ormolu lamp for oil, circa 1870, 2ft. 7in. high. £150

One of a pair of Louis XVI ormolu wall lights. £320

Victorian brass desk lamp with white shade. £36

LAMPS

George III cut-glass eight light chandelier, 43in. high.   £1,625

Late Victorian brass ship's mast lamp.
£35

Victorian brass argand lamp with white shades. £48

19th century crystal chandelier with ten scrolled ormolu arms, 3ft. 6in. high.   £400

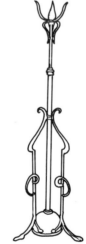

Adjustable lamp-stand of steel, brass and copper, about 1900.   £75

Mid 19th century ormolu candelabrum centrepiece, 48cm. high.   £295

Pond lily table lamp in Art Noveau style.
£48

Early 19th century six light brass chandelier of good patination.   £1,000

Brass and copper lamp, about 1905.
£85

Czechoslovakian peach hanging chandelier, 1920. £70

Early 20th century Ridsdale brass and copper ship's lantern, 1ft. 9in. high. £40

One of a pair of star shaped lanterns. £34

Louis XVI Tole peinte hanging lantern of hexagonal shape, 2ft. 1in. high. £520

Sevres pattern ormolu mounted lamp with contemporary shade, 6ft. high. £2,000

Small, late Victorian ormolu chandelier. £95

One of a pair of Louis XVI ormolu wall lights, 1ft. 10½in. high. £800

Mid 18th century gilt brass chandelier with frosted glass bowls. £340

Louis XVI ormolu wall light, 1ft. 9in. high, one of a pair. £1,500

457

LEAD SOLDIERS

'Jacks Band' of ten musicians each seated on a gilt chair, with conductor, in original box.   £30

A Napoleonic Dutch Lancer wearing a scarlet Kurtka with blue facings and a Czapska, 8in. high.   £18

A Napoleonic Dragoon guard with a brass helmet with red plume, 6in. high.   £18

Army wagon with soldiers and despatch rider, made in Japan, 1920.   £40

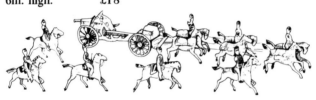

Royal Horse Artillery gun team with five outriders.£30

A Napoleonic eighth Hussar wearing a Shako with a red plume, 6in. high.£22

A Napoleonic Grenadier of the Imperial Guard wearing a black bearskin with scarlet plume, 6½in. high.   £25

A Britains complete boxed set of the Coronation display no. 1477, including Her Majesty's coronation state coach, 150 pieces.   £180

A soldier of the 24th South Wales Borderers of the 1880's, wearing a pith helmet, 5¼in. high.   £18

Royal Engineers pontoon section in original box no. 1254.   £35

Band of the Royal Horse Guards of twenty-five mounted figures and a few beefeaters, contained in a Britain's box.   £85

A Napoleonic officer of the Caribiniers wearing a brass helmet with a red plume, 6in. high.   £18

A Napoleonic Grenadier of the 'Young Guard' wearing a black bearskin with red plume, 6½in. high.   £20

Her Majesty's state coach drawn by eight horses, in original box.   £75

Life Guards, ten mounted figures with swords drawn.   £18

Boxed set of Montenegrin lead soldiers by Britain 1914. £390

MAGIC

'The Decapitated Princess', a throne designed to show a head with no body apparent, 6ft. 2in. high, circa 1890. £160

Collection of turned boxwood magic tricks, circa 1910. £48

A large 'Head Chopper' once the property of the 'Great Levante', 4ft. 4in. high. £35

  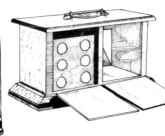 

A pair of magical sand and sugar containers. £10

An early sliding die box. £25

A Will Goldston penetration frame in which a photograph is magically penetrated by a pencil, circa 1905. £30

 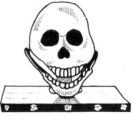 

A dolls house for production of a girl, 3ft. wide. £12

'The Talking Skull' which opens and closes its mouth at the will of the performer, circa 1920. £60

The 'Giant Bran Glass' trick in which the bran is transformed into a live dove, circa 1900. £58

Mid 19th century white marble figure of Venus, 28½in. wide. £300

Fine figured Blue John vase, on a square marble base, 13½in. high. £675

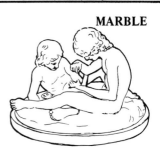

Marble group of two boys feeding birds. £1,000

Marble bust of the Prince Consort, 69cm. high. £38

One of a pair of Venetian marble blackamoors from the late 19th century. £32,000

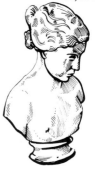

Mid 19th century marble bust of a lady by Joseph Mitchell, 20½in., high. £150

19th century Italian sculpture in white marble by P. Bivirtant, Florence, 39 x 78in. high. £500

Pair of Louis XVI red marble busts of a man and a woman, 6¼in. high, on green marble socles. £850

Blue John obelisk, circa 1820-30, 11½in. tall, one of a pair. £500

461

MARBLE

Russian or French blue marble vase, circa 1930, 8in. high.   £200

Late 19th century Italian bust of an old man, marble, 32in. high.   £90

White marble group of Leda and the Swan, probably French, mid 19th century.   £850

Marble bust of a young man, 55cm. high.   £48

One of a pair of Louis XVI ormolu mounted black and white marble obelisks, 1ft. 8in. high.   £580

Marble bust of Queen Victoria, 59cm. high. £38

Blue John vase, mounted on a square marble base.   £260

Late 17th century Italian marble gazebo.   £1,050

Late 18th century marble statue by Antonio Corradini, Italy.   £16,657

Mid 18th century
Venetian mirror,
3ft. 1in. wide.
£540

Queen Anne period
walnut framed toilet
mirror.   **£470**

Carved giltwood
mirror of the
Chippendale
period.   **£700**

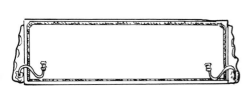

Unusual George I walnut and parcel
gilt overmantel mirror, about 1715.
£435

Chippendale period landscape mirror,
66 x 37in.   **£1,750**

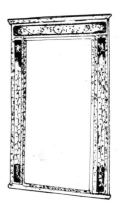

Mid 18th century
Gothic style maho-
gany mirror. **£1,500**

Early 18th century
mahogany and parcel
gilt mirror.   **£820**

George III gilt wood
and verre eglomise
mirror, 3ft. 1in. wide.
£450

MIRRORS

One of a pair of English George III period wall mirrors, 1.83m. high. £4,000

Unusual Georgian mahogany toilet mirror, 23in. wide, circa 1830. £95

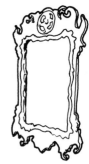

Carved mahogany and gilt wall mirror, circa 1750, 29½in. long. £225

19th century wall mirror, in the baroque style, 5ft. 6in. high, Italian. £10,000

Irish gilt wood framed pier glass, 86in. tall, circa 1760. £1,100

Large Georgian period convex mirror in gilt frame, 31in. wide, circa 1830. £195

Unusual Regency wood and gesso gilt wall mirror, circa 1825, 45in. high. £275

Queen Anne walnut mirror with three drawers in base. £255

18th century pier glass by Chippendale festooned with birds and foliage. £3,200

One of a pair of Chinese Chippendale giltwood miniature wall mirrors, painted with an Oriental scene. £560

Early 19th century inlaid swing mirror. £470

Regency convex looking glass, circa 1810. £68

Regency gilt framed convex mirror. £110

A superb 18th century walnut and parcel gilt mirror with broken arch pediment. £1,850

18th century carved wood mirror, probably Austrian, 4ft.4in. x 2ft.8in. £260

Early Neo-classical giltwood mirror with glass divided at the top, 92in. tall. £2,100

Late 19th century mahogany oval toilet mirror, 18in. wide. £20

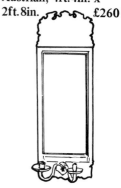

A small early 18th century walnut mirror with original bevelled glass. £275

MIRRORS

Mid 18th century
Venetian painted
mirror, 5ft. 10in.
high.   £1,450

Rectangular giltwood
wall mirror with
bevelled plate, 93cm.
wide.   £28

18th century walnut
toilet mirror on
drawered base, 21½in.
wide.   £250

George II mahogany
wall mirror, circa
1730.   £330

Mid 18th century
Venetian gilt mirror,
4ft. 9in. high. £500

Early George II
gilt gesso mirror
with arched plate,
2ft. 2in. wide.
          £680

Rare late 17th
century Dutch
mirror, 4ft. 3in.
high. £3,100

Early George III
giltwood mirror,
3ft. 8in. high.
          £1,050

Late 16th century Italian
giltwood frame with mirror
plate, 1ft. 8in. high, 1ft
4in. wide.   £285

Late George II
giltwood mirror
with oval plate,
4ft. 3in. high.
£1,050

Regency giltwood
circular convex mirror,
73cm. diameter.   £28

One of a pair of glass
and gilt metal girandoles
of Louis XIV style, 1ft.
5in. high.   £250

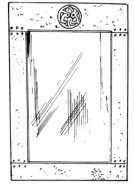

Late 17th century Flemish
walnut marquetry mirror,
2ft. 10in. wide.   £490

Regency gilt and
ebonised mirror.
           £125

Hammered pewter
mirror with enamel
blue decoration. £120

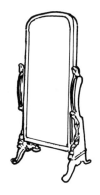

Victorian mahogany
cheval glass, 1.64m.
high.   £98

Carved and gilt
Chippendale period
pier glass.   £450

19th century
Continental
mirror. £250

MISCELLANEOUS

A 19th century entwined
dolphin copper powder
flask.   £50

An Indo Persian saddle
of mauve velvet covered
with gold bullion. £380

French enamel and
gold mounted rock
crystal cup in the
manner of Morel,
about 1840, 6in.
high.   £2,100

Louis XVI terra-
cotta bust, signed
Houdon 1779,
19½in. high.£2,600

Rare paper cut-out model
ship of the Defiance, by
Augustine Walker of Rye,
dated 1762.   £4,200

Victorian Sea-
forth Highlander's
sporran.   £45

Dummy board
figure.   £330

Badge and cipher of Edward
VI as Prince of Wales,
English, 16th century, 14½in.
diameter.   £250

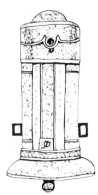

16th century car-
tridge holder, 5½in.
high.   £3,400

Kingfisher feather
hair ornament set
with coral, Chinese.
£15

A bowl in bowenite,
finely carved in one
piece, circa 1800.
£60

Signed and sealed 19th
century tsuba, pierced
with five rats with
golden eyes.   £80

Early 18th century
crab claw priming
flask, 7½in. high.
£180

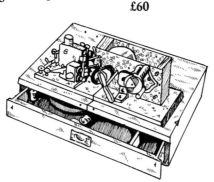

A telegraphic inkwriter
by Dent from the mid-
19th century.   £320

Early sampler
dated 1677.
£300

Victorian glove button
hook with mother-of-
pearl handle.   £7

Preserved human head
with tattoo ornament,
7½in. high.   £12,000

An unusual pair of
Indian betel nut
crushers.   £80

MISCELLANEOUS

One of a pair of maroon lacquer coasters decorated with flower sprays. £75

12th century Byzantine panel depicting the Virgin and Child between two Apostles. £1,150

19th century powder flask made from a coconut. £100

Egyptian, late XVIII-early XIX dynasty carved limestone figure of 'The Lady Of The House Enehey, 38.6cm. high. £70,000

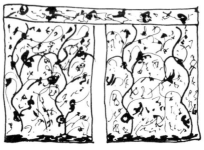

Pair of antique curtains, possibly 18th century, 5ft. 3in. x 7ft. 6in., complete with pelmet. £420

Ahrens automatic palmistry amusement machine, 193cm. high. £250

19th century Continental pine wood spinning wheel. £62

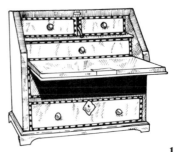

Early 19th century miniature bureau. £250

19th century stained fruitwood Biedermeier spinning frame, 7½in. wide. £40

19th century hip bath with brass fittings.   £205

'The Naval Achievements of Great Britain' from the year 1793-1817, by James Jenkins.   £1,250

Superb 17th century leather bottle, 2ft. high, 18in. wide.   £185

A large, Indian elephant goad.   £36

Late Renaissance limestone over-mantel carved in relief to show the race of Atalanta and Hippomenes.   £3,000

English cast iron football game, circa 1910, 5ft. 6in. high.   £140

18th century fruitwood spinning wheel.   £750

Mid 18th century Dutch marquetry miniature bureau cabinet with glazed doors, 28¾in. wide.   £3,400

19th century English miniature mandolin overlaid with tor-toiseshell, 5in. long.   £55

MISCELLANEOUS

Rare postcard
depicting a
balloon flight.
£400

Stevengraph of Radetzky
and King Victor Emanuel.
£125

Victorian black silk
parasol with embroid-
ered decoration. £20

19th century
wrought-iron
wellhead, 36in.
diameter.£280

Stevengraph of
Victoria and her
four sons. £400

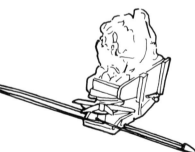

Small French
Provincial oak
bread press,
83cm.   £185

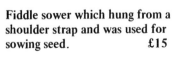

Pine and elm
dolly for
washing clothes.
£7.50

Fiddle sower which hung from a
shoulder strap and was used for
sowing seed.   £15

Early 17th century
powder flask, 8in.
high.   £350

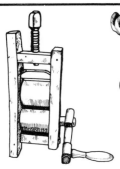

Scottish wooden
miniature mangle
for clerical bands.
£15

Bokhara wood saddle
painted in polychrome
with floral and foliate
designs, 16in. high. £200

19th century Oriental,
paper parasol.   £7

17th century Venetian
sedan chair with carved
gilt wood frame and
leather panels.   £1,000

Cast iron
mutoscope.
£650

Wurlitzer juke box
with twenty-four
records, 1946.
£1,900

Victorian ebonised pen
tray with various fittings.
£20

Tibetan trumpet made
from a human thigh
bone.   £55

An early oak mechan-
ical mousetrap. £130

MODELS

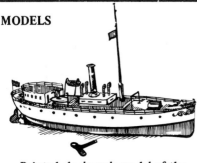

Painted clockwork model of the liner 'Provence' by Bing.   £620

Fine 2in. scale live steam coal-fired model Allchin Agricultural Traction engine, finished in red and black, 26in.   £1,000

Two sections of a glass case containing three scenes from 'Three Little Kittens', 58in. long. £200

Hand built and painted model of a London carriage with two open passenger seats, 1ft. 1in. wide. £60

Fine apprentice made model of a ship steam engine, 10 x 15in. £300

Hand built and painted model of an open Landau with folding hoods, cushioned seats and hinged doors, 1ft. 2in. wide.   £80

Model of the London-to-Brighton stagecoach 'The George'.   £110

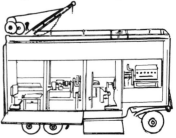

A well constructed six wheeled showman's mobile workshop trailer, 2ft. 2in. wide.   £100

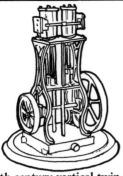

Late 19th century model of a Lord
Mayor's coach, 23in. long.   £210

Good 19th century vertical twin-
cylinder stationary steam engine in
brass and steel, 1ft. 3¼in. high, the
valve inscribed G. H. Joslin, 1880. £320

French sawmill model in a glass case.
                                £365

An exhibition class working model of
a Merryweather steam fire engine
built by Tyrer, Hastings.   £3,200

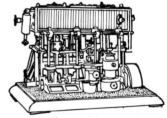

Scale model of a road haulage traction
engine, 2ft. 3in. long.   £620

Fine model of a triple expansion
marine steam engine finished in grey
and mounted on a chequered base-
board, 10¾in. long.   £260

A hand built and hand painted model
of the London-York Royal Mail
coach, 1ft. 3in. wide.   £110

Good 19th century model of a coal-
fired horse drawn steam fire engine,
14in. long, in a glass showcase. £480

MODEL SHIPS

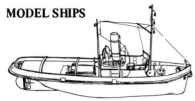

Fine live steam exhibition model of an ocean-going tug 'Margaret', 4ft. 8in. long, circa 1938-1942. £900

A Bassett-Lowke working model of a tug, 2ft. 1in. long. £140

The frigate 'Mars', a full rigged, pinned bone model ship, 19½in. long. £700

Mid 19th century model of the galleon 'Elizabeth Jonas', 1ft. 5in. wide. £200

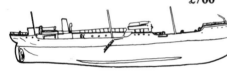

A half block model of the steamer 'Twingone', 6ft. 7in. long. £450

Mid 20th century English half block model of the tanker 'Bilswood', in a stained oak glazed case, 8ft. 5in. long. £430

Good English bone and wood model of a clipper ship, 1ft. 4in. wide, circa 1860. £420

French prisoner-of-war bone model of a frigate, 14in. long, circa 1810-15. £2,300

A Bassett-Lowke working model of a tanker, 2ft. 5in. wide. £200

Mid 20th century working model of a destroyer, 5ft. 6in. long. £225

'Pilot', a 2-2-0 live steam model engine with whistle and chequered footplate, 7in. £120

A Bing 4-2-2 live steam spirit-fired locomotive and tender, sold with several coaches. £720

A clockwork Ernst Plank 2-2-0 engine and tender with key, circa 1905, sold with three four-wheeled coaches. £120

Marklin clockwork 'precursor' 4-4-2 tank locomotive, 16¼in., sold with three coaches. £520

Working model brass 0-6-0 railway tank engine with steel wheels, 2in. gauge, 11½in. long. £185

2½in. gauge live steam coal-fired 4-6-2 locomotive 'Saint Lawrence' with tender, 3ft. 8in. long. £500

Carette live steam spirit-fired 4-4-0 locomotive with cast iron frames 13½in., lacking tender. £920

A 3½in. gauge working steam model of a Duchess Class locomotive and tender in maroon livery of L.M.S. £2,200

MONEY BOXES

20th century English cast iron 'Jonah and the Whale' money box, 9½in. wide. **£90**

Copper lighthouse money box, circa 1860, 9in. high. **£27**

A cold painted American cast iron money box 'always did 'spise a mule', 10in. long. **£120**

20th century English cast iron Artillery bank in the form of a cannon which fires coins into a pill box. **£85**

Cast iron Coronation chair money box, 1953. **£19**

A late 19th century American cold painted cast iron money box in the form of a soldier who fires a penny into a tree stump. **£110**

A 20th century English cold painted cast iron 'Stumps Speaker' money box, 10in. high. **£85**

An American cold painted cast iron 'Bucking Mule' money box, 8½in. long. **£85**

19th century Japanese wooden money box, 14cm. high. **£10**

German 9½in. Kallippe disc musical
box, 11½in. wide, with twelve discs,
circa 1905.   £220

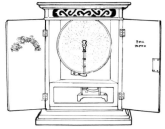

Swiss 11½in. Britannia disc musical
box, 2ft. high, with nine metal
discs, circa 1905.   £480

Nicole Freres cylinder musical box,
Swiss, circa 1842, 1ft. 3in. wide. £420

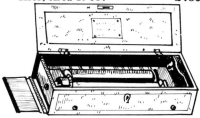

Swiss keywound Nicole Freres
cylinder musical box, 1ft. 8in. wide,
circa 1841.   £920

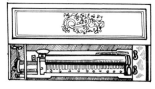

Swiss Mojon, Manger & Co. cylinder
musical box, 2ft. 8in. wide, circa
1880.   £520

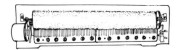

Swiss cylinder musical box by Nicole
Freres, circa 1875.   £260

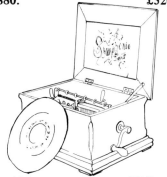

Late 19th century German, 10½in.
symphonium disc musical box, 1ft.
6in. wide, sold with nine metal
discs.   £340

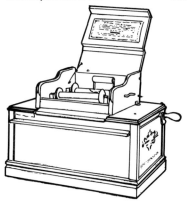

Late 19th century 'Fairy Musician'
twenty-note paper roll organette,
1ft. 4in. wide.   £230

MUSICAL BOXES

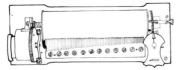

Good Paillard, Vaucher, Fils
'Mandoline' cylinder box, 1ft.8in.
wide, Swiss, late 19th century.£500

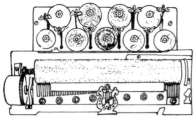

B.H. Abrahams 'Bells in Sight'
cylinder musical box, 38cm. wide,
Swiss, late 19th century.   £150

Good Nicole Freres hand wound
cylinder musical box, circa 1860,
1ft.8in. wide.   £480

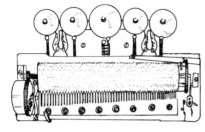

Swiss Bremond 'Bells in Sight'
cylinder musical box, 1ft.11in. wide,
circa 1880.   £580

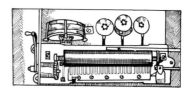

Good Nicole Freres pianoforte
cylinder musical box, Swiss, circa
1881, 2ft.4in. wide.   £1,000

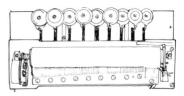

Late 19th century Swiss 'Bells in
Sight' cylinder musical box, 1ft.
11in. wide, in simulated rosewood
case.   £320

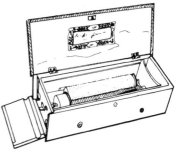

Swiss key wound cylinder musical
box, 1ft. wide, circa 1850. £240

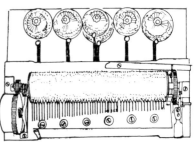

Late 19th century Swiss 'Bells in
Sight' cylinder musical box, 1ft.
7in. wide.   £165

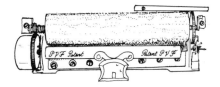

Swiss Nicole Freres cylinder musical box, circa 1900. £640

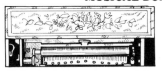

Late 19th century Swiss 'Bells and Drum in Sight' cylinder musical box, 1ft.8in. wide. £260

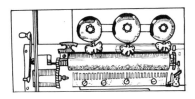

Late 19th century Swiss 'Bells in Sight' cylinder musical box in a rosewood case, 2ft.2in. wide.£510

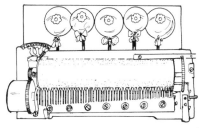

Swiss, late 19th century' 'Bells in Sight' cylinder musical box, 2ft.2in. wide. £320

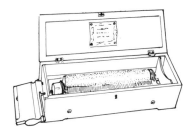

Good Nicole Freres key wound cylinder musical box, 1ft.2in. wide, Swiss, circa 1840. £440

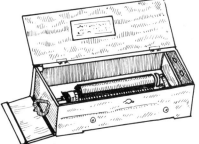

Mid 19th century Swiss key wound cylinder musical box in a rosewood case and reeded edged lid, 1ft.3in. wide. £320

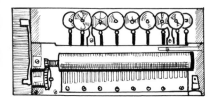

Late 19th century Swiss 'Bells in Sight' cylinder musical box in a rosewood case with fruitwood floral design, 1ft.8in. wide. £320

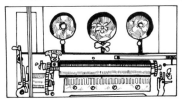

Late 19th century Swiss 'Bells in Sight' cylinder musical box which plays ten tunes, 1ft.10in. wide.£340

MUSICAL INSTRUMENTS

Fine eight keyed ivory flute by Louis Drouet, London, circa 1815, sounding length 23½in., in leather case.
£340

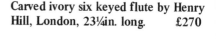

Unusual Japanese Lac Burgate violin case, 31½in. long. £510

American fiddle by Sylvanus J. Talbott, New Hampshire, circa 1887, total length 23¼in. £600

Carved ivory six keyed flute by Henry Hill, London, 23¼in. long. £270

Ten keyed ivory flute by Henry Hill, London, circa 1835, 24½in. long.
£780

Fine satinwood violin case by W. E. Hill & Sons, London, 30½in. long.
£900

Rare boxwood double flute flageolet by William Bainbridge, London, 23½in. long, circa 1830. £420

English brass horn, circa 1800, 7ft. 3in. long. £250

Important five keyed boxwood clarinet by Henry Kusder, London, circa 1865, 26¼in. long. £2,600

Rare ivory three keyed oboe by Klenig, mid 18th century, 22¾in. long. £3,400

Mid 18th century fine small Hurdy Gurdy in leather bound case, 14¼in. long. £900

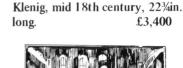

Late 19th century Italian virginals, 21¼in. wide. £725

Tenor sarrusophone, mid 19th century, 28in. long. £210

French one keyed ivory flute, mid 18th century, sounding length, 21½in., unstamped. £800

One keyed boxwood flute by Proser, London, late 18th century, 21¼in. long. £850

Mid 18th century German pochette, 19¼in. long. £780

Late 18th century Viennese Orphica, 41in. long in a case bound with red velvet. £1,700

Fine six keyed boxwood flute by Clementi & Co., London, circa 1810. £190

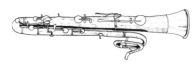

Mid 19th century ophicleide, 9ft. long. £360

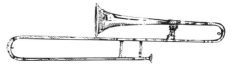

Rare Swiss sackbut by Jacob Steimer, Zofingen, early 18th century, length of tube without mouthpiece 105½in. £2,800

Six keyed rosewood flageolet by Monzani, London, circa 1815, total length 21½in. £90

Mid 18th century English flute or recorder, 24in. long. £650

French Hurdy Gurdy by Caron, Versailles, circa 1770, with S-shaped iron handle, 26in. long. £660

Rare Salterio Tedesco by Gion Zino, Brescia 1692, maximum length 3ft. 11in. £500

MUSICAL INSTRUMENTS

Symphonium by C. Wheatstone, London, circa 1830, 2¾in. high. £400

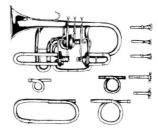

Brass cornopean by Henry Kohler, London, mid 19th century. £420

Late 19th century Faience model horn decorated in green, orange and blue on a white ground, probably French. £520

Early 18th century Mandora, unlabelled, length of body 11½in. £320

Silver plated cornet by Antoine Courtois, 1862, in original mahogany case. £275

English guitar or cittern by Michael Rauche, London 1766, length of back 13½in. £180

A horn in D engraved on the garland 'Iohann Wilhelm Haas in Nurnberg', 186in. long, early 18th century.£800

French pedal harp by Cousineau, Paris, circa 1775, 5ft. 3¾in. high. £850

Edinburgh made set of bagpipes with the Gordon tartan. £209

18th century horn by the Haas family in Nuremberg, 149½in. long.   £900

English serpent by D'Almaine & Co., London, early 19th century, length 7ft. 7in.   £460

Late 18th century English keyed guitar or cittern, length 28¾in.   £700

Attractive Dital harp by Edward Light, London, the simulated rosewood body in seven sections, circa 1815, 34½in. high.   £380

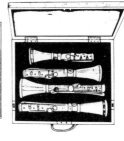

Rare set of four clarinets by Richard John Bolton, London, circa 1840.   £1,100

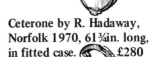

Ceterone by R. Hadaway, Norfolk 1970, 61¾in. long, in fitted case.   £280

Unusual English mute violin, 1874, length of body 14in.   £220

Late 17th century Italian virginals in a leather bound case.   £450

Mid 19th century Cecilium by Arthur Quentin de Gromard, Paris, 4ft. 1½in. high.   £300

MUSICAL INSTRUMENTS

Fine violin by Andrea Guarneri, Cremona, circa 1680, length of back 14in. £420

Violin by Omobono Stradivari, Cremona 1736, length of back 14in. £14,000

American violin circa 1900, length of back 14in. £275

French violin by Paul Bailly, Paris 1884, signed in ink, length of back 14in. £800

Italian violin by Tommaso Balestrieri, Mantua, length of back 14in. £10,500

Important violin by Francesco Ruggeri, Cremona 1691, length of back 14in. £12,500

Italian violin by A. Gagliano, Naples 1724, length of back 13½in. £4,800

Italian violin by Joseph Gagliano, Naples 1782, length of back 14in., sold with bow. £8,500

Italian violin by Joseph Gagliano, Naples 1769, length of back 14in. £5,600

486

French violin by C. A. Miremont, Paris 1873, length of back 14in. £200

Fine violin by Hannibal Fagnola of Turin, circa 1890, length of back 14in. £3,600

Fine violin by Dario D'Attili, New York 1963, length of back 14in. £2,100

Italian violin by Gartano Pollastri, Bologna 1951, length of back 14in. £1,200

Fine violin by Paul Bailly, signed, length of back 14in. £850

Violin by Arthur Richardson, Crediton, Devon 1921, length of back 14in. £550

'The Mackenzie Stradivari' violin, Cremona 1685, length of back 14in. £48,200

20th century Italian violin, length of back 14in. £480

Important violin by A. Stradivari, Cremona 1697, length of back 14in. £36,100

MUSICAL INSTRUMENTS

18th century French violin, length of back 14in. £480

French violoncello by Jean Baptiste Vuillaume, circa 1840, length of back 29½in. £9,600

Viola by Joannes Franciscus Pressenda, Turin 1826, length of back 15½in. £7,800

Mid 18th century Mittenwald violin, sold with bow, length of back 14in. £390

Attractive miniature violin by John Shaw, Manchester 1905, length of back 2¾in. £1,600

Mid 17th century violin by Jacob Stainer, Absam, length of back 14in. £1,650

Unlabelled German violin, Nurnberg School, length of back 14in. £650

Interesting violoncello labelled Fato in Gerona di Giacomo Zanoni 1751, length of back 29in. £900

Italian violin by Alexander Gagliano, Naples 1710, length of back 13¼in. £4,200

Italian violin by
Aloysi Soffriti
1892, length of
back 14in. £1,000

Violoncello by Henrick
Jacobs, Amsterdam
1676, length of back
21in.   £3,000

Italian violin by A.
and H. Amati, Cremona
1618, length of back
14in.   £7,800

Fine Italian viola by
Tomaso Eberle, Naples
1777, length of back
15½in.   £3,000

French violin by Charles
J. B. Collin-Mezin, Paris
1896, length of back
14¼in.   £900

American viola by W. H.
Patten, New Hampshire
1909, sold with two
bows, length of back
16¼in.   £420

Milanese violoncello labelled
'Paulo Antonio Testori
Milano Ao 1745', length of
back 13¼in.   £1,200

Fine viola by William
H. Luff, London 1969,
length of back 15¾in. £750

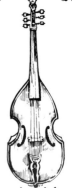

Interesting viola
bastarda, unlabelled,
length of back 25¾in.
£1,550

NETSUKE

Carved ivory netsuke of a mouse. £130

Superb horse and foal netsuke by Rantei. £1,500

Ivory netsuke of a mouse in a rope. £320

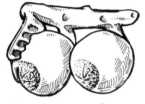

Netsuke group of two Biwa fruits by Mitsuhiro of Osaka. £450

Late 18th century early 19th century netsuke of the Kyoto school. £650

Ivory netsuke of a tiger, attributed to Tomotada. £1,500

Late 18th century Japanese ivory netsuke figure of Shoki. £6,000

Ivory signed netsuke, mouse in a husk of corn. £30

19th century Japanese ivory netsuke of Kirin and young by Ikkosai Toun. £6,800

Japanese ivory netsuke of a puppy pulling a string, signed. £780

Ivory basket of iris netsuke, 1920, by Kyokusai. £2,500

Finely carved wooden netsuke of a Kirin. £8,100

Carved ivory netsuke
of a monkey in a
shell.   £200

Carved ivory netsuke
of a cow lying down.
£400

Late 18th century
ivory netsuke by
Tomotada.£2,090

Carved ivory netsuke,
Tomotada school,
2¼in. long, unsigned,
Japanese.   £520

Superb ivory goat
netsuke by Okatomo.
£4,000

A wooden
netsuke.£180

Ivory netsuke of
mushrooms by
Okatomo. £500

19th century trick
netsuke by
Tomomasa.   £264

19th century ivory net-
suke of Ashinaga and
Tenaga by Tomoyasu.
£520

Ivory netsuke by
Masanao the 1st
of Kyoto, damaged.
£1,200

Japanese ivory netsuke
of a tiger preening its
tail, signed.   £780

Carved ivory netsuke
of a cow.   £270

NETSUKE

Ivory netsuke of
the Demon Warrior
on horseback, 1¾in.
high.   £160

Netsuke of Tamamo
No Mae and the Fox
with Nine Tails, 2in.
high.   £380

Ivory netsuke of
Soki doing battle
with four Oni,
2in. high.   £280

Signed ivory netsuke,
2¼in. high overall.
              £32

Ivory netsuke of
Longarms, 3in.
high.   £67

Ivory mask
netsuke. £40

Mitsuyuki musician,
signed.   £95

Netsuke group of
a bearded man and
an ox, 2in high.
              £380

Japanese fisherman
Sanichi, signed. £55

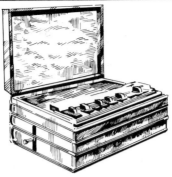

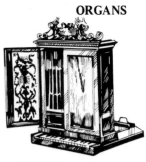

Mid 19th century portatine harmonium, by A.F. Debain, 2ft. 1in. high, on a tripod support with foot pedal at base. £210

Late 18th century French bible organ, 17in. long, 13¼in. wide. £450

Mid 18th century Italian positive organ with hand operated bellows at the rear, 37in. wide. £2,100

Fine Dutch chamber organ by T. Strumphler, Amsterdam, 1792, 43in. long. £2,700

Victorian ten-tune piano organ. £1,600

Late 18th century French barrel organ with painted panel, 25¾in. long. £1,025

Mid Victorian carved oak organ. £32

Late 18th century German positive organ on Regency style oak stand, 21in. wide. £1,385

Fine Aeolian Orchestrelle, circa 1899. £1,600

PEWTER

A good Stuart porringer of booged type, 7.7/8in. diameter, circa 1690.
£300

A Stuart plate, maker's mark R.B., 8.7/8in. diameter, late 17th century.
£130

Late 19th century German pewter vase.
£15

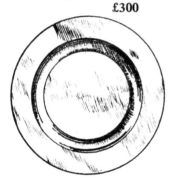

Pewter dish, touch marks rubbed, 16½in. diameter.
£50

One of a pair of Gothic altar candleholders, probably Dutch or North West German, about 1500, 26cm. high.
£1,600

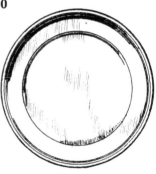

18th century pewter plate by Bush and Perkins, 9¾in. diameter.
£20

A rare Charles II flagon, 11.1/8in. tall, circa 1680.
£520

Late 19th century pewter jug, 6in. high.
£8

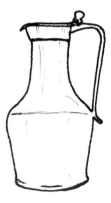

19th century baluster pewter quart measure by James Yates, 6½in. high.
£32

Mahogany cased pair of
Chinese pewter tea
canisters, circa 1780.
£175

Antique pewter
tankard with
lid. £422

18th century pewter
tureen on claw and
ball feet. £160

Pewter charger, maker I.S.,
engraved with initials H.R.B.,
18in. diameter. £105

Rare Queen Anne
period pewter
mace. £275

Hard metal dish,
16½in. diameter.
£30

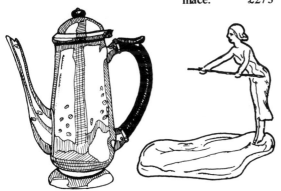

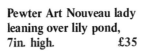

Early 20th century
pewter coffee pot
with ebony handle.
£15

Pewter Art Nouveau lady
leaning over lily pond,
7in. high. £35

Large 18th century
Scottish pewter
tappit hen measure.
£260

PEWTER

A porringer with booged sides and gutter and boss in the base by John Langford, 7¼in. diam., circa 1725. £220

Pewter oval tureen by John Jones, late 19th century. £450

A Queen Anne tankard by Adam Banks of Milngate, the drum encircled by a single fillet at waist, 17.5cm high, circa 1710. £390

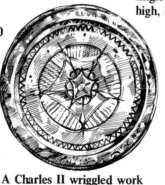

A slit top spoon with hexagonal stem, touch mark E.H., 6½in. long, circa 1600. £150

A Charles II wriggled work plate with narrow rim, maker F.B., 8½in. diam., circa 1665. £300

A slit top spoon with maker's mark ?¯. stamped in bowl, 6in. long, 16th century. £70

A good Swiss stegkanne, the cover with winged thumbpiece, 32cm. high, 18th century. £1,550

A gallon size bud measure with maker's mark E.S., 12¾in. high, circa 1680. £1,000

A Scots baluster measure of quart capacity by William Scott of Edinburgh, 20cm. high, circa 1800. £400

Trencher salt of squat form, 1½in. high, circa 1700. £130

Pewter hot water plate with engraved monogram. £23

Chinese repousse pewter medical box, 1850-60, 9in. long. £38

A rare medieval spoon with lion statant gardant top, 12.1cm. long, 15th century. £220

Pair of Queen Anne church flagons by Adam Banks of Milngate, 27cm. high, circa 1705. £950

A relief cast Queen Anne portrait spoon, with initials S.S., 7¼in. long, circa 1702. £260

James I flagon of plain drum and ovolo moulded foot and lip, 13½in. high, circa 1610. £1,200

Baluster shaped wine measure of gallon capacity by Thomas Stevens of London, 33.2cm. high, circa 1735. £900

A good Swiss wine can by Jakob Ganting, the bulbous body with floral decoration, 33.2cm. high, 18th century. £800

PEWTER

Porringer with finely pierced and shaped ear by Adam Banckes of Chester, 7½in. diam., circa 1700. £280

Early 18th century pewter charger, 19in. diam. £130

One of a pair of 19th century pewter candlesticks, 23cm. high. £36

An attractive strawberry dish, the booge fluted into eighteen petal-shaped panels, 5in. diam., circa 1720. £280

An extremely rare bell-based candlestick with central dished grease catch, 21.7cm. high, circa 1600. £2,000

A plain rimmed Stuart plate by Richard Fletcher, 9¼in. diam., circa 1690. £160

A James I flagon of small size dated 1614, with erect notched thumbpiece. £850

A wriggled work marriage plate by James Hitchman, engraved with a peacock, 8¼in. diam., circa 1718. £450

A pewter mutchkin tappit hen. £245

A Stuart plate with narrow triple reeded rim by Thomas Templeman, 8½in. diam., 17th century. £130

Bud baluster measure of half pint capacity, by John Carr, touch dated 1697, 5¼in. tall. £340

18th century pewter measure, handle engraved by N. Jodard, 10¾in. high. £115

A fine wavy-edged plate by Thomas Chamberlain, 9½in. diam., circa 1760. £210

A Bernese stegkanne by Daniel Hemman from the first half of the 18th century, 31.5cm. high. £1,550

One of a pair of Stuart plates by Edward Kent, 9½in. diam., circa 1690. £250

James I flagon with plain slightly tapering drum raised on an ovolo moulded foot, 34.5cm. high, circa 1610. £620

A large broad rimmed plate made by Edward Everett, 11¾in. diam., circa 1660. £580

A rare Irish gallon haystack measure by William Seymour, 29.5cm. high, circa 1825. £500

PEWTER

A good porringer with booged sides by I. L., 7.5/8in. diameter, circa 1725. £280

An octagonal salt with concave sides and oval salt depression, 3in. long, circa 1720. £120

A Charles II porringer with single fretted ear, 7¼in. diameter, circa 1675. £520

Charles II porringer with flat bottom by W. I., 7.7/8in. diameter, circa 1670. £600

Pair of Queen Anne church flagons for Dumfries Kirk, 27in. high, circa 1705. £850

A rare Charles I flagon of slender tapering form by T. P., 11½in. tall, circa 1625. £1,800

A wriggled work plate with single reeded rim by Chapman, 7.7/8in. diameter, circa 1720. £180

Charles II Beefeater flagon by R. B., 10.5/8in. tall, circa 1675. £1,150

Trencher salt with cylindrical sides, maker's mark I.H., 1½in. high, circa 1700.   £180

Charles II porringer of booged type, 7.1/8in. diameter, circa 1680.   £280

A rare trencher salt of bulbous type with incised reeding around waist, 1¾in. high, circa 1700.   £160

Pair of wriggled work marriage plates by Thomas Widmore, 8½in. diameter, circa 1715.   £800

One of a pair of late Stuart flagons by W. W., 9½in. high, circa 1690.   £1,500

A fine Stuart flagon by John Emes, 11¼in. high, circa 1680.   £1,300

One of a pair of broad rimmed 'Mount Edgecumbe' plates by W. H., 9¾in. diameter, circa 1670.   £440

A fine Beefeater flagon by Francis Seagood, 9¾in. high, circa 1600.   £1,450

PHONOGRAPHS

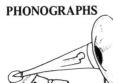

Reinhold & Co. Puck phonograph with conical nickel horn, German, circa 1904-1908.   £140

Good and rare Edison spring motor phonograph in oak cabinet, American, circa 1896-1900.   £640

Columbia Puck type phonograph, model AQ, American, circa 1900.   £140

Edison Bell gem phonograph model A, American 1908-1912.   £210

Small coin-operated phonograph, in an oak cabinet with hinged lid, possibly Continental, circa 1905-1910.   £250

Edison home phonograph in a light oak case, American, circa 1904.   £270

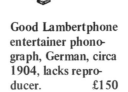

German G.C. & Co. phonograph with spun aluminium horn, circa 1900-1905.£150

Good Lambertphone entertainer phonograph, German, circa 1904, lacks reproducer.   £150

Swiss Paillards echophone phonograph, 12in. high, 30.5cm. diam. at mouth, circa 1905-1910.   £170

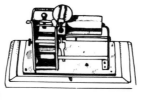

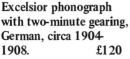

Excelsior phonograph with two-minute gearing, German, circa 1904-1908. £120

Britannia phonograph with key-wound open mechanism, German, circa 1903-1908. £85

Pathe democratic phonograph, model No. O, French, circa 1904. £140

Fine diamond disc phonograph in Chippendale style cabinet, American, circa 1925. £400

G.C. & Co. phonograph with Puck type mechanism, German, circa 1900-1905. £130

Edison gem phonograph with two and four minute gearing, American, 1905-1908. £210

American Edison home phonograph, 1906-08. £190

Lyrophonwerke Koh-I-Noor favourite phonograph - German, circa 1908. £140

Edison Bell gem phonograph with New Model reproducer, English, circa 1904-1908. £120

PIANOS

Square piano by John Broadwood, London 1792, 5ft. 2½in. long. £940

French combined piano and toilet table, circa 1820, 28in. wide. £635

Square piano by Longman & Broderip, London, circa 1795, length 5ft. 2in. £650

Unusual upright piano by Anton Martin Thym, Vienna, circa 1820, 5ft. 6¼in. high. £900

Sycamore cased baby grand by Strohmenger. £1,350

English grand pianoforte by John Broadwood & Son, London 1804, 7ft. 5½in. long. £2,000

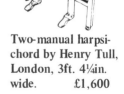

Square piano by Adam Beyer, London 1785, 4ft. 9¼in. long. £620

Mid 18th century French Regal piano in walnut case, 38½in. long. £1,200

Two-manual harpsichord by Henry Tull, London, 3ft. 4¼in. wide. £1,600

Grand pianoforte by
William Stodard &
Son, London, circa
1830, 6ft. 11in. long.
£420

Late 18th century German
clavichord in a walnut case,
36½in. long.   £1,570

Grand pianoforte by
John Broadwood &
Sons, London, circa
1815, 8ft. 1½in. long.
£1,600

French 'giraffe' piano,
circa 1830, 7ft. 6in.
high.   £2,000

Boudoir grand piano
by Collard & Collard,
rosewood case inlaid
with satinwood, 72in.
long.   £560

Mid 19th century
Viennese 'giraffe'
piano, 7ft. 7in.
high, in rosewood
case.   £780

Early 19th century
portable piano by
Joseph Klein, Vienna,
30in. long.   £600

Viennese grand pianoforte
by Anton Walter & Son,
circa 1815, 5ft. 11in. long.£800

17th century Italian
octavino in cypress
case, on oak Regency
style stand.   £1,385

PIPES

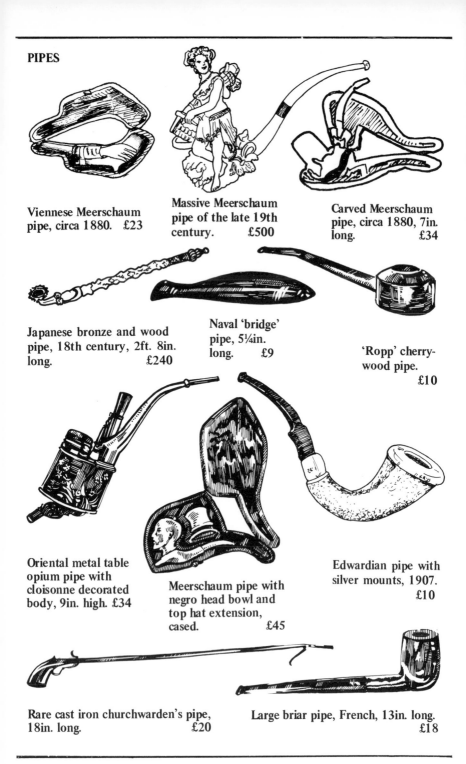

Viennese Meerschaum pipe, circa 1880.   £23

Massive Meerschaum pipe of the late 19th century.   £500

Carved Meerschaum pipe, circa 1880, 7in. long.   £34

Japanese bronze and wood pipe, 18th century, 2ft. 8in. long.   £240

Naval 'bridge' pipe, 5¼in. long.   £9

'Ropp' cherry-wood pipe.   £10

Oriental metal table opium pipe with cloisonne decorated body, 9in. high. £34

Meerschaum pipe with negro head bowl and top hat extension, cased.   £45

Edwardian pipe with silver mounts, 1907.   £10

Rare cast iron churchwarden's pipe, 18in. long.   £20

Large briar pipe, French, 13in. long.   £18

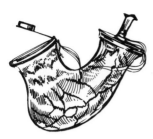

Early 19th century block Meerschaum pipe with silver mounts, bowl 9½in. long.   £50

Erotic Meerschaum pipe holder, about 1885, 10½in. long.   £230

Carved Meerschaum in the form of a tiger and a snake in combat, 6in. long.   £85

Victorian wickerwork pipe.   £3

Meerschaum pipe with bowl supported by carved claw. £28

Late 18th century pottery pipe with brown glaze, 8in. long. £22

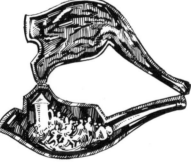

Opium pipe with coloured enamel cover.   £25

Meerschaum pipe carved with 16th century soldiers, 7½in. long, cased.   £90

19th century German pottery pipe, carved, with copper and mother-of-pearl stem.   £22

Cigar or cigarette case.   £5

Metal pipe in the form of a large briar, 13in. long.   £18

RED INDIAN WORK

Tongass wood mask, 10in. high, from the Cape Fox area. £20,000

Late 19th century Sioux eagle feather bonnet. £500

Tongass wood mask with winking eyes, 9in. high. £36,000

One of a pair of Indian women's gauntlets with floral designs in coloured beads. £60

American Indian soft sole mocassins from the Eastern Great Lakes. £750

Blackfoot painted parfleche, folded like a huge envelope to form a carrying case, 30in. long. £222

Indian hide wedding dress painted with warriors and buffalo. £75

Superb Tlingit wood frontlet head-dress, 7½in. high. £17,000

508

Pair of Sioux buck-
skin leggings, deco-
rated with beads
and fringes. **£200**

North American Haida
rattle, 26.5cm. long,
in carved and coloured
wood. **£32,000**

20th century Indian eagle
feather bonnet with bead
work band. **£40**

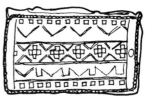

Nootka raven rattle, unusual for
having a curved handle, 12in.
long. **£600**

Cree needle case of felt with
silk lining, outside decorated
with porcupine quillwork,
5½in. long. **£300**

North American Indian
tomahawk pipe with
iron blade. **£130**

Teton Dakota deerskin
shirt bordered with
beadwork. **£5,000**

North American Sioux
breastplate section,
35in. long. **£450**

RUGS

Antique Caucasian 'Fertility' rug, 6ft. 3in. x 4ft.3in.£425

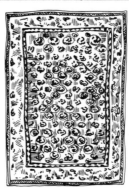

Late 19th century Old Derbend rug, 2.93 x 1.64m. £900

Mid 19th century South Persian antique Afshar rug, 2.02 x 1.68m.£600

20th century central Persian silk Quoom rug, 2.76 x 1.85m.£6,000

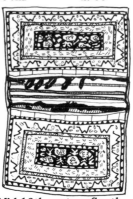

Mid 19th century South Persian antique Quashgai bag, 0.61 x 0.61m.£300

Fine part silk Ispahan rug with floral surrounds, 7ft.8in. x 4ft. 11in.   £2,250

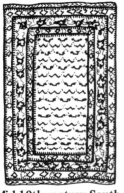

Mid 19th century South Persian antique Afshar rug, 1.64 x 1.16m.£350

Late 19th century central Persian Old Teheran rug, 2.14 x 1.17m.   £2,500

Late 19th century central Persian Old Silk Isphanan rug, 2.08 x 1.35m.   £3,500

Late 19th century
East Persian Old
Belouch rug, 1.17
x 0.91 m.   £220

Late 19th century South
Russian Old Pende rug,
1.32 x 0.89 m.   £650

Mid 19th century cen-
tral Anatolian antique
Bergama rug, 1.93 x
1.45 m.   £2.500

Mid 19th century
East Persian antique
Belouch rug, 1.87 x
1.09 m.   £180

Late 19th century Old
Shirvan rug, 3.43 x
1.44 m.   £1,200

Mid 19th century
antique Kazak rug,
2.70 x 1.13 m. £1,800

Late 19th century cen-
tral Persian Old Kashan
rug, 1.95 x 1.34 m. £1,400

Mid 19th century North-
West Persian antique silk
Heriz rug, 1.88 x 1.37 m.
£6,500

Early 20th century cen-
tral Anatolian Old Pan-
derma rug, 1.73 x 1.24 m.
£600

RUGS

A Bordjalou Kazak prayer rug, circa 1930, 4ft.5in. x 3ft.8in. £660

Karadagh rug, circa 1930, 9ft.3in. x 5ft. £250

Antique Karatchoph Kazak rug, circa 1900, 7ft.5in. x 5ft.1in.£4,000

Fine Daghestan prayer rug, 4ft.11in. x 3ft. 11in. £1,700

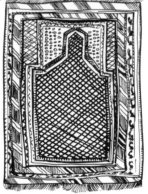

Herat Beluchistan prayer rug, 4ft.7in. x 3ft.6in.£240

Antique Peking rug, late 19th century, 7ft.1in. x 4ft.4in.£540

Modern Kashmir silk prayer rug, 4ft.1in. x 2ft.9in. £360

19th century Kashan Kelim rug. £58,000

Mid 19th century antique Shirvan rug, 3.10 x 1.19m.£1,600

Early 20th century
central Persian Old
Figural Kashan rug,
2.00 x 1.31m. £900

Rare Chi-Chi runner,
2.84 x 1.35m. £1,400

Early 20th century
central Persian Old
Kashan rug, 2.07 x
1.34m.   £2,000

Rare Pende prayer
rug, circa 1925, 4ft.
x 2ft.10in.   £420

Tabriz picture rug
with central lozenge,
10ft.3in. x 6ft.2in.
£2,500

Fine Isfahan rug with
cream field and rust
border, 7ft.4in. x 4ft.
9in.   £1,500

Early 20th century North
West Persian Old Tabriz
rug, 2.05 x 1.40m. £1,100

Early 19th century
antique Beshir rug,
7ft.7in. x 4ft.7in.
£1,250

Good Herez silk prayer
rug, 6ft.5in. x 4ft.7in.
£3,000

Late 19th century South Russian Old Yamout Hatchli rug, 1.64 x 1.32m. £1,300

Daghestan prayer rug, 1884, 4ft.7in. x 2ft. 11in. £550

Khamseh Shiraz rug, circa 1920, 8ft.9in. x 6ft.4in. £280

Late 19th century South Persian Old Figural Kirman rug, 0.72 x 0.60m. £600

Fine Saliani Baku runner, circa 1880, 11ft.10in. x 3ft. 11in. £820

Rare Kuba prayer rug, circa 1820, 4ft.5in. x 2ft.9in. £110

Bokhara Susani panel, late 19th century, 5ft. 4in. x 3ft.7in. £400

Tekke saddle bag, circa 1900, 3ft.5in. x 1ft.7in. £170

Daghestan prayer rug, circa 1900, 5ft.9in. x 3ft.10in. £450

Akstafa rug, circa 1880, 10ft. x 4ft. 4in. £2,800

One of a pair of Kashan rugs, circa 1930, 6ft.9in. x 4ft.4in. £950

Mid 19th century South Persian antique Shiraz rug, 2.35 x 1.67m. £600

Fine Kazak-Chelabird rug, circa 1880, 8ft. 9in. x 4ft.6in. £1,050

19th century Verne Kelim rug, 6ft.6in. x 5ft. £4,800

Fine modern Nain rug, 5ft.6in. x 3ft. 9in. £1,100

Yomut Turkman saddle bag, circa 1900, 3ft.8in. x 1ft.6in. £170

Unusual Yomut Ensi Turkman rug, circa 1880, 5ft.2in. x 4ft. 4in. £1,050

Pendi Juval rug, circa 1850, 3ft.4in. x 5ft. 9in. £900

515

SEALS

Early 18th century gold combined watch key and seal. £80

Rare Chelsea seal, 1in. high, about 1756. £160

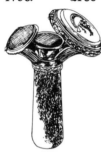

Faberge gold mounted desk seal with triple head. £1,600

Victorian gold and cornelian fob seal. £50

Victorian gold and bloodstone swivel seal. £50

Victorian brass, desk seal with fern decoration. £5

Late Victorian silver and agate fob seal. £25

A small mid Victorian combined watch key and seal. £40

Victorian pinchbeck fob seal. £10

Rare Chelsea seal, 7¼in. high, about 1758, possibly 'Girl in a Swing' style. £160

Victorian embossed silver desk seal. £15

Late Victorian pinchbeck fob seal. £10

English double-sided iron
tavern sign, 34in. x 39in.
£39

Courage counter model
of a cockerel on a plinth,
1ft. high, circa 1931. £30

Coloured poster for a
Chaplin film 'Madem-
oiselle Charlot.' £198

Double sided tavern
sign 'The Bell', 40in.
by 31in. £98

Victoria and Albert saxe-
Gotha Royal Coat of Arms
on wooden shield, 7½in.
high. £49

Fine raised lead Tavern
sign in wrought iron
frame, 38in. across,
circa 1850. £275

A rare English enamelled
advertising sign designed by
the 'Beggarstaffs', 21in. x
14in., circa 1900. £15

Whitbread counter model
of a spelter figure, 1ft. 4in.
high, circa 1930. £40

An English three-
dimensional cardboard
display, 4ft. high,
circa 1920. £22

BASKETS

George III silver boatshaped sweetmeat dish by Hester Bateman, London 1787, 7¼oz.   £240

Fine cake basket by Henry Wilkinson, Sheffield 1845, 10¾in. diameter, 22oz.   £375

George III oblong cake basket, 12½in. wide, by Thomas Robins, London 1806, 38oz. £520

George II shaped oval cake basket, by George Wickes, London 1740, 13¼in. wide, 61oz. 2dwt.   £2,200

Late 19th century plated sugar basket.   £15

George III silver cake basket by William Tuite, London 1773, 14in., 19½oz.   £440

George III silver sweetmeat basket by Henry Chawner, 1794.   £165

George II oval cake basket, 13in. wide, by James Schruder, London 1738, 51oz. 5dwt.   £2,500

George III sweetmeat basket, 6½in. wide, London 1798, 7oz. 15dwt.   £240

Silver George III sweet-meat basket, 6in. wide, by Charles Chesterman, 1784, London, 8oz. 4dwt. £220

One of a set of seven silver epergne baskets in graduated sizes, 120oz. £1,100

Silver George III cake basket, London 1770, 31oz. £300

George II cake basket by James Schruder, London 1742, 12¾in. wide, 55oz. 9dwt. £2,000

Fine silver sweet-meat basket by William Vincent, London 1786, 6in. wide, 8oz. 10dwt. £335

George III silver fruit basket, London 1815, 34oz. £360

Victorian silver cake basket, 46oz. £375

Pierced silver sugar basket, by Charles Chesterman, London 1784. £250

Early Victorian shaped circular cake basket with swing handle, 13in. diam., by Hardy, Bell & Co. Ltd., Sheffield 1839, 34oz. 17dwt. £320

BEAKERS

Russian silver gilt multi-colour enamel vodka beaker.   £220

Early 18th century German beaker, 4in. high, Augsburg, circa 1700, 6oz. 7dwt.   £700

Late 17th century Dutch beaker, 7in. high, 12oz.   £5,800

Engraved silver beaker, 8in. tall, made in Holland, early 18th century.   £5,800

18th century Scandinavian beaker and cover, 1717, 5½in. high, 7oz. 9dwt.£900

Provincial Dutch silver beaker, circa 1650.   £3,100

George IV silver beaker, by Charles Fox, London 1828, 4½in. high, 8oz. 15dwt.   £250

Plain silver beaker, John Horsley, London 1766.£140

One of a pair of George III beakers, 3½in. high, by Charles Wright, London 1778, 9oz. 14dwt.   £650

18th century Swedish beaker by Carl Fahlberg, Uppsala, 1777, 12oz. 4dwt., 7in. high. £1,200

Early George III Chester double beaker, 5½in. high, by Richard Richardson, 1767, 6oz. 11dwt. £500

Early Charles II silver beaker, 3½in. high, London 1671, 5oz. £850

17th century Dutch silver beaker, 7in. high, 1651, 10oz. 2dwt. £2,700

Set of three early 18th century parcel gilt tumbler cups, circa 1700, 9oz. 2dwt.£750

18th century Swedish parcel gilt beaker, 6in. high, by Friedrich Helinrich Klinck, Stockholm 1742, 8oz. 10dwt. £1,050

18th century German beaker, 4in. high, circa 1735, 3oz. 7dwt. £600

One of a pair of George II Chester beakers, 3in. high, by Richard Richardson, 1748, 9oz. 14dwt. £580

18th century Swedish parcel gilt beaker, by Ekfelt Zacharias, Arboga 1764, 13oz. 17dwt., 7in. high.£1,300

BOWLS

Large 18th century Sheffield monteith, 12in. high. £85

Continental silver covered bowl, 8½in., 41oz. £380

One of a pair of silver gilt bowls, 8½in. diam., 5in. high, Sheffield 1900, 48oz. £440

Small silver bowl by Thomas Farren, 1717, 8½in. diam., 916g. £5,800

Early 17th century Dutch tazza, 7in. high, 13oz. 12dwt. £3,000

George II Irish circular bowl, 6in. diam., by John Hamilton, Dublin 1737, 13oz. 2dwt. £820

Shallow sterling silver bowl, by J. Taylor, London 1836. £120

Early 19th century Russian sugar bowl, 6½in. wide, 1805, 17oz. 17dwt. £700

Circular silver rose bowl by Omar Ramsden, 1935, 70oz. 18dwt., 11¾in. wide. £1,600

A small monteith bowl with repousse decoration, by Charles Stuart Harris, London 1882. £300

William III small bowl and cover, 4¾in. diam., by Pierre Platel, London 1700, 12oz. 11dwt. £1,000

Large sterling silver monteith bowl with repousse decoration, with gilded lining, by Charles Harris, London 1876.£1,250

Irish punch bowl by Alexander Brown of Dublin 1735, 8¾in. diameter. £7,500

Early Charles II bleeding bowl, 5½in. diam., London 1664, 7oz. 6dwt. £1,200

Rare early American silver punch bowl by John Coney. £15,500

One of a pair of silver potato rings with blue glass liners, Dublin 1910, 6¼oz. £100

Silver sugar basin, York 1813. £95

Rare George II Scottish Provincial sugar bowl, 4in. diam., by Coline Allan, Aberdeen, circa 1750, 5oz. 19dwt. £420

BOXES

Early 18th century circular patch box, ¾in. diam., by Thomas Kedder, London, circa 1705.   £100

Ivory and blue enamel gold patch box, encrusted with sea pearls.   £85

A silver gilt Freedom box.   £1,000

Bean shaped sovereign case in silver, Birmingham 1904.   £65

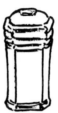

Small Maltese silver box, 1¾in. high, by Gio. Carlo Vella, circa 1730. £80

George III Irish silver gilt Freedom box, 3½in. wide, by James Warner, Cork, circa 1787.   £1,200

Silver box to hold a wax taper, about 1800, 1oz. 75dwt.   £125

George III silver gilt rectangular toilet box, by William Pitts, London 1815, 7in. long.   £550

Simple silver soap box, 1887.   £40

Silver counter box, about 1821, with ropework borders.   £130

Tortoiseshell piquet box, inlaid with silver and mother-of-pearl.   £72

George III Irish Freedom box, 3¼in. wide, by Alexander Ticknell, Dublin 1797.   £1,450

A silver gilt
Freedom
box.   £760

Seven silver thimbles engraved
with the names of the Lost
Boys from 'Peter Pan'.   £70

Miniature silver
patch box by
Samuel Pemberton,
Birmingham 1818.
£45

18th century Dutch
gilt tobacco box,
5in. wide.   £230

Oval French gilt
metal casket,
6½in. wide, Paris,
circa 1875, with
key.   £160

George III silver tooth-
brush and double
sided powder box,
Birmingham 1801.£90

George IV silver tooth-
pick case, 2½in. wide,
by Ledsam, Vale &
Wheeler, Birmingham
1827.   £75

George III Irish
Freedom box,
3in. wide,
unmarked, circa
1795.   £1,200

Silver tinder box,
Vienna, circa
1870.   £38

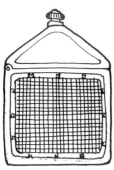

Silver vesta case,
1913.   £85

Silver violin shaped hinged box.
£95

Small cylindrical
box for gaming
counters, silver,
with slip top, 1680.
£150

BUTTONS

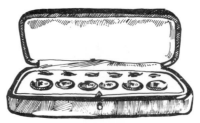

One of a set of twelve Georgian cut steel buttons, about 1800. £60

Box of six buttons with fasteners, 1920. £5

One of eight 18th century buttons, by Samuel Wheat, circa 1755. £130

Late 19th century chased gilt button. £6

Eight George III buttons, by Thomas Wallis, circa 1770. £260

Silver plated livery button £1

CANDELABRA

Victorian silver two-branch candelabrum by I.S. Hunt, 1845. £4,500

One of a pair of George III table candlesticks, 12in. high, by John Green & Co., Sheffield 1794, with plated branches. £490

Seven-light candelabrum by Edward Barnard & Sons, 1867. £1,150

One of a pair of George III table candlesticks, 16¾in. high, by Henry Hallsworth, London 1776, 44oz. 18dwt.£700

George III candelabrum by Smith Tate & Co., Sheffield, 1819, 29in., high.   £1,150

One of a pair of plated silver on copper three-light candelabra, 22in. high.   £150

One of a pair of Victorian silver candelabra, London 1892, 134oz.£1,800

Pair of two-light candelabra, 9in. high, by Carrington & Co., London 1971, 101oz.   £1,050

One of a pair of four-light candelabra, 23in. high, circa 1815. £620

One of a pair of three-light candelabra, 23½in. high, by R. and W. Sorley, Glasgow 1900.   £450

Victorian silver centrepiece candelabrum by Edward, Edward Jnr., John and Wm. Barnard, 1850, 24½in. high.   £1,500

One of a pair of large electroplated on copper five-light candelabra.   £400

One of a pair of early George III table candle-sticks, 9¾in. high, by William Cafe, London 1767, 36oz. 8dwt. £900

One of a pair of early 19th century Russian silver gilt dressing table candlesticks, 3¼in. high, by Johann Hermann Bewert, St. Petersburg, circa 1810, 18oz. 19dwt. £700

One of a set of four George III table candlesticks by Wm. Turton, London 1780, 99oz. 4dwt., 10½in. high. £1,800

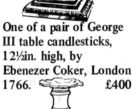

One of a pair of George III table candlesticks, 12½in. high, by Ebenezer Coker, London 1766. £400

One of a pair of early 19th century German table candlesticks, 9¼in. high, circa 1810, 16oz. 10dwt. £280

One of a pair of large George II table candle-sticks, 11¼in. high, by Simon le Sage, London 1759, 70oz. 2dwt. £2,300

One of a pair of George II table candlesticks by Thomas Parr II, London 1753, 29oz. 15dwt., 8½in. high. £850

One of a pair of George II table candlesticks, 9in. high, by John Cafe, London 1756, 42oz. 17dwt. £1,000

One of a pair of George II table candlesticks by Eliza Godfrey, London 1758, 10¼in. high, 48oz. 14dwt. £1,800

One of a pair of
Queen Anne table
candlesticks, 5¾in.
high, by Anthony
Nelme, London 1703,
22oz. 11dwt.   £1,500

One of a set of four late
Victorian silver candle-
sticks, 11½in. high.£360

One of a pair of
George I table
candlesticks, 6¼in.
high, by Joseph
Barbut, London
1719, 23oz. 1dwt.
                £1,350

One of a pair of
George II table
candlesticks by
Paul Crespin, London
1745, 44oz. 4dwt.,
10¼in. high.   £1,700

One of a pair of German
table candlesticks, 8¾in.
high, by Johann Rudolf
Haller, 1826, 20oz. 11dwt.
                £600

One of a pair of Louis
XVI table candlesticks,
11in. high, by J. T. van
Cauwenbergh, Paris
1779, 48oz. 8dwt.
              £2,400

One of a set of four George
III silver gilt table candlesticks, 10¾in. high, by J.
Winter & Co., Sheffield
1782.   £1,450

One of a pair of Queen
Anne table candlesticks,
7½in. high, by William
Denny, 1704, London,
30oz. 12dwt.   £1,900

One of a pair of early
George III tapersticks,
by Ebenezer Coker,
London 1760, 11oz.
13dwt., 5¼in. high.£650

CANDLESTICKS

One of a pair of silver Corinthian candlesticks, Sheffield 1899, 11½in. high. £265

One of a set of four pricket candlesticks, 12½in. high, London 1911, and four campana shaped sconces, 55oz. £450

One of a pair of George II table candlesticks, 7½in. high, by William Gould, London 1745, 33oz. 1dwt. £780

One of a pair of Queen Anne table candlesticks, 7½in. high, by Jonathan Newton, London 1713, 22oz. 8dwt. £2,000

One of a pair of George III cast candlesticks, by Ebenezer Coker. £680

One of a set of four 18th century silver candlesticks by Ebenezer Coker, London 1764. £1,280

One of a set of four Adam style candlesticks, Sheffield 1899, by JR. £480

One of a pair of 18th century Spanish table candlesticks, circa 1750, 6¾in. high, 17oz. 10dwt. £1,000

One of a pair of Victorian plated table candlesticks, 10½in. high. £28

One of a set of four
George III table candle-
sticks, by Matthew
Boulton, Birmingham
1805, 13½in. high.
£1,600

One of a pair of George
III table candlesticks,
By John Carter, London
1775, 11¾in. high. £440

One of a set of six
table candlesticks,
by Nicholas Clausen,
1718, 21.6cm. high,
160oz.   £16,000

One of a pair of George
IV silver table candle-
sticks, 13½in. high,
Sheffield 1823.   £500

One of a pair of George
I table candlesticks, by
David Willaume, London
1717, 6½in. high, 19oz.
£1,700

One of a pair of George
II cast candlesticks, by
John Perry, London
1759, 10¾in. high.£900

One of a set of four silver
table candlesticks, by
Simon le Sage, London
1759, 28.5cm. high,
141oz. 2dwt.   £8,600

One of a pair of Queen
Anne table candlesticks,
by Richard Syng, London
1706, 26oz. 12dwt., 9½in.
high.   £1,300

One of a pair of table
candlesticks, 9¼in.
high, by Hunt and
Roskell Ltd., London
1915, 46oz. 18dwt.£420

CARD CASES

Victorian tortoiseshell card case with silver string inlay, 4in. tall.
£16

Fine Victorian card case embossed with a view of King's College Chapel, Cambridge. £150

Victorian Tunbridge ware card case with geometric patterns.
£15

Oriental silver card case with embossed floral design, 4in. tall.
£25

Silver card case with floral engraving, Birmingham 1901.
£20

Oriental carved hardwood card case depicting a domestic scene.
£10

Victorian silver card case, Birmingham 1853.
£60

Victorian lacquered card case with mother-of-pearl decoration. £28

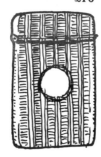

Edwardian engine turned silver card case, Birmingham 1905, 4in. tall. £18

Victorian engraved silver, shaped card case, 3½in. tall. **£40**

19th century transfer printed wooden card case. **£9**

Victorian tortoiseshell card case with pewter inlay. **£9**

Oriental lacquered card case with floral design, 4in. tall. **£22**

Silver card and notecase, with propelling pencil, by William Neale & Sons, Sheffield 1897. **£52**

Oriental wooden card case with sliding action. **£8**

Victorian mother-of-pearl card case with silver pique decoration. **£20**

Victorian diamond pattern mother-of-pearl card case, 4½in. tall. **£16**

19th century Tunbridge ware card case depicting a castle, 4½in. tall. **£35**

CASKETS

Silver presentation casket with lightly hammered surface, 5½in. long, by Omar Ramsden, London 1929. £320

Silver gilt Freedom casket given by Southampton to General Buller. £902

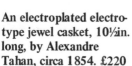

An electroplated electrotype jewel casket, 10½in. long, by Alexandre Tahan, circa 1854. £220

CASTERS

One of a pair of George II silver sugar casters, by Peter Lee Choaabe, 1729. £1,300

Set of three George II baluster casters, 8¾in. and 7¼in. high, by Samuel Wood, London 1751, 41oz. 9dwt. £1,400

One of a pair of George III casters by Hester Bateman, 5oz. £360

Queen Anne octagonal caster, 6¼in. high, by John Eckfourd I, London, 1708, 8oz. 10dwt. £850

Heavy George II baluster caster, 8¼in. high, London 1735, 17oz. 4dwt. £580

George I large plain caster by John Sanders, 1719, 23.5cm. high. £1,700

George I caster, by
Charles Adam, London
1716, 8oz. 4dwt., 7½in.
high.   £400

Silver caster in the shape of
a cock, 6in. high, Chester
1906, 6oz. 13dwt.   £80

Rare 18th century cape
caster, 6in. high, by
Gerhardus Lotter,
circa 1790, 6oz. 13dwt.
                         £900

Silver caster by
Samuel Hennell,
1806.   £95

Set of three silver sugar casters,
pair 7in. high, single 8½in. high,
26oz.   £230

One of a pair of
muffineers by
Hester Bateman,
London 1786,
5¾in. high. £440

George I vase-shaped
caster, 8¼in. high, by
Louis Cuny, London
1722, 14oz. 9dwt. £600

Silver sugar caster,
7in. high, London
1934, 7oz. 5dwt. £60

18th century Flemish vase
shaped caster, 7½in. high,
Malines, circa 1710, 8oz.
19dwt.   £1,300

CENTREPIECES

One of a pair of
Victorian silver table
centrepieces, London
1885, 50oz.   £320

Late Victorian silver
model of a Life
Guard, 30in. tall. £1,750

Silver centrepiece
by Benjamin
Smith, 1838. £475

Silver centrepiece, 15½in. high, by
James Dixon & Sons, Sheffield 1910,
139oz. 16dwt.   £880

George III epergne, 15¼in. high, by
Thomas Pitts, London 1774, 129oz.
12dwt.   £2,650

Silver epergne by
A.H. London
1864.   £2,250

George III table centre-
piece by Thomas Powell,
London 1768, 77oz.
                        £1,650

Victorian silver
centrepiece, 28oz.
              £160

George III silver gilt 'Gazebo' centrepiece, 21¼in. high, by Wm. Pitts and Joseph Preedy, London 1791, 111oz. 4dwt. £1,900

Silver table centrepiece by R. & S. Garrard, London 1837. £3,600

A fine silver George III centrepiece. £1,150

Regency style centrepiece by Walker and Hall, Sheffield 1900, 65oz. 13dwt. £500

Silver gilt epergne, 14in. high, by Elkington & Co., Birmingham 1906, 121oz. £1,500

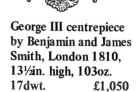

George III silver table centrepiece, Dublin 1801, 61oz., 21½in. wide. £400

George III silver gilt centrepiece by Paul Storr, 17½in. high, London 1809, 231oz. 2dwt. £15,000

George III centrepiece by Benjamin and James Smith, London 1810, 13½in. high, 103oz. 17dwt. £1,050

CHAMBERSTICKS

Fine silver chamber candle-stick by William Seaman, London 1806, 6½in. wide, 11oz. 14dwt.   £355

George III silver chamberstick, by John Schofield, 13½oz. London 1778.   £270

One of a pair of George III silver chamber candle-sticks and snuffers, 1810-11, 11oz. each.   £350

One of a pair of George III Scottish chamber candlesticks, 5½in. diam., by Patrick Robertson, Edinburgh 1786, 25oz. 1dwt.   £750

George III chamber-stick by John Moore, 1808, 9½oz.   £125

One of a pair of George III silver chamber candlesticks by Robert & Co., Sheffield 1809.   £390

One of a pair of chamber candlesticks in Sheffield Plate, circa 1815. £130

George III miniature chamberstick in silver and mother-of-pearl, Joseph Willmore.   £50

George III chamber candlestick, com-plete with snuffer.   £174

A silver chamber candlestick, circa 1790. £290

One of a pair of George III chamber candlesticks by William Stroud, 1805-06, 6in. diam., with pair of snuffers. £620

Silver chamber candlestick, circa 1790. £270

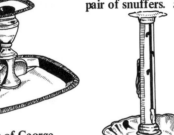

One of a pair of George III chamber candlesticks with snuffers by Emes and Barnard, London 1818, 24oz. 7dwt. £600

One of a pair of Swiss chamber candlesticks, 8½in. high, by Bossard of Luzern, circa 1880, 260oz. 7dwt. £850

One of a pair of King Adolphus of Sweden silver candlesticks by Mattias Grahl, Goteburg, 1752. £3,000

CHOCOLATE POTS

18th century German chocolate pot, 7¼in. high, by Johann Heinrich Menzel, Augsburg, circa 1735, 15oz. 1dwt. £1,450

Fine cylindrical silver chocolate pot, 1725, 9in. high, 26oz. 10dwt, made by Joseph Clare. £5,500

Short spouted chocolate jug by David Willaume, Jnr., 1744, 10¼in. high, 45oz. 10dwt., with wickerwork handle. £3,200

CIGARETTE CASES

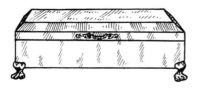

Edwardian plated cigarette box with wooden liner and claw feet.   £7.50

Edwardian silver cigarette box with hinged cover and ball feet, 8in. wide.   £28

Victorian elephant's foot cigar and cigarette casket with plated fittings.   £60

1930's hand carved aluminium cigarette case.   £12

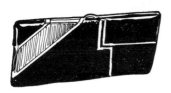

Art Deco enamelled cigarette case.   £14

Curved, silver cigarette case, Birmingham 1910, 4½oz. £10

CORERS

Silver apple corer by Joseph Willmore, Birmingham 1841.   £125

George III silver apple corer by Joseph Taylor, Birmingham 1818.   £86

Silver peeler and corer by Samuel Pemberton, 1803.   £135

Early 19th century apple corer, with ivory handle.   £16

Cut glass claret jug London 1902, 11¼in. high.   & £190

Edwardian silver mounted etched glass claret jug.   £75

Mid Victorian claret jug, Sheffield 1877.   £260

Victorian engraved silver claret jug by George Unite, Birmingham 1880.   £150

Late 19th century silver mounted cut glass claret jug.   £135

Late 19th century glass claret jug with plated mounts. £40

Victorian silver mounted clear glass 'Lotus' claret jug, 7¼in. high, by E.H. Stockwell, London 1880.   £280

Late Victorian glass claret jug, silver gilt handle and mount, maker F.B.M. London 1887, 10in. high.£255

Victorian silver mounted claret jug, 8in. high, by William Comyns, London 1895.£225

COASTERS

One of a pair of George III wine coasters, 5in. diam., by Philip Freeman, London 1773. £400

One of a set of four George III circular wine coasters, 4¼in. diam., by William Abdy I, London 1788.£520

One of a pair of George III coasters, London 1805. £180

Sheffield Plate decanter trolley, circa 1810, with ivory handle. £240

One of a pair of heavy openwork wine coasters by Robert Garrard, London 1836, 33oz. £550

A pair of George III silver gilt wine coasters on a gilt metal four-wheeled wagon, 5in. diam., by Michael Plummer, London 1792. £950

COFFEE POTS

George III vase-shaped coffee pot, 11in. high, by Peter Podio, London 1797, 29oz. 6dwt. £650

Early Georgian coffee pot by Abraham Buteaux, 1725, 26½oz. £2,800

George III silver coffee pot by Whipham & Wright, 29oz.£720

George II Irish coffee pot, 8½in. high, by William Townsend, Dublin, circa 1745, 28oz. 1dwt.   £800

18th century German coffee pot, 11¼in. high, by Diedrich Bockstover, Quakenbruck, circa 1755, 25oz. 18dwt.
                                £2,300

Victorian silver coffee pot by Robert Hennell, London 1842, 20oz.
                    £260

Sheffield plate coffee pot with attractive floral design chased on a matted ground, circa 1825.   £40

18th century Swiss coffee pot, 7¾in. high, maker's mark L.B.D., circa 1760, 11oz. 18dwt.   £1,050

George II tapered cylindrical coffee pot, 9in. high, by Thomas Whipham, London 1751, 21oz. 11dwt.   £1,100

George II coffee pot, 9in. high, by Thomas Tearle, London 1752, 24oz. 1dwt.   £1,400

George III baluster coffee pot, 11in. high, by John Angell, London 1817, 33oz. 2dwt.   £650

George II baluster coffee pot, 10¾in. high, by Samuel Welles, London 1759, 29oz. 16dwt. £1,100

COFFEE POTS

Victorian coffee pot by Edward, John and William Barnard, London 1843, 26cm. high, 26oz. £485

Early George III silver coffee pot. £300

18th century German coffee pot, 11¼in. high, by Johann Christian Neuss, Augsburg, 1799, 23oz.6dwt. £900

Individual coffee pot, 5½in. high, 8oz., 1727, by Peze Pilleau. £1,175

George III vase-shaped coffee pot, 11in. high, Edinburgh 1802, 25oz. 14dwt. £330

George II coffee pot, 9½in. high, by Christian Hillan, London 1740, 27oz.12dwt. £1,250

Russian vase-shaped small coffee pot, 8in. high, Moscow, circa 1790, 10oz. 2dwt. £300

George II coffee pot, 8½in. high, by Henry Brind, London 1742, 21oz.16dwt. £750

A fine George II silver coffee pot with ebony handle. £675

Silver straight sided coffee pot with stepped cover by Isaac Cookson, Newcastle, 9¼in. high, 22oz.16dwt. £2,500

Silver George IV heavy baluster coffee jug, 9½in. high, marked on base Glasgow 1820, 43oz. 12dwt. £380

Silver coffee pot by Thos. Farren, London 1736, 9¼in. high, 24oz.10dwt. £1,600

George II Newcastle coffee pot. £400

George II pear-shaped coffee pot, 11in. high, by William Dempster, Edinburgh 1758, 37oz.11dwt. £850

Silver George III baluster coffee pot, 10½in. high, by W. & P. Cunningham, Edinburgh 1818, 34oz. 2dwt. £500

George II baluster coffee pot, 10in. high, London 1757, 21oz. £450

18th century Swiss coffee pot, 8¼in. high, Geneva, circa 1770, 16oz. £1,300

Silver coffee pot by James Schruder, 1741, with scrolling work on base, 8¾in. high, 25oz.3dwt. £1,150

COFFEE POTS

Victorian silver coffee pot, Sheffield 1851, 11in. high. £500

Silver gilt coffee pot, 1823, on a heater stand, 8in. high, by William Eley. £900

Silver coffee pot in the rococo style by John Fray, 1760, 29 oz., with domed cover £1,350

George III baluster coffee pot, 13¼in. high, by John Mitchison, Newcastle, 1788, 30oz.2dwt. £850

Victorian coffee pot by John Smyth, Dublin 1867, 24cm. high, 28oz. £465

George II coffee pot, 8¾in. high, by William Williamson, Dublin 1732, 20oz.12dwt. £1,250

George II silver coffee pot with repousse decoration, marked Newcastle 1751, 27oz. £400

Side-handled coffee pot by David Tanqueray, 9½in. high, 33oz.10dwt. £3,250

Vase-shaped silver coffee pot by Daniel Smith and Robert Sharp, 1776, 11in. high, 24oz. £1,300

Silver rococo coffee pot by John Swift, 1750, with shell, scroll, foliage and marine motifs, 13in. high. £6,000

Half-fluted silver coffee pot by W. & P. Cunningham, Edinburgh, 11in. high, with an engraved border of oak leaves. £950

George II baluster coffee pot, 11in. high, by Wm. Cripps, London 1754, 29oz.7dwt. £500

George III coffee jug, vase shaped, 12¾in. high, by John Denziloe, London 1789, 24oz. 7dwt. £580

Unusual early 19th century German parcel gilt coffee pot and milk jug, by Johann George Daniel Fournie, Berlin, circa 1800, 29oz.10dwt. £1,300

Vase shaped silver coffee pot made in 1785 by Samuel Godbehere, outlined with beading. £1,000

Unusual pear shaped coffee pot by T.J. & N. Creswick of Sheffield 1855, 9½in. high, 25oz. £550

Silver coffee pot by Thomas Farren, 1732, 8¼ in. high, 20 oz. 12 dwt. £2,500

Baluster shaped silver coffee pot by Samuel Walker, Dublin 1758, 11½in. high, 26oz.10dwt. £1,250

CREAM JUGS

George II cream jug formed as a cow, by John Schuppe, 1759. £1,150

Cream jug, embossed with garden scene, William Sampel, London 1756. £130

George II cream boat, 5¼in., by William Cripps, London 1743, 6oz. 2dwt. £420

Elkington silver plate cream jug, about 1890, 3½in. high.£10

Georgian silver cream jug, 3½oz., circa 1820. £75

Georgian cream jug, London 1801. £90

CRUETS

18th century German two-bottle cruet frame, 9½in. high, by Elias Adam, Augsburg, circa 1735, 8oz. 13dwt.£1,500

Silver George II cinque-foil cruet frame, 8½in. high, by Samuel Wood, London 1749, 47oz. 12dwt. £900

George IV seven bottle silver cruet stand, maker E.F., London 1824. £280

George II cinquefoil cruet frame, by S. Wood, London 1737, 9¼in. high, 59oz.   £1,350

George III egg cruet for six, rectangular, 7½in. wide, by R. Emes and E. Barnard, London 1810, 33oz. 8dwt.   £360

George III oval cruet frame and bottles, by Robert and David Hennell, London 1799.   £450

CUPS

Late 16th century silver gilt standing cup and cover, 11¾in. high, by K. Erb, Augsburg, 11oz. 18dwt. £2,000

Queen Anne Britannia silver two-handled cup, London 1706, 4oz., 2¾in. high.   £150

Early 17th century silver gilt standing cup, 11¼in. high, by A. Tittecke, Nuremberg, circa 1600, 11oz. 11dwt.   £2,100

Standing cup by Omar Ramsden, 7¼in. high, London 1938, 24oz. 15dwt.   £230

Queen Anne two-handled cup, 12oz.   £490

18th century silver mounted coconut cup and cover, 1799.   £150

CUPS

German silver trophy cup, 18in. tall, inscribed 1908. £210

George II Irish provincial two-handled cup, 5in. high, by George Hodder, Cork, circa 1750, 11oz. 14dwt. £270

James I silver gilt wine cup, 8in. high, London 1610, 10oz. 12dwt. £2,400

George III large cup and cover, 17½in. high, by Robert and Samuel Hennell, London 1810, 101oz. 8dwt. £500

George III cup and cover, by Paul Storr, London 1814, 59oz. 5dwt., 12½in. high. £820

George I silver gilt cup and cover, 12in. high, by Edward Vincent, London 1723, 78oz. 1dwt. £600

Charles II caudle cup, 2½in. high, London 1664, 2oz. 9dwt. £500

Early 18th century German parcel gilt standing cup and cover, 14in. high, Nuremberg, circa 1700, 12oz. 16dwt. £1,600

Silver font cup, 1920. £40

George III wine cup, 6in. high, by Hester Bateman, London 1787, 5oz. 19dwt. £310

Silver Victorian christening cup, by J. Angel, 1851, 4oz. £48

One of a pair of fine silver double handled cups, by Peter and William Bateman, 8¾in. high, 41oz., 1812-1813. £750

Queen Anne two-handled cup and cover, 10½in. high, by David Willaume, London 1712, 54oz. 16dwt. £850

One of a pair of George III two-handled cups and covers, 13¼in. high, by William Grundy, London 1768, 96oz. 16dwt. £850

Heavy George II cup and cover by John Jacob, London 1753, 14¼in. high, 90oz. 18dwt. £1,700

Early Charles II caudle cup and cover, 5½in. high, maker's mark G.V., London 1666, 19oz. 7dwt. £3,000

Victorian silver presentation cup, 7½ins. high, 7ozs. £40

Louis XV marriage cup, 5in. diameter, circa 1770, 9oz. 7dwt. £700

DISHES

One of a pair of Victorian silver entree dishes by Garrards, London 1865, 102oz.   £770

One of three George III oval meat dishes, 12in. wide, by Wm. Cripps, London 1760, 61oz.3dwt.£750

Victorian silver meat dish, London 1860, 92oz.   £510

Danish silver dessert bowl, 10½in. high, by Georg Jensen, Denmark, 38oz.9dwt.   £310

One of a pair of George III silver gilt dessert dishes, 15in. wide, by Wm. Fountain, London 1816, 44oz.8dwt.   £650

16th century German alms dish, 1ft.3in. diameter.   £360

One of a set of fourteen William IV silver soup dishes, 9½in. diam., by Paul Storr, London 1835, 238oz.   £2,000

George IV oval meat dish, domed cover and mazarin, 20in. wide, by Robert Garrard II, London 1827, 231oz.10dwt.   £1,500

One of a set of four George II second course dishes, 11in. diam., by Shuder, London 1739, 135oz. 14dwt.   £2,000

George IV meat dish by Paul Storr, 21¼in. wide, London 1820, 78oz. 3dwt. **£980**

One of four silver dessert dishes by Benjamin Pyne, 6½in. diam., 35oz. 2dwt. **£5,000**

One of a pair of George III shaped oval meat dishes, 13in. wide, London 1762, 51oz. 18dwt. **£750**

One of a pair of George IV silver gilt strawberry dishes, 8½in. diam., by Phillip Rundell, London 1820, 26oz. **£950**

One of a pair of Victorian silver embossed fruit stands, 40oz. **£230**

One of a pair of George I silver gilt strawberry dishes, 8½in. diam., London 1719, 24oz. 18dwt. **£750**

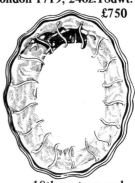

George III oval meat dish, 13¾in. wide, by Wm. Burwash, London 1818, 32oz. 11dwt. **£275**

Breakfast dish and cover in Sheffield Plate, about 1820. **£200**

18th century oval dessert dish, 11¼in. wide, circa 1765, 21oz. 8dwt. **£270**

DISHES

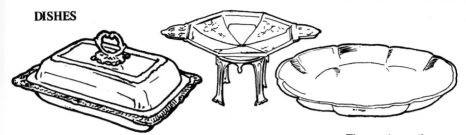

One of a pair of fine entree dishes and covers in Sheffield plate, circa 1815.
£350

One of three silver dessert dishes, 12¾in. and 11½in. wide, maker's mark A.R., London 1903, 73oz.
£360

Fine antique silver strawberry dish by Robert Garrard, London 1836, 10oz. 18dwt. £220

One of a pair of George II shaped oval meat dishes, 16¼in. wide, by George Methuen, London 1751, 74oz. £780

George III altar dish, 21¼in. diam., by Robert Gaze, London 1796.
£720

One of a pair of George III shaped oval meat dishes, 13in. wide, by George Heming and William Chawner, London 1776, 50oz. 15dwt. £700

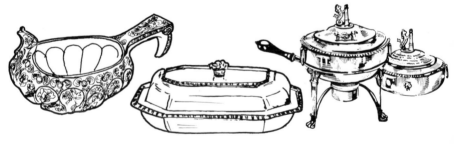

Superb silver Russian kovsh, probably by Maria Somenova.
£11,000

One of a pair of George III entree dishes and covers by Paul Storr, 12¼in. wide, London 1800, 105oz. 8dwt.
£1,900

Pair of George III circular entree dishes and covers, 9¼in. diam., and one stand, London 1808, 156oz. 8dwt. £1,450

One of a pair of
American 7¾in.
circular silver
dishes.   £70

One of a set of four
pedestal dessert
dishes, 7¾in. high,
by H. Wilkinson &
Co. Ltd., London
1901, 102oz.
10dwt.   £1,000

One of a pair of
George III silver
entree dishes,
London 1809,
98oz.   £560

George III oval
meat dish, 16in.
wide, by William
Burwash, London
1817, 49oz. 10dwt.
        £400

Circular dish by Omar
Ramsden, London
1930, 6in. diam., 6oz.
9dwt.   £220

William IV, shaped
circular entree dish
and cover, 11¾in.
diam., by Benjamin
Smith, London 1830,
69oz. 8dwt.   £500

One of a pair of
French Empire
rectangular dishes,
Paris 1805. £600

George IV circular
dish and cover by
Edward Barton,
London 1825, 92oz.
13dwt., 13¼in. diam.£800

19th century
Russian kovsh
in silver and
enamel inlaid
with green and
red stones.
        £3,400

DRESSING TABLE SETS

Late 19th century embossed silver hand mirror, hallmarked 1895.   £40

Edwardian silver hand mirror, Birmingham 1910.   £15

French Empire silver gilt rectangular toilet box, 4¾in. wide, by Martin-Guillaume Riennais, Paris, circa 1800.   £290

Small toilet box by Nathaniel Mills, Birmingham 1850.   £40

Late 19th century silver backed manicure set in a fitted case. £18

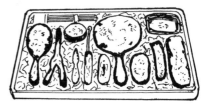

Turtle shell toilet set with Chinese dragon design, circa 1900-1910.   £100

George IV dressing set, silver gilt mounts by John and Archibald Douglas, London 1822, 19oz.5dwt.   £240

Victorian silver dressing table set, comprising two brushes, a mirror and matching pin tray in the rococo style, Sheffield 1880.   £75

Late Victorian silver pin tray by
W.C., Birmingham, 4oz.   £14

Heavily embossed Victorian silver
hand mirror.   £45

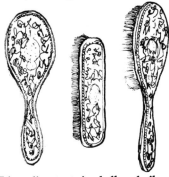

Edwardian tortoiseshell and silver
niello dressing table set.   £35

Victorian cased set of silver hatpins.
£10

Small Victorian vanity case with
silver fittings, contained in a burr
walnut box.   £95

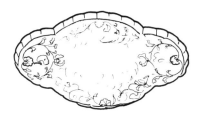

Late 19th century shaped silver
pin tray, 7oz.   £24

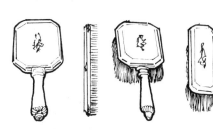

Victorian silver backed dressing table
set, comprising two brushes, a mirror
and comb.   £55

Victorian mahogany vanity case with
silver plated fittings, circa 1860. £45

EWERS

Silver presentation ewer by R. & S. Garrard in the Louis XIV style.
£13,200

Silver Victorian 'Cellini' pattern wine ewer, 12in. high, by C. Boyton, London 1898, 34oz. 7dwt.
£220

Early 17th century Dutch silver gilt ewer.
£164,686

17th century helmet shaped ewer, 7¼in. high, 21oz. 4dwt.
£8,700

Spanish parcel gilt ewer, 11in. high, mid 16th century, 34oz. 16dwt.
£6,500

18th century Spanish baluster, covered ewer, 11in. high, probably Cadiz 1787, 23oz. 10dwt.
£1,100

FLASKS

17th century silver flask, 3½in. high, circa 1675, 2oz. 13dwt.
£340

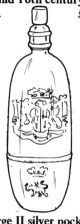

George II silver pocket flask, 7¼in. high, London 1759, 7oz. 8dwt.
£600

Cylindrical scent flask by Ramsden and Carr, 3½in. high, London 1906.
£105

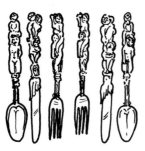

A George IV silver-gilt dessert service, by William Traies, London 1829, 39oz. 6dwt. £1,250

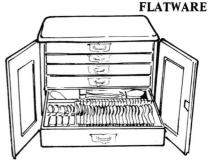

A canteen of cutlery by Francis Higgins, in an oak case, 1900. £1,350

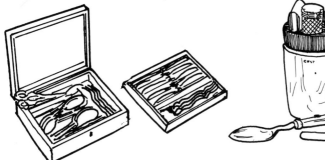

Canteen of silver, London 1810, 1814, and a pair of grape scissors, all by Paul Storr. £640

George III picnic set in a leather case. £330

Part of an extensive canteen of table silver contained in two wooden chests, 114 pieces in all. £15,000

Part of a George IV King's pattern table service. £3,200

FLATWARE

Fine George II silver Hanoverian pattern basting or ragout spoon.
£280

Silver pickle fork with ivory handle, about 1820.   £6

Silver six-pronged serving fork, Simon Harris, London 1808. £62

One of a pair of silver gilt serving spoons, London 1883.   £67

Part of a set of eighteen German fruit knives and forks, 19th century, with porcelain handles.   £1,200

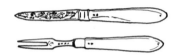

A knife and fork by Harrison Bros., and Howson, Sheffield 1890.   £4

Early 18th century knife and fork, probably German, circa 1710. £110

James I Maidenhead spoon, London 1607.   £340

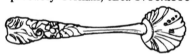

Silver sauce spoon with floral decoration, 1854.   £8

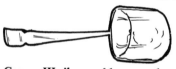

George III silver caddy spoon by Samuel Pemberton, London 1807.
£34

Fine tortoiseshell knife and fork, circa 1800, Sheffield, in leather case.   £50

Part of a Victorian silver and ivory canteen by Frederick Elkington, Birmingham, in a fitted wooden case.   £210

Early 18th century Norwegian spoon, by Johannes Johannesen Reimers of Bergen, circa 1705. £280

George II mote spoon, circa 1750. £45

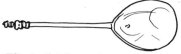

Elizabeth I lion sejant spoon, circa 1620, maker's mark IG in shield. £450

Victorian silver sifter spoon, London 1863. £38

Knife and fork with base cap and engraved handles, Sheffield 1810. £30

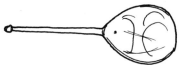

Late 15th century diamond top spoon, maker's mark RO in shaped shield. £500

Late 16th century provincial baluster top spoon, circa 1580. £850

Bright cut tablespoon by Thomas Northcote, London 1787. £17

Bright cut silver tablespoon by Charles Houghan, London 1789. £17

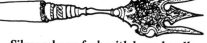

Silver salmon fork with bone handle, late Victorian. £6

Victorian rat-tail pattern table silver by Martin, Hall & Co. Ltd., Sheffield 1897, 157oz. 6dwt. £620

Part of a canteen of Salisbury pattern table silver, maker's mark RWB, London 1935, 98oz. 10dwt., sold in a fitted wooden case. £650

561

FLATWARE

Butter knife by Joseph Taylor, Birmingham 1790. £20

Butter knife (crested) by Edward Morley, London 1808. £20

20th century penknife by H.W. Ltd., Sheffield, with fluted cap. £3

17th century lion's head finial spoon, English Provincial, circa 1630. £245

French straining spoon by Alexis Jacob, Paris, circa 1715, 3oz. 17dwt. £780

18th century Dutch serving slice, 15¼in. long, by William Pont, Amsterdam 1772, 6oz. 14dwt. £560

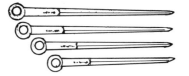

Set of George IV Scottish meat skewers. £240

Sterling silver cake knife and fork, Birmingham 1867. £115

Part of a silver gilt dessert service, 1824-32, 118oz. 15dwt. £2,100

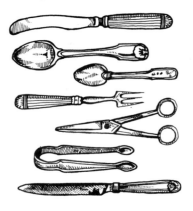

Part of a Georgian silver gilt dessert service by different makers. £1,800

George IV silver goblet with embossed acorn leaf decoration, London 1823, 12oz. £130

One of a pair of silver gilt German goblets, 17th century. £2,100

Engraved silver goblet, 19½oz. £105

Rare Elizabeth I chalice, 6in. high, circa 1580, 6oz. 14dwt. £550

One of a pair of silver goblets by Stephen Smith, 1867. £712

Rare Elizabethan Provincial chalice, 5¾in. high, Norwich 1567, 6oz. 18dwt. £2,400

HONEY POTS

William IV 'skep' honey pot, 4in. high, by Joseph and John Angell, London 1836, 9oz. 12dwt. £400

Silver plated honey pot with green glass body. £65

George III silver gilt honey pot, cover and stand by Paul Storr, 4¾in. high, 1798, 14oz. 8dwt. £2,200

INKSTANDS

Fine George II silver gilt inkstand, circa 1750, 12in. wide. £2,400

George IV silver gilt inkstand by John Bridge, 1824. £800

Walter Jordan naturalistic inkwell, London 1834. £270

Victorian silver oval shaped inkstand with two cut glass and silver mounted bottles, London 1870. £100

Edwardian silver plated inkwell by Mappin and Webb, about 1910. £38

William IV silver inkwell by Joseph Willmore, Birmingham 1829. £305

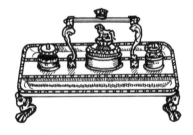

George III silver inkstand by Paul Storr, London 1803, 14¼in. wide. £4,000

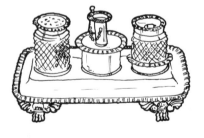

George III oblong inkstand, 9in. wide, London 1818, 26oz. 5dwt. £520

George IV campana-shaped jug, 9¼in. high, by Wm. Bateman, London 1823, 28oz. 1dwt. £270

Victorian 'Cellini' jug with hinged lid, 14½in. high, London 1884, 42oz. £750

George II Irish, covered jug, 9¾in. high, by Andrew Goodwin, Dublin, circa 1747, 41oz. 8dwt. £700

George III beer jug and three mugs by Thomas Moore II, London 1759, 75oz. 2dwt. £2,300

George II baluster beer jug, 9¼in. high, by Wm. Shaw and Wm. Priest, London 1752, 34oz. £1,700

George III coffee jug on stand, 12in. high, by Paul Storr, London 1807, 54oz. 11dwt. £1,700

George IV small brandy jug on stand with burner, 7¾in. high, by J. Angell, London 1825, 16oz. 19dwt. £400

Tiger-ware jug with Elizabeth I silver gilt mounts, 8½in. high, circa 1580. £1,750

LADLES

Old English silver spice spoon, William Sumner, London 1800.   £22

Circular punch ladle with everted lip and turned wood handle, 1730. £140

One of a pair of silver shell bowl sauce ladles, William Sumner and Richard Crossley, London 1776.   £78

Silver punch ladle with oval bowl by Edward Cornock, 1733. £165

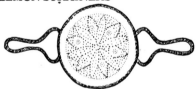

Georgian sifter spoon, London 1797.
£35

LEMON STRAINERS

Late 18th century, bright cut silver strainer, 10in. across.   £135

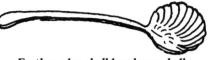

Feather edge shell bowl soup ladle, Walter Tweedie, London 1776. £120

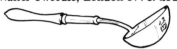

George II toddy ladle with mother-of-pearl handle by John Gamon, London 1731.   £120

Silver Old English cream ladle, Richard Crossley, London 1800.   £26

Georgian ladle, Charles Murray, Perth.
£120

Punch ladle with turned wood handle by William Justis, 13in. long.
£120

Early 18th century silver lemon strainer by Thomas Bamford, 6in. long, 2oz. 4dwt.   £450

George III lemon strainer by Hester Bateman, London 1777, 4in. diam., 2oz. 17dwt.   £260

Silver George I lemon strainer, Francis Nelme, London 1727.   £125

LEMON STRAINERS

Large silver strainer by Robert Calderwood, Dublin 1752, 11½in. long. £340

LEMON STRAINERS

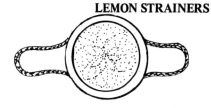

Silver lemon strainer by H. Northcote, 1799. £150

Silver lemon strainer, makers IW/TB, London, circa 1750. £145

MENU HOLDERS

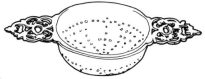

George I lemon strainer, 6½in. wide, London 1718, 3oz. 2dwt. £280

Victorian silver menu holder in the form of a snipe. £26

Victorian silver, pheasant menu holder. £26

MILK JUGS

Mid 18th century Irish milk jug, 4¼in. high, Dublin, 4oz. 15dwt. £190

George I hot milk jug, 4¾in. high, by Samuel Margas, London 1717, 5oz. 3dwt. £800

Swiss milk jug, 7¾in. high, Lausanne 1800, 12oz. 16dwt. £300

567

MISCELLANEOUS

18th century Dutch
silver gilt bag mount,
maker's mark I.V.I.,
Amsterdam 1749, 3oz.
15dwt.   £190

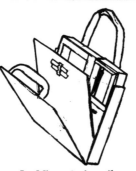

La Minauderie; silver
engine-turned evening
bag by C. van Cleef
and Arpels, about 1935.
                    £480

Silver belt
buckle, circa
1897.   £12

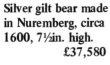

Silver gilt bear made
in Nuremberg, circa
1600, 7½in. high.
            £37,580

Cast and chased oblong plaque
depicting Marsyas and Apollo,
6½in. wide.   £420

Miniature Maltese coffee
pot, 1¾in. high, by
Francescot Fenech,
1797-98.   £240

Victorian plated mussel
server.   £12

Prayer book with
an ivory and
silver inlaid case. £9

French circular brazier,
6½in. diam., Paris 1825,
23oz. 2dwt.   £360

Queen Anne snuffers stand and a pair of snuffers, by Thomas Prichard, London 1704, 11oz. 17dwt. £1,900

One of a pair of silver table ornaments in the form of dolphins, 34in. long, Continental, circa 1870, 200oz. £1,000

Early 19th century Persian rectangular amulet, engraved in Hebrew, 3½in. high. £280

Silver model of a stag, Glasgow 1902, 143oz. 14dwt., 23½in. high. £2,100

Victorian desk calendar with silver hallmarked base, 6cm. high. £10

Victorian silver book-mark in the shape of a dagger, 7.5cm. long. £10

18th century Saxon model of a miner, 7in. high, by Andreas Muller, Freiberg, circa 1710, 12oz. 18dwt. £1,000

George IV butter cooler, 5¼in. diam., by R. Emes and E. Barnard, London 1824, 12oz. 11dwt.£270

Silver portrait bust on moulded pedestal base, 11¾in. high, engraved W. Grant Stevenson, R.S.A., Sc., 54oz. 5dwt. £260

MISCELLANEOUS

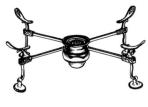

George III ear trumpet, 6in. long, by J. Hampston and J. Prince, York 1791, 3oz. 2dwt. £500

Georgian silver lorgnette with tortoiseshell case, about 1820. £30

George III dish cross, 12in. wide, by Robert Hennell, London 1782, 14oz. 16dwt. £460

Victorian toast rack by Robert Garrard, London 1869. £85

Victorian silver plated tantalus with three cut glass decanters. £75

Silver hunting horn, 1923.£38

Pair of silver flagons, London 1687 and 1690, 22.8cm. high, 56oz. 7dwt. £5,500

A plated shell design biscuit box on pierced end supports. £40

Early 19th century
oblong shaped casket,
5¾in. high, 16oz.
19dwt.   £95

One of a pair of George
II silver spurs, 3in. wide,
London 1729.   £1,050

Silver napkin ring,
by Marshall & Sons,
Edinburgh 1857.£8

One of a pair of dish covers by
Thomas Chawner, London,
1783, 128oz. 1dwt.   £520

One of a pair of George III decanter
wagons, 12¾in. wide, by Nathaniel
Smith & Co., Sheffield 1799.£1,900

Sheffield plated
Argyle in a vase
shape, about
1790.   £150

One of two late 17th
century small flagons,
9in. high, 56oz. 7dwt.
             £5,500

E.P.N.S. oak biscuit
barrel with ceramic
lining, circa 1910.
                £10

MODEL BIRDS

Silver model of a
sparrow, 6in.
high, 4oz. 6dwt.
£55

One of a pair of
ravens, 7¾in.
overall, London
13oz. 10dwt.
£100

Silver model of a snipe,
6½in. overall, 6oz.
18dwt.   £85

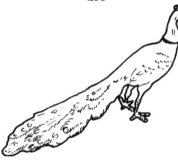

Silver model of a peacock, 11½in.
overall, by Berthold Muller, 6oz.
13dwt.   £105

Silver model of a pheasant, 11½in.
overall, London 1938, 9oz. 19dwt.
£80

Silver model of a
cock pheasant,
1911, 56oz.
13dwt., 16¼in.
high.   £800

German silver gilt
owl drinking cup,
7in. high, late
16th century.
£2,400

A silver coloured
metal model of a
bird, 6in. high,
Dutch, 4oz. 14dwt.
£55

Victorian silver
christening mug,
London 1853,
5oz.   £70

One of a pair of 18th
century silver Channel
Islands christening
mugs.   £520

George III silver
christening mug,
London 1798, by
John Emes, 3oz.
            £85

Silver mug, W. F. &
Co., Edinburgh 1829.
            £82

Victorian silver gilt
mug, 4in. high, by
J. Charles Edington,
London 1861, 6oz.
19dwt.   £120

One of a pair of
George III Scottish
mugs, 4in. high, by
Patrick Robertson,
Edinburgh 1777,
16oz. 16dwt. £350

One of a pair of
George II Irish
mugs by Michael
Fowler, Dublin,
circa 1750, 4in.
high, 16oz. 18dwt.£700

One of a pair of
George III silver
christening mugs,
London 1813.
            £140

One of a pair of early
George II Irish mugs,
4in. high, by Henry
Daniell, Dublin 1728,
12oz. 19dwt.   £620

MUSTARD POTS

Silver oval fluted
mustard pot,
Bernard Brothers,
London 1883.£48

Victorian mustard
pot with blue liner
by F.S., Exeter
1873, 3½in.   £80

One of a pair of
Victorian cylindrical
mustard pots, 2in.
high, maker's mark
overstruck, 10oz.
9dwt.   £150

One of a pair of
Victorian mustard
pots by I.S. Hunt,
London 1850,
18oz.   £250

Victorian mustard
pot by R. Peppin,
1856, 8½oz. £145

Victorian mustard
pot by Burrows
and Pearce, London
1841.   £95

George III vase-shaped
mustard pot, 5in. high,
by Robert Hennell I,
London 1790, and
spoon, 5oz. 1dwt.£160

George III silver gilt
mustard pot by Paul
Storr, 2½in. high,
1812, 6oz. 2dwt.£320

Victorian mustard
pot by W. & H.
Stratford, 1863.£78

Horn snuff mull, probably Tain, circa 1837. £58

Silver mounted ram's head table snuff mull, about 1880, 13½in. high.   £340

Scottish snuff mull, circa 1800.   £85

NUTMEG GRATERS

Silver screw top egg-shaped grater, maker KS, circa 1800. £85

Late 18th century egg-shaped nutmeg grater by Samuel Meriton.   £150

A small silver nutmeg grater made by Samuel Pemberton, Birmingham 1819.   £38

Early 18th century oct-agonel silver nutmeg grater by K.S.   £125

Rare Sheffield plated cylindrical nutmeg grater case with grater inside, about 1790.£70

George III silver gilt oval memorial nut-meg grater, 2in. wide, by John Reily, London 1793. £400

PANS

Plain silver brandy saucepan. £50

George I brandy saucepan, 2¼in. high, by William Fleming, London 1720, 5oz. 17dwt. £410

Early George III brandy saucepan, 4½in. high, by Benjamin Brewood II, London 1766, 19oz. 1dwt. £650

Silver saucepan by James Scott, Dublin 1824.£825

George III silver gilt brandy saucepan, 2¾in. high, by Walter Brind, London 1763, 5oz. 16dwt. £350

George IV brandy saucepan and cover, 4½in. high, by Emes and Barnard, London 1823, 11oz. 3dwt. £340

PEPPERS

Pepper caster by Duncan Urquart and Naphthalie Hart, London 1810. £78

George I kitchen pepper, 3¼in. high, London 1724, 2oz. 1dwt. £400

George III pepper by Stephen Adams, London 1809. £75

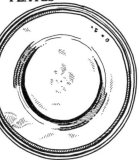

James II alms plate with reeded border, London 1685, 14oz. £900

One of twelve George III shaped circular dinner plates, 9¾in. diam., by Lewis Herne and Francis Butty, London 1762, 212oz. 15dwt. £2,600

One of twelve George II dinner plates, 9¾in. diam., by George Methuen, London 1756, 196oz. 6dwt. £2,600

PORRINGERS AND QUAICH

One of a pair of George II Scottish Provincial porringers, 3in. high, by James Glen, Glasgow, circa 1745, 15oz. 1dwt. £1,700

A typical Stuart quaich, 7¾in. diam., unmarked, Scottish, circa 1675. £1,050

Queen Anne porringer, 4in. high, by Robert Peake, London 1708, 8oz. 17dwt. £360

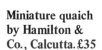

Queen Anne silver porringer by Gabriel Sleath, London 1713, 9cm. high. £420

Miniature quaich by Hamilton & Co., Calcutta. £35

Charles II silver porringer, by R.A., London 1663, 14oz. £920

SALTS

One of a pair of embossed circular salts by Edward and John Barnard, London 1859. £80

One of a set of six George III boat shaped salt cellars by Solomon Hougham, London 1801, 16oz. 12dwt., 5¼in. wide overall. £600

One of a pair of George III salts, London 1777. £95

One of a pair of pierced salts by P. & W. Bateman, London 1813. £150

One of a set of six George III silver salts, London 1802, 21½oz., by Hannah Northcote. £420

One of a set of four George II capstan salts London 1754, by G. Wickes, 32oz. £980

One of a pair of silver Victorian salts, 1875. £45

One of a pair of early 18th century Danish trencher salts, 3¼in. wide, by Gottfred Bolch, Copenhagen 1708, 6oz. £1,100

One of a set of four George III salt cellars by H. Nutting, 3¾in. diam., London 1806, 38oz. 14dwt. £680

Cased set of George III silver salts with gilt interiors, with four matching spoons, London 1820. £190

One of a pair of salt cellars and a mustard pot, 3¼in. diam., circa 1875, 19oz. 2dwt. £240

Inscribed standing silver salt, 1909, 76oz. £500

George III pierced salt by Fenton Creswick & Co., Sheffield, 1776. £55

One of a pair of silver boat shaped salts, James Young, London 1787. £150

One of six oval salt cellars, 3¼in. wide, Paris 1860, 21oz. 17dwt. £210

One of a pair of circular silver salts by Hester Bateman, London 1774. £190

One of a pair of silver George III salt cellars, by Paul Storr, London 1812, 8oz. 1dwt., 3½in. diameter. £600

One of a pair of rectangular shaped George III silver salts, London 1814, 6¼oz. £60

One of a set of six George III salt cellars, 4¾in. wide, by D. Smith & R. Sharp, London 1785, 28oz. 18dwt. £900

One of a pair of silver scallop shell salts on dolphin feet, by Robert Hennell, London 1872. £100

One of a pair of George II compressed silver salts, London 1756, 2½oz., 2¼in. diam. £36

One of a pair of silver salts in the Adam style, by Dobson & Sons, London 1917, 21oz.£230

One of a pair of George III silver salts of spool-shape, London 1792, 6oz. £55

Early 17th century Spanish standing salt, 8½in. high, 21oz. 2dwt.£1,250

SAUCEBOATS

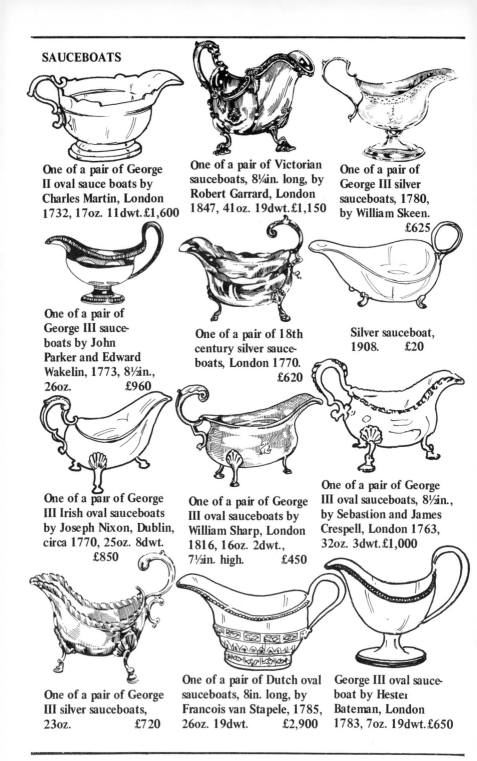

One of a pair of George II oval sauce boats by Charles Martin, London 1732, 17oz. 11dwt. £1,600

One of a pair of Victorian sauceboats, 8¼in. long, by Robert Garrard, London 1847, 41oz. 19dwt. £1,150

One of a pair of George III silver sauceboats, 1780, by William Skeen. £625

One of a pair of George III sauceboats by John Parker and Edward Wakelin, 1773, 8½in., 26oz. £960

One of a pair of 18th century silver sauceboats, London 1770. £620

Silver sauceboat, 1908. £20

One of a pair of George III Irish oval sauceboats by Joseph Nixon, Dublin, circa 1770, 25oz. 8dwt. £850

One of a pair of George III oval sauceboats by William Sharp, London 1816, 16oz. 2dwt., 7½in. high. £450

One of a pair of George III oval sauceboats, 8½in., by Sebastion and James Crespell, London 1763, 32oz. 3dwt. £1,000

One of a pair of George III silver sauceboats, 23oz. £720

One of a pair of Dutch oval sauceboats, 8in. long, by Francois van Stapele, 1785, 26oz. 19dwt. £2,900

George III oval sauceboat by Hester Bateman, London 1783, 7oz. 19dwt. £650

T'ang silver gilt scissors, 7½in. long. £8,000

Gilt and silver metal scissors and paper knife, circa 1935. £6

Ornate Victorian silver scissors and matching thimble, Birmingham 1890. £40

SCOOPS

Stilton cheese scoop with ejector slide, Joseph Taylor, Birmingham 1803. £52

Silver Stilton cheese scoop, 1931. £34

Silver shovel caddy spoon, Edinburgh 1797. £48

Irish silver cheese scoop, John Dalrymple, Dublin 1793. £62

Silver plated marrow scoop. £4

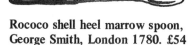

Rococo shell heel marrow spoon, George Smith, London 1780. £54

STIRRUP CUPS

Silver fox mask drinking cup by Thomas Daniel Leader, Sheffield 1807. £1,050

19th century silver stirrup cup. £210

Sterling silver stirrup cup, by Charles Gordon, 1833. £1,750

SNUFF BOXES

James Nasmyth rectangular snuff box, Edinburgh 1838. £150

Circular gold mounted tortoiseshell snuff box, 3in. diam., circa 1780. £140

Victorian silver rectangular snuff box, 4in. long, maker's mark TE, London 1838, 6oz. 17dwt. £180

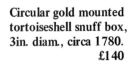

Early 17th century Jacobite snuff box, 2¼in. diam., circa 1715. £690

Continental snuff box with repousse decoration on lid and sides, Chester 1901. £75

Early 19th century Swiss musical box, snuff box and watch, 7cm. wide. £4,500

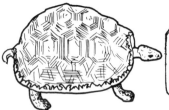
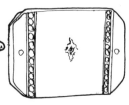

Curved snuff box by Joseph Taylor, Birmingham 1806, in silver. £90

Silver snuff box in the form of a tortoise, by Wallis and Hayne, London 1820, 1822, 3¼in. long. £1,100

Silver pocket snuff box by Ambrose Stevenson, circa 1720. £135

582

Circular French Pollard elm snuff box, lid inset with a plaque, tortoiseshell lined, 3½in. diam., circa 1800.   £100

Silver snuff box in the shape of a fox's head, 3¼in. long, by Joseph Willmore, Birmingham 1834.   £900

Circular ivory snuff box with lacquered lid, tortoiseshell lined, 2¾in. diam., early 19th century.   £95

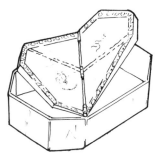

George IV snuff box by John Betteridge, Birmingham 1827.   £85

Cowrie shell snuff box with one side of mother-of-pearl, about 1750.   £135

Octagonal silver snuff box by Phipps & Robinson, London 1791, 3oz. 25dwt.£225

Early 19th century silver snuff box by Charles Rawlings, 1820, 3in. long.   £140

George III circular snuff box by Ruddock & Jennings, London 1809, 5oz. 12dwt., 2¾in. diam.   £250

Russian oblong Neillo snuff box, 3¼in. wide, maker's mark Goldberg No. 812, Moscow, circa 1868.   £440

TANKARDS

Charles II tankard, 6¾in. high, London 1681, 28oz.16dwt. £1,800

George III baluster tankard by Simeon Coley, London 1763, 24oz. 15dwt. £750

Dutch silver mounted horn tankard with silver lining, with portrait of William and Mary on side. £520

George II baluster tankard, 8in. high, by Fuller White, London 1746, 28oz. 7dwt. £900

Early 17th century Danish peg tankard, 7¼in. high, by Mads Clausson, Copenhagen, circa 1610, 28oz. 10dwt. £4,500

Charles II silver tankard, London 1683, possibly by J. Buck, 6in. high, 21½oz. £980

17th century Norwegian peg tankard. £300

Charles I lidded silver tankard. £4,900

Elizabethan silver gilt tankard, 8in. high, 19¾oz., maker's mark IR. £21,000

Early George II cylindrical tankard, 7in. high, by R. Gurney & T. Cooke, London 1729, 26oz. 2dwt.
£820

Fine 19th century ivory and silver gilt German tankard.   £3,600

Charles II York tankard, 6½in. high, by John Plummer, circa 1669, 20oz. 12dwt.   £3,200

Queen Anne tapering cylindrical tankard, 7¼in. high, by Wm. Gamble, London 1712, 25oz. 13dwt.
£980

Early 17th century Norwegian tankard, 8in. high, by Jost Albertszenn, Bergen, circa 1610, 19oz. 1dwt.   £5,500

One of a pair of George II silver quart tankards with lids, by Thomas Heming, London 1746, 7½in. high, 68oz.
£2,600

Silver Queen Anne tankard, 7¼in. high, by Jonathan Crutchfield, London 1704, 23oz. 8dwt.
£650

German 17th century chased and lidded tankard.   £6,400

Heavy tankard by Joseph Rondo, Calcutta, circa 1820, 14oz. 2dwt.   £245

TANKARDS

Attractive Chinese silver 'George III' tankard.   £190

Silver Augsburg tankard, circa 1700, 33oz., with embossed decoration.
£2,500

George III tankard by John Robins, London 1777, 27oz. 17dwt.
£450

George I cylindical tankard by William Pearson, London 1715.
£850

Early George II baluster tankard, 7½in. high, by Edward Vincent, London 1732, 34oz. 5dwt.   £1,700

George II, Irish, tankard by William Williamson, circa 1735, 28oz.   £900

George III baluster tankard, 8½in. high, by Benjamin Laver, London 1781, 28oz. 3dwt.   £850

Large Charles II cylindrical tankard, 8¾in. high, by Ralph Leake, London 1679, 50oz. 6dwt.   £4,000

Early 18th century silver tankard by Nathaniel Lock, 22½oz.   £580

Magnificent silver tazza by Robert Garrard, London 1812, 8in. diam., 6oz. 2dwt. £295

Early 17th century Spanish tazza, 10in. wide, circa 1630, 19oz. £1,300

One of two ornate silver tazzas, 10in. diam., 44oz. £300

TEA CADDIES

One of a set of three George II silver caddies by Lewis Herne and Francis Butty, 1758, 24.8oz. £1,125

George III oval tea caddy, 6¼in. high, by Henry Chawner, London 1794, 18oz. 16dwt. £520

George III octagonal tea caddy by Hester Bateman, 11oz. £590

Victorian copper, plated tea caddy, 7in. high. £25

Fine embossed tea caddy, maker T.B., London 1891, 8½oz. £120

George II oval tea caddy. £290

TEA CADDIES

George II silver tea caddy, of bombe form, embossed and chased with scrolls and foliage, 10oz., London 1752, 5¼in. high, made by S. Herbert & Co. £230

Sheffield plate caddy with a solid silver plate engraved with a crest set into the front, 1800-10, 4½in. high. £45

Oval Sheffield plate tea caddy, 4½in. wide, with bright cut engraving. £140

Set of three George II tea caddies, maker Samuel Taylor, London 1746/7. £920

Set of three George II rectangular tea caddies, 4½in. high, by Paul Crespin, London 1743, 37oz. £1,600

One of a pair of George II tea caddies, 5½in. high, by Samuel Taylor, London 1752, 17oz. 18dwt. £550

George III silver tea caddy by Peter and Anne Bateman, 1794.£750

Queen Anne octagonal tea caddy, 5in. high, by Thomas Ash, London 1711, 8oz. 5dwt. £520

George III cylindrical tea caddy, 4¾in. high, marked on base and lid by Augustin le Sage, London 1767, 15oz. 13dwt. £550

Early 19th century Swiss tea caddy, 6in. high, Berne, 12oz. 7dwt. £400

Silver caddy by George Fox, London 1898, 4in. high. £65

Pair of early George III tea caddies in marquetry box, 5½in. high, by Emick Romer, London, 1763, 15oz. 14dwt. £680

George II pair of silver tea canisters and matching sugar bowl which were contained in an inlaid satinwood tea caddy. £780

Late 19th century silver plated caddy. £18

Sheffield plate caddy, about 1775-80, with typical Adam decoration and a lock.£85

Silver plate Victorian tea caddy, circa 1890, 6½in. high. £20

589

TEA AND COFFEE SETS

George III three-piece tea set by Benjamin Smith, London 1808, 52oz. 4dwt. £880

Victorian silver four-piece tea and cofffee set by Martin and Hall, London 1887, 61¾oz. £460

George III three-piece tea set, by John Robins, 1804, London, 30oz. 6dwt. £430

William IV silver tea and coffee service, London 1833, 73oz. £1,200

Superb George IV tea service, Emes and Barnard, London 1826, embossed with flowers and leaves, 50oz.   **£725**

Silver George III tea and coffee service.   **£1,100**

George III silver tea set by Peter and Anne Bateman, London 1798, 33oz. 16dwt.   **£900**

Plated tea set by Elkington, circa 1860.   **£240**

TEA AND COFFEE SETS

Late Victorian silver teaset, by George Fox, London 1896, with hot water jug by Mappin & Webb, 84oz., together with oak box. £760

George III three-piece tea set by Emes and Barnard, London 1811, 38oz. 8dwt. £480

Fine quality William IV three-piece tea service, 1831-33, by John, Henry and Charles Lias, 47oz. £770

Victorian silver tea service with floral and festoon engraving, London 1870. £720

Victorian silver four-piece tea and coffee service, 82oz. £1,175

Four-piece tea and coffee set by the Barnards, London 1901/19, 84oz. 14dwt. £420

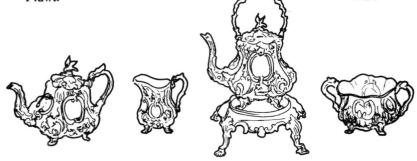

Late Victorian silver tea service by Walker and Hall, Sheffield 1896. £1,550

Victorian circular silver tea and coffee set, Glasgow 1866, 75oz.5dwt. £680

George IV Irish three-piece tea set, maker's mark F.M. & S., Dublin 1828, 52oz. 17dwt. £640

George IV teapot and coffee jug on stand, 6in. and 9½in. high, by J. Angell, London 1826-28, 51oz. 4dwt. £580

Three-piece silver tea service, London 1907, 24½oz. £175

Victorian plated tea and coffee set by Elkington & Co., circa 1878. £140

Three-piece tea set in George I style, 8in. high, by R. & W. Sorley, Glasgow 1930. 56oz. 15dwt. £450

Silver gilt Empire travelling tea, coffee and toilet set, by Martin Guillaume Biennais, Paris, circa 1810. £44,440

Victorian silver coffee pot and teapot, 10in. and 7¾in. high, 60oz. 2dwt. £580

George III three-piece tea set by Burwash & Sibley, London 1807, 47oz. 9dwt. £460

TEA AND COFFEE SETS

George IV silver four-piece tea and coffee service, by Jonathan Hayne, London 1824, 78oz.11dwt.   £700

Victorian silver four-piece tea and coffee set by Robert Hennell IV, London 1872, 83oz.7dwt.   £850

Four-piece tea and coffee set by Z. Barraclough & Sons, Sheffield, 1913, 88oz.7dwt.   £720

George III tea set and matching coffee pot by Emes and Barnard, London, circa 1810, 57oz.8dwt.   £920

Silver tea and coffee service with tray, by Atkin Brothers, Sheffield, 1926-7, 206oz.19dwt.   £1,000

Late Victorian five-piece silver tea and coffee set by Charles Stuart Harris, London 1898/9, 132oz.   £820

TEA AND COFFEE SETS

Victorian tea and coffee service by J. Round & Son, Sheffield 1884. £500

Fine three-piece Victorian tea set by Marshall & Sons, Edinburgh 1864. £625

George IV coffee pot and teapot by William Eley II, London 1825-27, 49oz. 1dwt. £550

George IV four-piece tea and coffee set by Solomon Royes, London 1820-21, 81oz. 1dwt. £1,400

Hammered silver three-piece tea set by Liberty & Co. £120

Victorian tea and coffee service, Sheffield 1898, 70oz. £620

George III tea kettle by F. Butty and N. Dumee, London 1766, 16in. high, 65oz. 2dwt. £820

George III silver tea kettle by S. Whitford, London 1816, 40cm. high. £1,050

Silver teapot on spirit stand. £350

George III tea kettle on stand, 18in. high, by Wm. Elliott, London 1817, 105oz. 15dwt. £900

18th century Dutch tea kettle, 15¾in. high, 67oz. 19dwt. £2,900

George II tea kettle on stand, 13¼in. high overall, by Christian Hillan, London 1741, 51oz. 17dwt. £680

George I tea kettle on stand, 14in. high, by John White, London circa 1720, 73oz. 9dwt. £1,200

Victorian silver tea kettle and stand by W. Mann, London 1843, 13in. high. £900

Silver tea kettle, maker D. Smith and R. Sharp, London 1761, 14in. high, 65oz. £1,150

599

George IV silver teapot of melon segmented form by Paul Storr, 22oz. £610

George II bullet shaped teapot, 15oz. £350

George III Irish silver oval teapot, 7¼in. high, by Richard Sawyer, Dublin 1799, 18oz. 18dwt. £400

George IV teapot, 7in. high, by George Fox, London 1825, 26oz. 2dwt. £270

18th century German teapot, 4¼in. high, stamped KROL, probably Dresden, circa 1745, 13oz. £1,050

George IV silver teapot of compressed pumpkin shape, London 1828, 12oz., maker W.E. £85

Unusual hexagonal teapot by Paul Storr, London 1832, 4¾in. high, 14oz. 1dwt. £850

George III oval teapot by Hester Bateman, 4¾in. high, London 1779, 13oz. £450

18th century American teapot, 4¾in. high, probably by William Pollard of Boston, circa 1730, 15oz. 5dwt.
£2,400

Victorian silver bullet-shaped teapot with crest and motto engraved, 6in. high, maker's mark W. C., Edinburgh 1843, 7oz. £160

Early George II bullet shaped teapot, 5½in. high, by John Main, Edinburgh 1731, 20oz. 16dwt.£750

Irish George IV silver teapot, Dublin 1823, by Edward Power, 33oz. £310

George III silver teapot and waiter.
£210

George II Scottish teapot, 6¾in. high, by Ker and Dempster, Edinburgh 1754, 21oz. 1dwt.£480

Irish George IV silver teapot, Dublin 1823, by Edward Twycross, 38oz.£310

A presentation teapot, inscribed and engraved, by Mappin & Webb, Sheffield 1896, 4¾in. high, 10oz. 12dwt.£85

TRAYS AND SALVERS

Silver George III oval two-handled tray by Robert and Thomas Makepeace, London, 1794, 83oz. 15dwt., 23¼in. wide. **£900**

One of a pair of George III silver salvers, 8in. diam., by Thomas Hannam and John Crouch, London, 1801, 26oz. **£280**

George III oval two-handled tray by William Bennet, London, 1796, 68oz. 9dwt., 21¾in. wide. **£1,250**

Three salvers with the Royal Arms of George III, 14in. and 9in. diam., London 1792-93, 76oz. 2dwt. **£1,150**

George III oval coffee tray by Hannam & Crouch, London, 1804, 50oz., 20in. wide. **£820**

Large silver salver, 12in. diam., by Ebenezer Coker, London, 1765, 24oz. **£320**

One of a pair of silver salvers by Ebenezer Coker, 9½in diam., London, 1761, 28oz. **£450**

George III oval salver, 18in. wide, by D. Smith and R. Sharp, London, 1785, 65oz. 16dwt. **£1,050**

George III oval salver, 16¼in. wide, by Walter Tweedie, London, 1788, 38oz. 5dwt. £720

Victorian silver plated tray with pierced gallery, 25in. long, circa 1845. £200

Victorian silver tray, 19in. diam., London, 1854, 82oz. £700

One of a pair of George III oval two-handled trays, by Timothy Renou, London, 1802, 124oz. 13dwt., 21¼in. wide. £1,900

Silver two-handled tea tray, with Chippendale border, 27½in., by Mappin & Webb, Sheffield, 1922, 109oz. 6dwt. £360

One of a pair of George III oval meat dishes, 13in. wide, by Lewis Herne and Francis Butty, London, 1762, 48oz. 2dwt. £580

George II oval meat dish, by Edward Feline, London, 1752, 52oz. 1dwt., 17¼in. wide. £550

Square silver salver, 9½in., 25oz. 3dwt., by Abraham Buteux, 1726. £1,100

TRAYS AND SALVERS

George II waiter by Dennis Langton, London 1736, 6oz. 18dwt. £230

George IV shaped circular salver, by S.C. Younge & Co., Sheffield, 18½in. diam., 1821, 83oz.3dwt. £540

Early 18th century German silver gilt circular dish, 9¼in. diam., Nuremberg, circa 1720, 6oz. 11dwt. £340

Silver salver by Crouch and Hannam, London 1796, 39oz.£530

Victorian circular silver salver, 15in. diam., by James Forrest, Glasgow 1896, 41oz.6dwt.£140

One of six silver dinner plates, 11in. diam., by Georg Jensen, Denmark, 136oz. £600

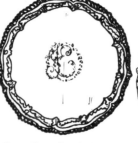

George IV circular salver, 18½in. diam., by R. Emes and E. Barnard, London 1827, 89oz. 15dwt. £750

One of a pair of George III circular salvers, 8in. diam., by Richard Rugg, London 1768, 24oz. 18dwt. £320

Shaped gadrooned silver waiter by Paul Storr, 23oz.6dwt. £950

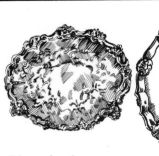

Silver salver by
Emes and Barnard.
£460

George II circular salver, 10in.
diam., by Robert Abercromby,
London 1743, 18oz.7dwt.
£300

George III Irish Pro-
vincial large silver
salver, by John
Nicholson, Cork,
circa 1760, 111oz.
10dwt.   £850

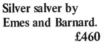

Fine silver salver with
moulded border, 1688,
24oz.7dwt., 12in.
diameter.   £4,800

Large silver salver,
1784, by Joseph
Heriot, 15in.
diameter, 54oz.
£1,350

One of a pair of Vic-
torian, shaped circular
salvers, 16in. diam.,
by G.M. Jackson,
London 1892, 117oz.
9dwt.   £400

George II Irish, shaped
circular salver, 17¾in.
diam., by John William-
son, 1745, 91oz.15dwt.
£1,050

Rococo silver salver,
by Alexander
Edmonston, Edin-
burgh 1830, 12in.
diam., 29oz.   £540

One of a pair of George II,
shaped circular salvers,
10½in. diam., by Thomas
Gilpin, London 56oz. 9dwt.
£950

TRAYS AND SALVERS

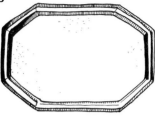

George III silver salver. £220

Oblong octagonal silver salver, 9in. long, 14oz., 1790, by John Crouch and Thomas Hannam. £500

Engraved silver pin tray decorated with scrolls and foliage, 1890. £60

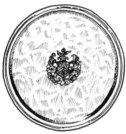

George II circular salver, by Robert Abercromby, London 1737, 41oz. 11dwt., 12¾in. diameter. £900

George II, shaped circular salver, 14in. diam., by John Robinson, London 1742, 41oz. 4dwt. £560

Queen Anne Irish salver on foot, 8in. diam., by Thomas Walker, Dublin, circa 1712, 10oz. 14dwt. £420

Circular silver salver, 20¾in. diam., circa 1820. £280

George III rectangular two-handled tea tray, 30½in. wide, by Peter and William Bateman, London 1809, 153oz. 5dwt. £980

One of a set of twelve George III dinner plates, 9½in. diam., by Thomas Heming, London 1778, 232oz. 10dwt. £2,600

Silver tea tray, 28 x 16in.
£520

One of a pair of George
III silver gilt circular
salvers, 8in. diam., by
John Edwards, London
1796, 29oz. 16dwt. £600

One of a pair of George
III waiters, 6in. diam.,
by James Young, London
1791, 13oz. 6dwt. £290

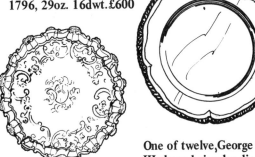

George II circular
salver by Ebenezer
Coker, 1757, 14¾in.
diam., 45oz. 9dwt.
£480

One of twelve, George
III, shaped circular dinner
plates, 9¾in. diam., by
Lewis Herne and Francis
Butty, London 1762,
216oz. 5dwt. £2,600

George II second course
dish, by Edward Feline,
London 1752, 36oz.
12dwt, 12¾in. diam.
£450

George III oval salver,
16in. wide, by William
Bennett, London 1798,
40oz. 10dwt. £520

George IV shaped circular
salver, 13½in. diam., by
William Bateman, London
1826, 38oz. 6dwt. £460

One of a pair of George
III oval salvers, 9½in.
wide, by D. Smith and
R. Sharp, London
1785, 31oz. £650

TUREENS

George IV oval silver soup tureen
and cover, 16¾in. wide, 1823,
82oz. 4dwt.   £1,550

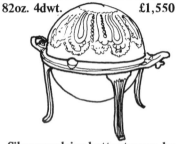

Silver revolving butter tureen, by
Atkin Brothers, Sheffield 1893.
                               £550

One of a pair of George III boat
shaped sauce tureens and covers by
Paul Storr, London 1798, 9½in.
wide, 46oz. 14dwt.   £1,200

Silver Edinburgh tureen with beading
round rim, 1796.   £1,300

One of a set of four silver entree
dishes by Paul Storr, 1829, 216oz.
                               £2,800

George III soup tureen and cover,
15in. wide, by Benjamin Smith II,
London 1818, 256oz.   £2,800

One of a pair of George III silver gilt
sauce tureens and covers, 11½in.
wide, by John Langlands and John
Robertson, Newcastle 1788, 46oz.
5dwt.   £850

George III sauce tureen and cover,
9in. wide, by Robert Garrard,
London 1815, 46oz. 10dwt.   £680

One of a pair of George IV sauce tureens and covers by Paul Storr, 8in. high, London 1821-22, 90oz. 17dwt. £2,800

One of a pair of 18th century German small soup tureens and covers, 9½in. wide, circa 1730, 69oz. 15dwt.£2,750

One of a pair of George III oval sauce tureens and covers, 9¼in. wide, by Daniel Smith and Robert Sharpe, London 1778, 47oz. 7dwt. £950

George IV oval soup tureen and cover, 16¾in. wide, by J. Craddock and W. Reid, London 1820, 183oz. 1dwt. £2,600

Silver plated bacon warmer. £45

French silver soup tureen, cover and stand, by Thomas Germain, Paris, one of a pair. £391,300

One of a set of four George III sauce tureens and covers by Paul Storr, London 1797, 101oz. 2dwt., 9in. wide overall. £4,400

One of a pair of George III boat shaped sauce tureens and covers, 9in. wide, by Thomas Pitts II, London 1805, 44oz. 2dwt. £1,500

TONGS AND NIPS

Pair of openwork silver tongs by
Benjamin Montague, London 1760.
£40

Pair of Irish sugar nippers, Dublin,
circa 1760.   £75

George III silver sugar nips, by
Richard Mills, circa 1760.   £36

Irish chased sugar tongs, by C.
Cummings, Dublin 1837.   £30

Silver asparagus tongs by G. W. Adams,
1864.   £75

George III sugar nips, by Henry
Plumpton, circa 1760.   £70

URNS

George III coffee urn,
14in. high, by Daniel
Smith and Robert
Sharp, London 1778,
24oz. 12dwt.   £650

Silver George III vase
shaped urn, 17¼in. high,
by James McKay,
Edinburgh 1802, 93oz.
18dwt.   £500

George III tea urn,
19¾in. high, by D.
Smith and R. Sharp,
London 1764, 88oz.
8dwt.   £620

Sheffield plate tea urn, by Thomas Holland, London 1810, 14½in. high.   £185

VASES

George III vase shaped tea urn, 20in. high, by Parker and Wakelin, London 1774, 89oz. 8dwt.   £680

Large melon shaped Irish water urn, by T. Smyth, Dublin 1854.   £1,250

One of a pair of George III sugar vases and covers, 7in. high, by Pierre Gillois, London 1775, 17oz. 6dwt.   £450

George II baluster tea vase, 4¾in. high, by Peze Pilleau, 1747, 7oz. 15dwt.   £320

One of a pair of George III silver gilt sugar vases, 8¼in. high, by Digby Scott and B. Smith, London 1806, 64oz. 4dwt.   £130

One of a set of three George II sugar vases in sizes by D. Piers, London 1752, 43oz. 1dwt.   £800

One of a pair of silver oblong vases, 8in. high, by W. Comyns & Sons, London 1913, 45oz. 3dwt.   £450

One of a set of three George III covered sugar vases, 9in. and 8in. high, by D. Smith and R. Sharp, London 1785, 45oz. 6dwt.   £680

VINAIGRETTES

George III oblong vinaigrette, 1½in. wide, by John Shaw, Birmingham 1812. £55

George IV rectangular silver gilt vinaigrette, 1¾in. wide, fully marked, by William Ellerby, London 1825. £140

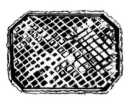

Early 19th century agate vinaigrette, 2in. wide, circa 1835. £280

Swiss gold vinaigrette, circa 1830, 1in. diam. £210

George III articulated fish vinaigrette, 3½in. wide, by W. Lea & Co., Birmingham 1817. £290

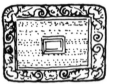

George IV silver gilt vinaigrette, 1in. wide, maker's mark W.S., Birmingham 1826. £120

George IV vinaigrette, 1in. wide, by Joseph Willmore, Birmingham 1820. £165

George IV silver gilt vinaigrette, 1½in. diam., by Joseph Willmore, Birmingham 1824. £180

17th century silver gilt pomander, German, circa 1620, 1¾in. high. £450

George IV rectangular vinaigrette, 1½in. wide, probably by Edward Edwards, London 1828. £105

William IV vinaigrette, 2in. wide, by Nathaniel Mills, Birmingham 1834. £90

George III rectangular vinaigrette, 2in. wide, by Wm. Eley, London 1815. £120

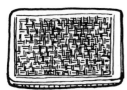

George III vinaigrette, 1½in. wide, by Phipps, Robinson and Phipps, London 1811. £90

Miniature book-shaped vinaigrette, London 1818, 19dwt., 1½in. long. £130

Early 19th century rectangular vinaigrette, 1¼in. wide, circa 1820. £400

Early 19th century gold vinaigrette, 1¼in. wide, circa 1800. £230

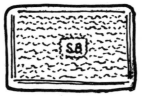

George IV silver vinaigrette, 1¼in. wide, possibly by Thomas Ellerton, London 1822. £60

Continental silver articulated fish, 7½in. long. £190

George III rectangular vinaigrette, 1¼in. wide, by Thomas Holland, London 1799. £90

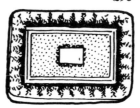

William IV silver vinaigrette, 1½in. wide, by Thomas Ellerton, London 1836. £90

George III snuff box cum vinaigrette, 2¼in. wide, by R. Lockwood and J. Douglas, London 1802. £165

Silver vinaigrette by Nathaniel Mills, Birmingham 1837. £460

George III silver gilt vinaigrette, 1½in. overall, by Joseph Taylor, Birmingham 1816. £95

George III vinaigrette, 1½in. wide, by Matthew Linwood, Birmingham 1806. £200

VINAIGRETTES

William IV rectangular vinaigrette, 1¾in. wide, by Nathaniel Mills, Birmingham 1830.   £230

Georgian purse shaped vinaigrette, 1in. wide, by J. Lawrence & Co., Birmingham, circa 1820.   £130

George III rectangular agate vinaigrette, by Phipps & Robinson, London 1810, 1¼in. wide.   £250

George IV rectangular vinaigrette, 1¼in. wide, by William Eley, London 1822.   £70

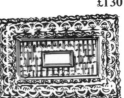

George IV silver gilt vinaigrette, 1¾in. wide, by Thomas Shaw, Birmingham 1828.   £210

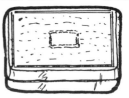

Engine-turned vinaigrette with ring end, 1¼in. long, London 1821, maker W.E.   £90

George IV oblong vinaigrette, 1½in. wide, by Samuel Pemberton, Birmingham 1821.£130

French gold snuff box with blue enamel top, painted with animals and figures.   £1,600

George IV silver gilt rectangular vinaigrette, 1¼in. wide, by W.S., Birmingham 1826.   £160

George IV rectangular vinaigrette, 1¼in. wide, by Joseph Willmore, Birmingham 1821.   £80

Early 19th century gold-mounted agate vinaigrette, 1¼in. wide, circa 1820.   £280

George IV silver gilt rectangular vinaigrette, 1½in. wide, by Nathaniel Mills, Birmingham 1828.   £140

George III gold-mounted agate vinaigrette, 1in. diam. circa 1780.£680

Georgian purse shaped vinaigrette, 1¼in. wide, by Ledsam, Vale and Wheeler, Birmingham, circa 1820.£140

George III rectangular vinaigrette, 1¼in. wide, by Joseph Willmore, Birmingham 1814.£125

George III rectangular vinaigrette, 1½in. wide, by Joseph Willmore, Birmingham 1815.   £95

Early 19th century silver gilt shell-shaped vinaigrette by Thomas Willmore. £150

George III rectangular vinaigrette, 1¾in. wide, by Joseph Willmore, Birmingham 1813.   £400

George III oval silver gilt vinaigrette, 1¼in. wide, London 1800.   £110

Victorian mussel-shell vinaigrette, stamped S. Mordan & Co., London 1876, 1¾in. wide.   £200

George III oblong vinaigrette, 1½in. wide, by Joseph Willmore, Birmingham 1815.   £140

George III oval vinaigrette, 1¼in. wide, circa 1800.   £360

George III gold-mounted agate vinaigrette, 1¼in. diameter, circa 1789.£160

George III oval vinaigrette, 1¼in. wide, circa 1810.   £150

WINE COOLERS

Russian silver wine cooler by Alexander Jaschinkov.   £5,250

One of a pair of George III Irish wine coolers, 7¾in. high, by James le Bass, 96oz. 5dwt.
£1,150

Immaculate Old Sheffield wine cooler.   £155

One of a pair of silver wine coolers, 8¾in. high, circa 1820. £580

One of a pair of Sheffield plated wine buckets.
£275

French vase shaped wine cooler, 10in. high, circa 1890, 65oz.   £520

French Empire silver gilt vase shaped wine cooler, 10¼in. high, by Jean-Nicholas Boulanger, Paris, circa 1800, 60oz. 19dwt.
£1,300

One of a pair of vase shaped wine coolers with half fluted bodies in Sheffield plate.   £600

One of a pair of vase shaped wine coolers, by E., E., J. & W. Barnard, London 1829, 306oz. 10dwt. 12¼in. high.   £3,800

George II wine cooler
by Edward Wakelin,
London 1754, 65oz.
5dwt. £2,800

Old Sheffield wine cooler
with revolving interior ,
circa 1800. £155

One of four George
III wine coolers by
Benjamin Smith III,
10¾in. high, London
1818-19, 467oz.
2dwt. £7,800

WINE FUNNELS

Wine funnel by Paul
Storr, 6in. high,
London 1830, 4oz.
12dwt. £200

George III silver
wine funnel,
London 1800,
5oz., with filter.
£115

Sheffield plate wine
funnel, about 1810,
with unusual ribbed
strengthening section
on spout. £40

WINE TASTERS

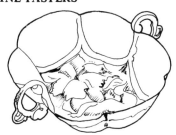

Early parcel gilt wine
taster, 3½in. wide. £110

Louis XV wine taster with shell
thumbpiece, 3¼in. diam., circa
1740, 4oz. 4dwt. £650

WINE LABELS

One of four George III
wine labels by J.L.,
Birmingham, 1817.
£160

George III urn shaped
wine label on pedestal
base, by James Atkins,
London 1801.   £75

One of two George IV
wine labels by Ledsham,
Vale and Wheeler,
Birmingham 1827. £85

Victorian wine label in
the shape of a vine
leaf, by Reily and
Storer, London 1839.
£22

George III oblong wine
label by William Bate-
man, London 1817.£85

One of two George IV
wine labels in the form
of leaves by John
Reily, London 1825.
£85

George III oblong wine
label by Hester Bate-
man, London, circa
1780.   £135

One of three banner
wine labels with
feather edge borders,
circa 1820.   £110

George III oval wine
label by Hester
Bateman, London,
circa 1780.   £115

One of two George III
wine labels by Hester
Bateman, London,
circa 1780.   £110

Victorian wine label
in the form of a vine
leaf, by Yapp and
Woodward, Birming-
ham, 1854.   £20

One of two William IV
Scottish wine labels by
Robert Gray & Son,
1836.   £65

One of two George III
wine labels by Peter,
Anne and William
Bateman, 1800.   £65

George III silver crescent
shaped wine label by
Hester Bateman, London,
circa 1780.   £80

One of two George III
crescent wine labels
by Susanna Barker,
London 1780.   £70

One of two William IV
wine labels in the form
of vine leaves by Reily
and Storer, London
1837.   £75

Fine George III silver-
gilt wine label by
Paul Storr, London,
circa 1818.   £320

One of two George III
wine labels by John
McDonald, Edinburgh,
circa 1810.   £95

One of two mid 18th
century wine labels by
Mary Binley, London,
circa 1760.   £140

One of four 18th century
wine labels by Sandilands
Drinkwater, London,
circa 1745.   £170

George III navette-
shaped wine label
by Susanna Barker,
London, circa
1785.   £45

One of two cast wine
labels in the mid 18th
century style.   £95

Sheffield plate wine label
decorated with cherubs
and grapes, about 1820.
                              £10

George III wine label
with ribbonwork sur-
round, maker's mark
J.K., probably Irish,
circa 1800.   £70

WINE LABELS

George III wine label by Edward Morley, London 1813, sold with a similar label. £28

One of two Georgian wine labels in the form of vine leaves, King's head and thistle mark, probably Edinburgh, circa 1825. £40

One of two George III wine labels, by Phipps and Robinson, 1808. £28

A George III crescent shaped wine label by Peter and Ann Bateman, 1794, sold with another. £40

One of three George III wine labels with gadrooned borders, by G. McHattie, Edinburgh, circa 1810. £40

George III silver crescent shaped wine label, by Joseph Willmore, Birmingham 1817. £22

Silver sherry label, Mary Binley, London, circa 1765. £36

One of a pair of George III wine labels by Hester Bateman, circa 1780. £80

Unmarked silver decanter label 'Lisbon'. £18

Unusual George IV wine label by Charles Rawlings, London 1822. £75

Two of six William IV initial wine labels, maker's mark G. M. H., Birmingham 1830. £160

George III banner shaped wine label by Godbehere, Wigan and Bult, circa 1800, one of two.   £55

Small George IV oval wine label, one of two, by William Kingdom, London 1829.   £45

George III wine label engraved for claret, by Margaret Binley, London, circa 1770.   £40

George III octagonal wine label by Phipps and Robinson, London 1811.   £45

One of two rare George III wine labels, feather edged, by James Erskine, Aberdeen, circa 1800.   £140

One of two urn-shaped wine labels by Phipps and Robinson, London, circa 1790.   £105

Rare 18th century wine label apparently unmarked, circa 1780.   £210

One of three rare Victorian wine labels, maker's mark F. & M., by Ferguson and McBean, Inverness, circa 1870.   £140

One of a pair of William IV wine labels by C. Reily and G. Storer, London 1836.   £125

Two George IV silver gilt wine labels by Digby Scott and Benjamin Smith, London.   £95

George III wine label by T. Phipps and E. Robinson, London 1809, sold with another similar.   £70

TOYS

Tin, mechanical
toy bear, circa
1930, 6in. high.
£28

A model of the 'Ancient House'
Ipswich, circa 1920.   £150

Clockwork 'Boy on
a Swing', English,
1937, 3½in. wide.
£50

German acrobatic clown
toy.   £15

Clockwork Steak-
house Joe, made
in Japan.   £15

German 'Man on a Pig'
toy.   £75

A Lehmann's clockwork
tricycle, circa 1910,
16.5cm. long.   £120

Fully furnished
Victorian dolls
house.   £490

Clockwork 'Old Shaker
Car', Japan 1936, with
flashing headlights,
11in. long.   £35

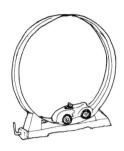

Clockwork 'Wheel of Death', Russian, 1896, 9in. high. **£100**

Victorian wooden dolls house, 47in. wide, 44in. high, with contents. **£1,070**

Schoenhuts crackerjack clown with original box and chair. **£60**

English clockwork toy 'Home James', circa 1900. **£55**

French 'Walking Clown' toy, 9in. high. **£150**

Old London 1925 double decker omnibus with light-up lamps, 22in. long. **£65**

Painted tin clockwork motor car with the driver holding a balloon, 6in. long. **£14**

A large Triang toy dolls house, circa 1930, 3ft. 8in. wide. **£125**

Clockwork guardsman with cymbals, made by Britain in 1890, 6½in. high. **£40**

An unusual Chad Valley clockwork
biscuit tin, 1947, 10in. long.   £70

Schuco Lady sports car, German,
1951, 9in. long.   £35

A good Georges Carette clockwork
omnibus, 1ft. 1in. wide.   £400

Fire Rescue tender, French, 1933,
ringing bell and extending ladder,
7in. long.   £40

Climbing monkey, made in France,
1872, fully extended 4½in.   £100

Painted tin clockwork ship, 7½in.
long.   £8

A Lehmann's clockwork delivery
van, circa 1910, 18in. long.   £55

French mid 20th century clockwork
tiger, 1ft. 6in. long.   £85

Marx clockwork mouse orchestra, 23cm. wide. £145

A living marionette theatre complete with thirteen puppets. £22

Clockwork Pirate ship, made in Japan in 1950, with firing cannons, 12in. long. £15

A Moko clockwork six cylinder saloon, 9½in. long. £50

Mid 20th century clockwork cat, 1ft. 3in. long. £70

Late 19th century model of a horse drawn milkcart, 1ft. 11in. long. £170

Electrical tin plate motor car. £150

Schuco Police Patrol car, German, 1952, 8in. long. £40

Toy model of a 1920's P2 Alfa Romeo. £360

19th century wind-up toy depicting a young boy on a tricycle, 11in. wide, 9in. high. £160

A model of a Royal Mail van of the 1920's period, 11¼in. high. £45

A Line's Brothers clockwork open sports car with front wheeled steering. £38

A good fully furnished 19th century doll's house. £470

Clockwork dancing Prince and Princess, 1936, 4½in. high. £30

Builders and Merchants Truck, made by Triang in 1951, 9in. long. £15

A Lehmann's clockwork donkey and cart, circa 1910, 7½in. long. £140

Four wheel carriage.   £380

4½ litre Lagonda sports car, first
registered in 1933.   £6,800

Superb 1935 Mercedes-Benz, type
500K, two-seater roadster.£18,000

Rudge Whitworth tricycle with 5ft.
5in. black frame, circa 1899.   £85

Charles Burrell single-crank compound,
two-speed, three shaft agricultural
traction engine, 1921.   £6,000

Invalid carriage with detachable
steering tiller and pony shafts. £110

1924 Model T Ford with original
engine with bread van body.£2,250

Early 19th century velocipede. £400

TRANSPORT

Brougham carriage by Mulliner of Birmingham. £775

Late 19th century Russian painted wooden sledge. £300

Penny farthing bicycle. £560

Late 19th century English bicycle, large wheel 130cm. diam., with adjustable pedals and straight handlebars. £450

A push chair with cast iron frame with leaf suspension, English, 3ft. 7in. long, mid 19th century. £50

Late 18th century hard-topped surrey with iron rimmed wheels. £2,750

Beale's 'Facile' bicycle of 1874. £560

Early 19th century child's three-wheeled carriage. £280

Victorian papier mache tray with painted scene. £140

Chinese Canton enamel tray, decorated with European ship in riverscape, Ch'ien Lung, 11½in. £150

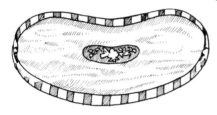

Edwardian mahogany kidney-shaped tray with marquetry centre, 23in. wide. £25

Tomonōbu Shibayama letter tray inlaid with mother-of-pearl and ivory, Japanese, circa 1900. £440

A good Jennens and Bettridge papier mache tray with floral decoration. £250

George III papier mache tray by Henry Clay, 27in. wide, with matching tea-pot stand. £96

Circular lobed papier mache tray with a painted view. £145

Victorian papier mache tray, 25in. £90

INDEX